Abolishing Poverty

Abolishing Poverty

TOWARD PLURIVERSE FUTURES
AND POLITICS

VICTORIA LAWSON, SARAH ELWOOD,
MICHELLE DAIGLE, YOLANDA GONZÁLEZ MENDOZA,
ANA P. GUTIÉRREZ GARZA, JUAN HERRERA,
ELLEN KOHL, JOVAN SCOTT LEWIS,
AARON MALLORY, PRISCILLA MCCUTCHEON,
MARGARET MARIETTA RAMÍREZ,
AND CHANDAN REDDY

THE UNIVERSITY OF GEORGIA PRESS
Athens

© 2023 by the University of Georgia Press
Athens, Georgia 30602
www.ugapress.org
All rights reserved
Set in 10.25/13.5 Minion Pro Regular
by Classic City Composition

Most University of Georgia Press titles are
available from popular e-book vendors.

Printed digitally

Library of Congress Cataloging-in-Publication Data
Names: Lawson, Victoria A., author.
Title: Abolishing poverty : toward pluriverse futures and politics / Victoria Lawson [and others].
Description: Athens : The University of Georgia Press, [2023] | Series: Geographies of justice and
    social transformation ; volume 58 | Includes bibliographical references and index.
Identifiers: LCCN 2022061284 | ISBN 9780820364377 (hardback) | ISBN 9780820364391 (paperback) |
    ISBN 9780820364384 (epub) | ISBN 9780820364407 (pdf) | ISBN 9780820364452 (other)
Subjects: LCSH: Poverty—Political aspects—North America. | Racism—North America.
Classification: LCC HC95.Z9 P6253 2023 | DDC 339.4/6097—dc23/eng/20230308
LC record available at https://lccn.loc.gov/2022061284

CONTENTS

ACKNOWLEDGMENTS

Victoria Lawson and Sarah Elwood

This book is the outcome of relationships of care and community spanning many years. We have been so lucky to be deeply challenged, inspired, and supported by brilliant thinking partners along our careers. We are deeply indebted to all the collaborators who created this volume together, who believed in our collective ability to argue that impoverishment can never be understood within the language and frames of liberal poverty knowledge. We are so grateful to students and colleagues/friends who generously shared ideas that opened space for many flights to the future that arise from histories of knowing and working for freedoms. We are grateful to all those graduate students who push us, both through their own work and in geography seminars on relational poverty knowledge. Some of them are coauthors in this book, and many others inspired our thinking through their brilliant interventions in our classes. Most particularly, we are grateful for the generosity of Magie Ramírez, Michelle Daigle, Yolanda González Mendoza, Katie Gillespie, Monica Farias, Tish Lopez, Eddy Sandoval, Eli Shoffner, Isaac Rivera, Austin Crane, Natalie Vaughan-Wynn, Amy Piedalue, Becky Burnett, Emma Slager, Anne Bonds, Sam Fredman, Samantha Thompson, and Aliyah Abu-Hazeem Turner. Danielle Brown inspires us not only with her thinking but also with her beautiful and prescient artwork that graces the cover or our book. We are also indebted to Ananya Roy, LaShawnDa Pittman, Jack Gieseking, David Giles, Amy Hagopian, Ed Taylor, Judy Howard, George Lovell, Tim Harris, and Jon Williams for their many insightful and supportive interventions along this journey. We are also very grateful to Mick Gusinde-Duffy for his immediate understanding of, and ongoing support for, the ethics and politics of collective recognition in the creation of our book. We are grateful for constructive feedback from reviewers of the proposal and full manuscript.

Vicky is also grateful to Dian Million. Dian engaged me in conversations that blew my mind and shifted the entire frame of my understanding and led me to this project! I am deeply grateful for my colleague Chandan Reddy who, at every step of this and many other projects, has been both the most brilliant and the most caring human. And then there is Sarah. Sarah Elwood has been my coconspirator for well over a decade. Sarah is my intellectual partner and colleague who shares all the joys and all the burdens of this work. But above all, Sarah is my dear friend who not only makes the work meaningful but makes life better through all the great meals, the trips, the hikes, the laughter.

Sarah thanks Chandan Reddy for being with us on this journey, inspiring and reenergizing us at every turn. Today and every day, I'm grateful to Lisa Faustino, whose politics, steadfastness, and generosity of spirit sustain me. For Vicky: Our collaboration has been one of the greatest gifts of my career. All should be so lucky to get to think and write, teach and learn, laugh and love so deeply with a cherished friend, for so many years. This book has come into being in the midst of joys and struggles of many kinds, and I am so grateful for you, in all of it.

Chandan Reddy

I want to express thanks to all the authors whose work and deep thinking are the source of this collective project. Above all, I thank Vicky and Sarah first for their generous invitation to think together about the critique of the political that Indigenous and critical ethnic studies thinkers of relationality chart and open up. Their vision to submit poverty studies to this critique opened the doors for the gatherings that created this book. They have been abiding guardians and sage interlocutors for us all, doing the crucial infrastructural work necessary for over two years without pause during these difficult and politically dark times to move this project from a shared set of ideas and conversations to a completed book. It is my honor to work beside them and consider myself their colleague at UW.

Yolanda González Mendoza

My multiple relations define who I am and how I make and experience communities and places across space and generations. I am of Indigenous descent from the lands of the Purépecha peoples in Michoacán, Mexico. I am also an uninvited guest in the lands of the Piscataway and Susquehannock peoples that is home to UMBC, which I joined in 2019 as assistant professor of geography and environmental systems. My deepest gratitude to all collaborators—authors/friends/colleagues, editors, and reviewers—of this collective abolitionist book. Especial thanks to Victoria Lawson, Sarah Elwood, and Chandan Reddy for your guidance, love, and energy in this project. I dedicate my contribution to my community in El Rancho (our powerful root in Mexico) who, as they wait for the return of their children and grandchildren, are aging, dying, and becoming soil alongside our ancestors. To my prim@s (cousins) who mourn at a distance—legally trapped in the United States—the deaths of their parents and loved ones in El Rancho due to the violence of white supremacists' laws that control and criminalize our mobilities. To this illegalized community who are making relations and roots in the northern part of Abya Yala (aka the United States) as uninvited guest. Overall, I dedicate this book to my present, past, and future generations across space. To you: Arisbeth, Anelsy, mis grandes amores y gran inspiration. Yours in the ongoing struggle to abolish all conditions of oppression.

Ana P. Gutiérrez Garza and Jovan Scott Lewis

We were hired by Tulsa native Charles Stafford and his colleague Rita Astuti, both anthropology professors at the London School of Economics, to research the relationship between cooperation and inequality among Black, Mexican American, and white Tulsans. We are incredibly thankful to Charles for introducing Tulsa to us and making available to us his family there. We also thank Professor Joseph Grzywacz and his staff at the Center for Family Resilience of Oklahoma State University–Tulsa and especially the Mexican and African American women who worked with the community for the center. Without them, we may never have truly come to know Tulsa. And therefore, we are most grateful to Tulsa's residents, who shared their lives, struggles, and hopes with us.

Aaron Mallory

I would like to thank the Houston Public Library System and the Rose Library at Emory University who provided archival support to work with Fabian Bridges's story. Additionally, I would like to thank Atlanta-based Queers who took the time to chat with me and show me their great city. Also, I want to shout out my WASC crew who read early drafts of the chapter. Finally, I want to acknowledge Fabian Bridges and others who lived, loved, and transitioned during the HIV/AIDS epidemic.

Juan Herrera

I would like to thank the members of the Fruitvale History Project, a collective of sixties and seventies activists who continue to inspire me in so many ways. These activists, along with those featured in my contribution to this book, showed me the power of collective organizing and how social movements mobilize to transform underserved communities. I thank them for their dedication to community care and their efforts to raise awareness about the history of the social movement in the Bay Area, and Oakland's Fruitvale neighborhood more specifically. They include Andres Alegria, Regina Chavarín, Mariano Contreras, Lenor De Cruz, Joel Garcia, Judi Garcia, Connie Jubb, Selia Melero, Elizabeth Meza, Annette Dolores Oropeza, and Beatriz M. Pesquera. I hope that more people can learn about their struggle for spatial justice. I also thank all those who contributed to this edited volume for having the courage to engage in work that is radically transforming a predominantly white discipline like geography. I especially thank Sarah Elwood and Vicky Lawson for paving the way to these conversations and for supporting us all throughout this journey. I also thank the reviewers for their generous feedback. I have learned so much through this collective endeavor and thank those who made this work possible. And I am especially grateful for the support from loved ones near and far.

Priscilla McCutcheon and Ellen Kohl

We would like to thank the members of the Wheat Street Baptist Church Action Mission Ministry and the Newtown Florist Club for sharing their time, stories, and wisdom with us. They continue to inspire and motivate our work. We would also like to thank Sarah Elwood, Vicky Lawson, Yolanda Valencia, and the anonymous reviewers for their suggestions on our chapter. Lastly, we would like to thank each other. We continue to learn and grow together in this work.

Margaret Marietta Ramírez and Michelle Daigle

Thank you to all those we have been in conversation with over the years, who have storied their relations with us with care and generosity. Thank you to Vicky Lawson and Sarah Elwood for inviting us to be in conversation on decolonization and liberation for the Relational Poverty Network's podcast in

2019, for allowing us to build on this conversation for this edited collection, and for providing leadership and guidance along with Chandan Reddy. Thank you to Austin Crane for his editorial guidance throughout the writing process and to all contributors for their conversation and insights as we envisioned the themes and spirit of this collective writing project. Meegwetch!

Abolishing Poverty

Abolishing Poverty

Toward Pluriverse Futures and Politics

SARAH ELWOOD, VICTORIA LAWSON,
YOLANDA GONZÁLEZ MENDOZA, AND CHANDAN REDDY

> We are living in a moment with this . . . [racist] capitalist economy, [a] failure
> when it comes to delivering [people's] needs. The nation-state failure to protect.
> The criminal justice system's failure to be fair. . . . We are more concerned about
> property . . . than poverty, decrepit school systems, dilapidated housing, massive
> unemployment and underemployment. . . . What we need is a non-violent revolutionary
> project of full-scale democratic sharing—power, wealth, resources, respect.
> —Cornel West (2020)

Speaking about the confluence of COVID-19-intensified ongoing inequality
with antiracist massed protests, Cornel West lays out a core principle of our
book: in the United States, a racial property regime protects white supremacy
and is more important than some groups of people. We argue that this must
be challenged with a revolutionary project for humanity. This viral moment,
as disease, antiracist movements, and violent responses to both spread ever
more rapidly, underscores the urgency of attending to the voices in this volume. This collection makes an urgent case for moving beyond "poverty thinking" (see Roy and Crane 2015; Lawson and Elwood 2018) to address the violences of the poverty relation under North American lethal liberalism and to
learn from long-standing politics of racialized, dispossessed groups that catalyze profoundly different relationalities and practices that fundamentally challenge poverty knowledge and action.[1]

These moves are utterly crucial in a moment in the United States that many
are referring to as a "dual pandemic" of COVID-19 and enduring racism. The
pandemic's massive economic devastation, tremendous burdens of death and
ill health, and the distinct concentration of these harms upon BIPOC communities make plain the stakes of inequality. This crisis is a powerful political opening: actions that policy makers have long dismissed as impossible

suddenly seem to be minimally possible. In 2020, the Trump administration issued a moratorium on evictions, state prison systems released some incarcerated people, and cities across the country took action to house unsheltered people in hotels and public buildings. Yet these moves must not be seen as some sudden sea change in the white-supremacist regimes of life in the United States. These efforts should have happened long ago—as initial steps—in the name of racial justice, yet only when COVID-19 translated the structural racism manifested in eviction, incarceration, and homelessness into a public health threat against relatively privileged people did governments feel compelled to act. Only in the face of the failure of the liberal government repertoire have policy makers been willing to take some actions that prison abolition, land/housing occupation, and other BIPOC liberation movements have called for across generations—an unspoken admission that these justice movements have answers that the liberal state does not. In this book, we center theorizations, politics, and histories that offer a vital framework for understanding this moment and amplifying its disruptions to the racial-economic regimes of life in the United States.

Our book interrupts liberal framings and makings of poverty that transact and reproduce white supremacy. We explore this through a focus on North American institutionalizations of global lethal liberalisms (Baldwin and Crane 2020). Liberalisms have long been lethal for those who are constructed as "surplus" and marked for premature death (Gilmore 2002, 2007). The foundational premise of our collection is that poverty is a predatory relation that in the North American context has historically advanced white supremacy and the false promises of the liberal nation. Belying its supposed promise for all, the "self-actualized, property-holding" liberal subject in fact depends upon the production of subordinate Others through logics of racialized difference (Goldstein 2012; Alexander 2010; Wynter 2003). Further, we begin from the premise that poverty studies' renditions of impoverishment rest on violent ontological and political claims of individualism, meritocracy, and white supremacy and on the techniques of categorization, measurement, and control at the heart of poverty research and poverty governance. Said another way, the ontological-ideological production of the liberal subject and the epistemologies and methodologies of knowing and acting upon "poverty" are intimately connected with one another, *and* with the material projects and institutional workings of liberal states. In contrast, this collection learns from political thought and action articulated by racialized dispossessed communities, joining a conversation with denied and disavowed knowledges that reject liberal violences. We argue for a reorientation away from diagnosing the violences of liberal poverty studies and instead offer a humble engagement with long-standing dialogues that are working for a relational politics of racial justice and equity. Specifically, our book is inspired by ongoing conversations between Indigenous cultural resurgence politics, abolitionist politics, and resistance and liberation movements within Black and Latinx communities.

The poverty relation resides in the entanglements of liberal and racial-capitalist ideologies and materialities of property and personhood. Within liberalism's frame, poverty is rendered as a failure to self-actualize and to attain "propertied personhood." Property within liberal governance can be understood as possessive individualism (Roy 2017, A3), wherein social life and material value are organized through ownership of the self—a logic of self-actualization—and through individual ownership of private property (Bhandar 2018). Prescient critiques of North American liberalism show how "the sovereign self is . . . a precondition for the claiming of rights . . . who is authorized to be this sovereign self? Who has the historical permission for such sovereignty? . . . [and] draw attention to the constitution of freedom through unfreedom" (Roy 2017, A9). These fundamental relations of property and personhood constitute the poverty relation within North American liberalism. That is, full personhood entails rights to hold and dispose property, to profit from property, and to be recognized by the state in the regulation of property (Byrd et al. 2018; Roy 2003, 2017; Blomley 2004; Bhandar 2018). The poverty relation sustains racial capitalism and reproduces its rights-bearing subjects. Racialized others are rendered ineligible for propertied personhood because both liberal governance and poverty studies ontology obscure the devaluation of much social life through ongoing forms of colonization arising from racialized histories of subjectification and dispossession (Roy 2003; Ranganathan 2016; Byrd et al. 2018; Bhandar 2018; Bledsoe and Wright 2019b). Racialized and impoverished subjects cannot be incorporated into liberal orders—precisely because those very orders depend on their difference and subordination (Cacho 2012; Espiritu 2003; McKittrick 2013; Bhandar 2018). Our book disorganizes this liberal framing of poverty, arguing instead that the poverty relation is produced and circulated through practices of racialized dispossession, the denial of personhood through differential social valuation, and the establishment of racial caste systems of social control, all of which rest on original and ongoing dispossessions of stolen lands and stolen labor in (settler) colonial and racial-capitalist sites.

North American liberalism is, of course, a multivalent and multiscalar project of enormous complexity. At its broadest, our book explores myriad ways in which liberal governance in North America is advanced through the lens of poverty studies / poverty knowledge to reinscribe racialized social control. Contributors reveal the ways in which white-supremacist capitalist power in North America depends on forms of actually existing liberalism that govern by simultaneously naturalizing and erasing racial difference, resulting in impoverishment and premature death (Gilmore 2007). Baldwin and Crane (2020, 369) term this "lethal liberalism," a project of governance that understands "inclusion and opportunity . . . as finite commodities for a deserving majority [that] . . . extinguish certain modes of life." We reveal the intersections between the discursive field of poverty thinking grounded in ideologies of individualism and deservingness that reinforce the legitimacy of North Atlantic academic poverty studies, and specific policies/practices this authorizes, to normalize violence against racialized communities. Contributors examine grounded expressions of liberal ontological power exercised through poverty governance, discourses representing "poor subjects," and a constructed hierarchy of racialized social (de)valuation. For instance, Gutiérrez Garza and Lewis (chapter 1) trace how liberal poverty policies set up tensions between communities of Mexican migrants and African Americans in Tulsa, Oklahoma, highlighting their different investments in racialized identities of relative social value arising as they seek access to social services, overlayered with gendered ideologies of motherhood and family. Lawson and Elwood (chapter 2) unpack how liberal poverty studies reproduces racialized dispossession, setting conditions for whiteness as a system of property that confers material and political advantages. One striking example is the toxic trope of the "welfare queen" that constructs welfare recipients as Black, morally bankrupt, disgusting women.

Our goals in this collection are a recentering neither of North American liberalism writ large nor of poverty studies per se. Rather, our project *disorganizes* poverty studies, precisely because this body of knowledge reinscribes liberal violences. Our methodology for disorganizing poverty studies has three intertwined dimensions: epistemological-terminological tactics that avoid reinscribing the established terms of liberal social-scientific discourse, a focus upon forms and imaginations of politics that overspill the objects and terms of liberal (poverty) governance, and an insistence that liberal life depends on racial orders configured by white supremacy. Disorganizing liberal poverty studies at an epistemological-terminological level involves refusing forms of critique and argumentation that reiterate white-supremacist framings of knowledge, governance, and power (Lawson and Elwood, chapter 2). For instance, in all chapters we intentionally do not rehearse citational genealogies of academic writing on liberalism (even through critique) or trace permutations of liberalism across time and place. Authors' analyses refuse the problem-solution and evaluation-judgment frameworks that script how liberal poverty studies is written and read. The chapters consider *various diverse struggles* toward survival, liberation, and thriving on terms that emphasize racialized and dispossessed communities as productive of alternative knowledges. We eschew arguments aimed at convincing readers that these politics are sufficiently radical, lasting, "effective," appropriate, co-optation proof, and so on. These modes of writing and the many voices (not always in alignment) across chapters will unsettle some readers. Indeed, this is part of the point. Disruptions to the (impossible) neat conclusions, tools for action, and definitive outcomes that liberal poverty studies purports to offer are imperative, as is subverting the epistemological foreclosure move of constantly questioning whether these politics are "enough." Instead, we invite readers into active reflection on what possibilities these chapters suggest for knowledge, imagination, action, and politics of accountable relationality within their own places, knowledge projects, and communities.

Our methodology for disorganizing poverty studies further involves centering our analysis on politics that elude and confound liberal governance and *not* calibrating this analysis back to liberalism. Authors *do* expose operations of actually existing liberalisms, yet their central focus is on articulating politics and actions that express and actualize resistance and survival that are not referential to liberalism. Rather than recounting yet again the politics of differential incorporation that characterize liberal poverty knowledge and practice, contributors instead disrupt liberalism's politics (in the here and now) by amplifying politics *beyond what liberalism allows*. Herrera's essay (chapter 5) uncovers a politics beyond the "suffering racialized body" to reveal how Chicano Movement activism in Fruitvale, Oakland, built solidarities around care provision for disenfranchised people. In so doing, Herrera explores antiracist mobilizations that transcend rigid identity boundaries, engaging in cooperative human efforts to care that forge what he terms *nepantla* identities of shared humanity. Ramírez and Daigle (chapter 7) envision a decolonial relational methodology for collective liberation. They argue for radical relationality among BIPOC people through storytelling and deep listening that embrace solidarities and also reckon with points of contention that can constrain the possibilities for fully engaging desires and movements for liberation. Our intention is precisely to disrupt lethal liberalism by engaging with political ideas and movements beyond liberal frames, ones that the academy too often ignores.

Further, our methodology for disorganizing poverty studies rests upon race as a foundational construct that prefigures some lives as "remainder" or "surplus" across extended geohistories and that shapes how social life becomes translated into liberal orders. Much of poverty studies situates race as one of multiple vectors of differentiation to be parsed and analyzed—an orientation that ultimately stabilizes the very abstractions through which liberal poverty governance operates. Our collection disorganizes these categorical modes of thought and action. As authors trace the multiplex formations of lethal liberalisms, they center racial orders of life. Importantly, they theorize racial formations as always already gendered, sexualized, and produced within larger geohistories of white supremacy and premature death. For instance, González Mendoza (chapter 3) illustrates how Mexico's national ontologies "include" through racial formations like *mestizaje* that arise from disavowed histories of violent exclusion and are sustained by institutions of liberal governance such as schools. Further, she shows how transnational migration to the United States exposes these racialized subjects to another national project that relies on different categories of liberal governance (such as "illegal") expressed in different registers (bordering, labor exploitation) but still operates in service of white-supremacist capitalism. Mallory (chapter 4) exposes the foundational anti-Blackness of the homonormative sexual citizenship through which many LGBTQIA+ movements seek inclusion into the benefits and protections of a white-supremacist liberal welfare state. Importantly, all these relational analyses think through geometries of complex social formations, rather than, for example, trying to tick through a series of coherent categories upon which liberal governance depends (race, class, gender, and so on). In so doing, these categories reproduce the naturalization of the nation-state as the basis of analysis and policy. For instance, national censuses organize populations into these categories as if they were inclusive, while simultaneously erasing the relations that create possibilities for politics beyond liberalism.

We join with scholars and activists who are working to abolish projects that expose racialized persons and Indigenous peoples to banishment, erasure, or premature death or that demand adverse incorporation into racial-capitalist extractivism and financialized capitalism (Gilmore 2002; Goldstein 2012; Byrd et al. 2018; Alexander 2010; Robinson 1983). In the United States and Canada, the production of discrete objects of social control, necessary to the poverty relation, arises from the devaluation of Indigenous life, lands, and livelihoods in a constant and restless effort to exclude racialized lives that hold memories of the original violence of this settler state. The poverty relation continues to be reproduced through discourses and practices of liberal governance, practices that conform social life to racial capitalism (Gilmore 2002), operate through heteropatriarchal norms (L. Simpson 2017), racialize processes of devaluation, dispossession, and social disappearance (Baldwin and Crane 2020; De Genova and Roy 2020; Cacho 2012), erase past and present takings of lands, natural resources, and labor, and disrespect Indigenous and postcolonial ontologies and sovereignty (Alexander 2010; L. Simpson 2017; Ybarra 2017). The poverty relation is constantly reinstantiated in subjects and places through bordering, norming, and property regimes that produce racial and heteropatriarchal categories to consolidate white capitalist power as it expresses in particular time and places (Goldstein 2012; Byrd et al. 2018; Alexander 2010; De Genova and Roy 2020).

In North America, the poverty relation has deep roots in dispossessive capitalist exploitation under settler colonialism, expressed through the taking of lands, stolen labor, and refusal of treaty obligations, all to secure white power (A. Simpson 2014; Moreton-Robinson 2015; L. Simpson 2017). The poverty relation upholds a racial caste system that secures white power through propertied personhood, through the financialization of homes and lands, and through myriad practices of settler-colonial governance, and its cultural productions, that normalize racial and gender hierarchies (Park 2021). For instance, the monetization of lands and homes defines propertied personhood and excludes people from shelter through urban redevelopment, eviction, and racial banishment (Baldwin and Crane 2020). As Roy (2017, A9) concludes in research on eviction on Chicago's South Side, "Racialization . . . is much more than racial discrimination and racial exclusion. It is about foundational dispossession—the subject whose claims to personhood are tenuous and whose claims to property are thus always a lived experience of loss." The monetization of lands, homes, and labor concentrates wealth through exclusionary banking and indebtedness that deepens differential devaluation of racialized people through mortgage foreclosure and other financialized practices (Byrd et al. 2018). Governance practices produce impoverishment through the denial of voting rights and access to food and housing, racial profiling in policing, and disproportionate sentencing and incarceration (Alexander 2010). Poverty governance and the social control of racialized subjects is also always exercised through the regulation of gender and sexuality enforced by, for example, limiting access to the U.S. social safety net to subjects who conform to heteropatriarchal gender identities and behaviors (Spade 2006). In North American states, borders further operate as a racial categorization scheme, deepening the poverty relation by designating some people as illegal and deportable or detainable (De Genova and Roy 2020). These political, material, and governmental tactics that reinstantiate the poverty relation are normalized and legitimated through academic and cultural productions and circulations of poverty knowledge (Lawson and Elwood 2018).

Our collection foregrounds disavowed knowledges and politics through forms of radical relationality, as an inquiry that challenges liberal concepts of individual personhood and private property that sustain the poverty relation. We bring together traditions of thought, politics, and worldings from Black, Latinx, queer, Indigenous, and diasporic subjects to disrupt the twinned logics of poverty studies and lethal liberalisms. Through our collective thinking, this book nourishes forms of relationality that provide openings for conversations about the potentials of reparative politics. Our volume explores the political possibilities that arise from reading against thinkable, that is, liberal poverty politics, to center and understand the workings of politics rendered unthinkable under settler-colonial and racial-capitalist liberalism in North America.

The contribution of this collection is more than only abolishing poverty studies' role in validating the liberal state and its fictions of equal opportunity, universality, meritocracy, and so on. We illuminate how "poverty" is materially and institutionally embedded with U.S. liberalism and racial capitalism, ensuring the reproduction of white supremacy. But further, this collection opens up new politics and futures by learning from knowledge projects, politics, and worlds that abolish the poverty relation and by refusing to reproduce poverty studies and its ontological, epistemological, and governing techniques. This collection is a call for material projects aimed at shattering racial-capitalist and settler-colonial relations in specific places and times, with constant attention to the ways that racialized dispossessed groups are always already producing politics and possibilities for thriving beyond the poverty relation.

Learning from Political Traditions of Racialized Communities

Theorizing the poverty relation and the ways it reproduces white-supremacist logics of property and personhood lays plain the urgency of disorganizing liberal poverty knowledge and poverty governance. This collection opens paths for learning from and across political thought and action that seek "a present future beyond the imaginative and territorial bounds of colonialism" (Martineau and Ritskes 2014, 4). We start from the premise that long-standing politics of racialized, dispossessed groups catalyze profoundly different relationalities and practices that are crucial resources for this work (Daigle and Ramírez 2019; Valencia 2019; McCutcheon 2016; Herrera 2012; McCutcheon and Kohl 2019; Lewis 2018; Gutiérrez 2018, 2019). This collection examines ways of being, knowing, and doing from the Black Radical Tradition, Black, Latinx, Indigenous, and queer geographies, Indigenous resurgence politics, and decolonial geographies that refuse the ontologies and epistemologies of liberal poverty studies/governance and instead re-root from other relations and reroute toward other futures. Our book creates openings for learning from and across these politics, while also insisting on deep attention to both the possibilities and limits of doing so. Scholar-activists working in these traditions underscore pluralities within the politics forged by (differently) racialized dispossessed peoples as well as incommensurabilities within and between these movements and communities, while also charting possibilities for accountable relations and ethical engagements (Bledsoe and Wright 2019a; Byrd et al. 2018; Daigle and Ramírez 2019; Pulido and De Lara 2018; Pulido 2018; Ybarra 2017).

We argue that a politics of disorganizing liberal poverty studies starts from engagement with long-standing traditions of thought and action by racialized dispossessed peoples, precisely because these very politics have long critiqued the forms of racialized personhood and possession that sustain the poverty relation. Black Marxism and antecedent work by Du Bois, C. L. R. James, and others situate racialization as a fundamental precursor to capitalism (Robinson 1983; Johnson and Lubin 2017; Kelley 2002). Black, Chicanx, queer, and feminist thinkers make arguments about subordinate racialized, gendered heteropatriarchal personhoods as inherent to global capitalism (Combahee River Collective 1977; Moraga and Anzaldúa 1983; Lorde 2007). Dené thinker Glen Coulthard (2014) argues against a politics of recognition and accommodation with the settler-colonial state because this reproduces colonial power. Coulthard (2014), Corntassel (Tsalagi, Cherokee Nation) and Scow (Kwakwaka'wakw and Snuneymuxw) (2017), and Leanne Simpson (Michi Saagiig Nishnaabeg) (2017) argue for building a politics of individual and collective resurgence in loving relations with particular lands, rather than engaging with white, heteropatriarchal settler-colonial framings of property, personhood, and nation. Simpson argues for resurgence politics that are generative, arising from collective subjects engaging diverse ontologies and grounded normativities (A. Simpson 2014; Coulthard 2014; Daigle 2016). These critiques resonate across the challenges to racial-capitalist productions of space that Pulido and De Lara (2018) find within decolonial and queer epistemologies from Latinx geopolitics and abolition politics from the Black Radical Tradition and in Daigle (Mushkegowuk, Cree, Constance Lake First Nation) and Ramírez's (2019) invitation to further explore the possibilities for co-resistance by abolition, decolonization, and anticapitalist movements.

Importantly, many of these politics diagnose racialized propertied personhood as the wellspring of "systemic inequality and endemic social suffering" (Million 2013, 6) yet do not explicitly name or examine "poverty." They illuminate the poverty relation without reproducing the liberal violence of the category of "poverty." Further, they foreground sites and forms of politics that reject racialized propertied personhood. Robinson (1983) points to refusal as a fundamental expression of Black radicalism, rooted in the act of running away, of removing one's body from the system of chattel slavery. Gilroy (1993) argues that collective self-affirmation of Blackness refuses multisystemic violent erasures of Black being (also McKittrick and Woods 2007), while Kelley (2017, 262) frames Black radicalism as including everyday acts of "ontological affirmation of Blackness that consistently beat back the prevailing logic of Black inferiority." Related to this, Corntassel and Scow (2017) argue that everyday acts of resurgence renew Indigenous *peoplehood*—articulating a collective subject in relation to land and life that at base rejects Western individualism, heteropatriarchy, and liberal assertions of propertied personhood (see also Herrera 2012 on Mexican American antipoverty politics oriented around collective subjects). Indigenous scholar-activists have drawn particular attention to forms of life and action that reject settler-colonial formulations of property/territory and their harnessing up to personhood. Audra Simpson (2014, 73) traces Mohawk membership rules, practices for crossing international borders, and land claims that reject the legitimacy of settler-colonial nation-states and territories, framing these as refusals that "enunciate repeatedly to ourselves and to outsiders that 'this is who we are, this is who you are, these are my rights.'" Daigle and Ramírez (2019) trace Indigenous activism practices such as radical hospitality (Coulthard 2014) that welcome other dispossessed people (such as racialized immigrants) and in so doing call out the illegitimacy of settler-colonial states and territorial claims and instead reassert Indigenous peoples as those with legitimate position to welcome newcomers.

Across the complexity and pluralism of abolition politics, Indigenous resurgence politics, decolonization movements, Black and queer liberation struggles, and Latinx geographies, their forms of refusal lead to generative politics that are always already rooted in other relations and worlds across multiple realms of social and economic life. Cree artist-theorist Jarrett Martineau (2015) names this both "affirmative refusal" and "creative negation," noting that Indigenous artists whose work refuses colonial logics are always also creating visual forms that give rise to other subjects and worlds (see also Barnd 2017). Daigle and Ramírez (2019) emphasize the world-making/transforming possibilities of refusal and reparative politics. Reading across Black and Indigenous thought, they find resistance politics that refuse settler-colonial, racial-capitalist systems of oppression and foster modes of life and action aimed at restoration, repair, and relations of accountability. For instance, prison abolition movements not only refuse the racial violence of carceral systems but also call for wholesale transformations in housing, education, employment, and care and health systems as well as in normative social imaginaries around "crime," "justice," and more (Gilmore 2007, 2017). Indigenous resurgence politics also seek wholesale remaking of worlds and relations, as in Leanne Simpson's (2016, 22) framing: "Indigenous resurgence, in its most radical form, is nation building . . . by centring, amplifying, animating, and actualizing the processes of [Nishnaabeg] grounded normativity as flight paths or fugitive escapes from the violences of settler colonialism." Coulthard (2014), Corntassel (2012), and Simpson (2017) conceive of resurgence as a profound reorientation around grounded practices of ethical relation to lands, waters, communities, and human and animal lives on Indigenous peoples' own terms.

While these diverse politics are engaged in affirmative refusals of liberal ontologies, epistemologies, and social formations at the heart of the poverty relation, we argue for the crucial importance of also giving sustained attention to their incommensurabilities. For instance, abolition politics that envision civil rights conferred by nation-states and/or Black self-determination through land/property stand in tension with decolonial politics that reject the legitimacy of nation-states and seek repatriation of Indigenous lands (Tuck and Yang 2012; Pulido and De Lara 2018; Daigle and Ramírez 2019). Latinx politics grapple with the complexity of social and political subjecthoods that may involve being both settler and racialized other within and across places and times (Pulido 2018; Ybarra 2017). Learning across these and other political traditions requires ongoing questioning of "what is distinct, what . . . portions of these projects simply cannot speak to one another, cannot be aligned or allied" (Tuck and Yang 2012, 28). For instance Daigle and Ramírez's chapter argues for constellations of radical relationality, produced through holding presence, care, and embodied and accountable connections to those we are in dialogue with. We join with others who insist that learning from and across movements of racialized dispossessed peoples must start from grounded accountable relations and reflexive questioning of when, where, and how diverse politics might be practiced in distinction from one another and whether they reproduce anti-Blackness, heteropatriarchy, Indigenous dispossession, and other forms of domination (Walia 2013; L. Simpson 2017; Byrd et al. 2018; Pulido 2018; Daigle and Ramírez 2019).

We employ relational analysis to explore refusals and flights to the future as vital ways of being and relating. Specifically, we articulate a relational politics that challenges "fatal couplings of power and difference" (Gilmore 2002, 15) that have rendered numerous racialized and Indigenous political imaginaries, and the subjects who make them, illegible to hegemonic forms of power. What is rendered unimaginable (or, in our framing, unthinkable) is based on "an ontology, an implicit organization of the world and its inhabitants" (Trouillot 1991, 37, quoted in Baldwin and Crane 2020, 373) that continually centers white supremacy and settler-colonial capitalist power. Unthinkable politics, in all their complexity, entail the "subjects, meanings, claims, relations and actions formed *outside the terms of what can be* under existing racial capitalist social orders" (Baldwin and Crane 2020, 373). Our collection centers the premise that unthinkable politics destabilize the poverty relation by rejecting its projects of erasure, otherness, dispossession, appropriation, incorporation, and banishment associated with predatory/extractive capitalism. At the same time, we argue that unthinkability also entails forms of relationality that open the possibility for pluriversal projects of world making and political futurities. Our collection explores creative reworkings of subjectivity, pluriverse futures, and politics, beyond propertied personhood, made by persons who have been erased or dispossessed within thinkable liberal racial capitalism and settler-colonial states.

Unthinkability and Relational Politics

Unthinkability in our book is *not* concerned with putting rebellious politics into an idiom that is legible to Western hegemonic orders. Rather, we raise vital questions about the conditions that produce forms of unthinkability and for whom. We use unthinkability as an analytic to open up questions about how it is possible that myriad forms of activism, communities of survival and persistence, fights for sovereignty, and much more are all vibrantly happening in our midst but remain unthinkable to so many people. We argue that the condition of possibility for unthinkability is a denial of relationality, which sustains racial-capitalist politics of division, difference, and impoverishment. By contrast, centering relational analyses of unthinkability turns our attention away from poverty as object and category and toward ways of being and knowing that destabilize the poverty relation and its lethal frames of personhood and property. That is, unthinkability focuses on the relational politics of imagination and liberation that are the heart of this collection. This book pushes beyond liberal projects of recognition, diversity, and inclusivity, calling for flights to the future not yet fully imagined (Coulthard 2014; L. Simpson 2017). This collection enacts three registers of relational politics. First, we challenge the limits of hegemonic knowledge in poverty studies by foregrounding how Black, Brown, Indigenous, and queer communities continue to be in dialogue with one another across time and space, revealing the ruptures and incompleteness of white supremacy/liberalism. We trace how knowledges and politics that refuse liberal and racial-capitalist forms of discipline and dispossession counter "a collective inarticulation due to colonial histories of erasure" (Daigle and Ramírez 2019, 81) by bringing into view that which the poverty relation violently eliminates. A fundamental challenge in this work is to grapple with the ways in which unthinkable forms of knowledge production and political struggles are so dominated by liberal orders of thought that it is difficult to think and speak beyond such disciplining frames. That is, our collection contends with the ways in which radical relationalities exist and thrive yet often are rendered unthinkable and unspeakable by lethal liberalisms. Second, we organize our project through a collective writing subject, disrupting academic orders of merit and individualism, offering a model for rebuilding academic spaces/relations. Our collaborative writing subject unsettles the white, masculinist, middle-classed knowledge and authority that dominate liberal knowledge projects and help sustain the historical erasures of racial capitalism, land dispossession, and impoverishment. Inspired by feminist slow scholarship, we build deliberate practices of ethical collaboration that account for differences in power and identity and resist the speedup of the neoliberal university (Moraga and Anzaldúa 1983; Mahtani 2006; Hunt and Holmes 2015; Mountz et al. 2015). Third, beyond unthinkability as marking the limits of hegemonic knowledge, our collection explores complex iterations of unthinkability within pluriverse movements and politics themselves. For instance, some forms of politics are intentionally veiled, so that everyday, embodied practices of social survival and thriving can enable those targeted for premature death to build and sustain strong communities (McCutcheon 2016; L. Simpson 2017; see also Mallory's chapter 4). At the same time unthinkable politics is a way to mark the challenges movements face within themselves, as with anti-Blackness or heteropatriarchal refusals of sexual agency that may arise within justice struggles. Being in relation entails working with the incommensurabilities within and between movements and communities as we/they articulate political identities and build politics.

A first strand of our relational politics begins from the ways in which poverty studies has reproduced racialized exclusions from personhood, foregrounded a settler-colonial property relation, and reinscribed social difference. Chapters by Gutiérrez Garza and Lewis and by Lawson and Elwood trace how poverty studies itself is an expression of the power effects of violent liberal erasures that assert individualism, categorization, and meritocracy through violent and ongoing dispossession of land and labor. Our collection challenges these limits through relational forms of knowing and being. Contributors articulate a plurality of political visions and practices that have been rendered unrecognizable under the ideological terms of liberalism and hegemonic thinkable poverty knowledge and practices. Our collection builds creative analyses of diverse political traditions to explore the relations between political futures/imaginations that have been violently separated from each other (Woods, Camp, and Pulido 2017; Byrd et al. 2018). The chapters engage with histories of collective activisms, grounded ontologies of place-based worlding, and imaginations of pluriverse futures that fight for self-determination, renewal, and reclaimings of land and liberation. Our aim is to mount a conversation and a learning from juxtaposing the grounded, lively brilliance of Indigenous, Black, queer of color, and Latinx political traditions, imaginings, and world makings and their creative politics of self-determination and reparations.

Second, we forge relational politics by working toward creating a collective writing subject. This form has largely been unthinkable in North Atlantic academic traditions that reward solo authorship, speedy production, and "disciplinary analysis" that denies relations to the lives, lands, communities, and politics from which the work arises. We are inspired by the Sangtin Writers and Nagar (2006), the Athena Co-Learning Collective (2018), and others who write in sustained relation, as collectives. Our collective writing subject coalesces around relations of coauthorship in many of the chapters, the long-standing relations of authors to the communities, social movements, lands, and lives centered in their chapters, as well as our efforts to imagine and articulate this project together. For years, as various of us have convened electronically and in person to imagine the project, discuss, and write and rewrite the chapters of our book, we have read and responded to one another's work (the chapters presented here and also other work in progress). The relational politics of this project are enacted not just through long-standing relations of co-creating but also in the genre of its presentation. This collection is *not* a volume presented by *coeditors*. Rather, it is a *coauthored* collection, committed to cross-disciplinary (boundary-shattering) scholarship, with all contributors invited to be coauthors on the book—one way of signaling the relations of its making.

Yet it must be said up front that our effort to forge a collective writing subject remains incomplete, aspirational, and fraught. As Black-, Latinx-, Indigenous-, Asian-, white-, queer-, and straight-identified scholars whose lives are linked to many places, we have different relationships to the concept of poverty and the violences of impoverishment. Imagining this collection together has meant wrestling with our differences. Our collaboration carries, and struggles with, the material stakes and lived experiences of dispossession, banishment, and loss of lands and livelihoods and the inevitable tensions of working with white settler-colonial subjects. We have sought to make ideas together iteratively and intentionally, learning across our different research projects and lives, yet it is also true that this knowing across difference is also tentative, frustrating, and painful. This is especially so because we are differently situated within white supremacy and settler colonialism and are at different stages of unlearning the ways they inflect our research, epistemological reflexes, politics of citation, and more. Writing in this context involves the hard work of crafting constructive critique while feeling frustrated or hurt by what someone else wrote (or overlooked), hearing critiques of the limits to our analysis that are painful to recognize, and sustaining accountable relations to one another.

Our ambition for cowriting this project and refusing the demands and expectations of neoliberal academic productivity stands in tension to the reality that all authors are (differently) positioned within the academy. Only a few of us have career seniority and institutional security. Most of us are navigating the stark difficulties of surviving the early career years—living far from home communities, feeling isolated personally and politically, and writing under intense publish-or-perish imperatives—struggles now amplified by unequally distributed burdens of care, loss, and precarity that both the pandemic and the even deeper intensification of racial injustice are prompting in our own lives. In preparing this collection, we have sought to practice a grounded care ethics of welcoming differences in what and how much each of us could contribute to collective thinking and writing for the overall project. Some of us contributed more, others less; some were able to join our collective conversations often, others less often—and still the overall project reflects creative insights from all coauthors.

The genre of this collection, our writing practices, and our wrestling with these inherent tensions are informed by a commitment to remaining in accountable relation with one another and with the social movement groups whose politics are at the heart of our analysis. Many of us are deeply involved in social movements that refuse whitened ways of being and knowing together. We learn from these relationships that care is a condition of possibility for the kind of knowledge politics we seek to build. Our collective writing subject is assembled through ethics of care that involve trust and openness, to allow for expressions of pain and the difficult work of learning across differences. We have been building these relationships as advisers, students, peers, friends, allies, and colleagues. Indeed, this work is possible in this emotional and inter-personal register only because of our accountable (but still fraught) relation-ships to each other and to those whom we collaborate with in our work. We are attempting to practice the politics we explore in the volume: of working across differences to be in accountable relation with each other, and with our multiple communities, in order to build futures not yet realized.

Third, our volume reads for complex iterations of relational politics within and between movements forging political futures beyond lethal liberalisms, racial capitalism, and settler colonialism. These collective imaginations are ur-gent, and yet we also recognize they are not new nor uncomplicated. Scholar-activists have long traced the co-emerging critiques of colonialism and vi-sions of liberation as well as articulations of Indigenous presence in Central and North Atlantic and in African spaces (Robinson 1983; McKittrick 2006; Woods 1998; Kelley 2002; Gilroy 1993; Coulthard 2014; L. Simpson 2017; Goe-man 2013; Daigle and Ramírez 2019; Bonfil Batalla and Dennis 1996; Luna 2015; Dahl-Bredine and Hicken 2008). In the spirit of unsettling hegemo-nies, relational analysis entails thinking through incommensurabilities within and between the political imaginaries of racialized peoples. Here again, we employ unthinkability as an analytic, asking to whom unthinkable politics are legible. This question shifts from unthinkability as marking the limits of hegemonic knowledge to unthinkability as (il)legibilities produced through diverse politics themselves. For instance, in some chapters this relational anal-ysis illuminates how anti-Blackness and homo/transphobia circulate within communities and their politics. Other chapters trace how settler colonial-ism and racial capitalism set up mutual misrecognitions between racialized groups struggling against dispossession, caging, and social and literal death. The political imaginations expressed by other authors open the conversation about the possibility that "The decolonial . . . [could be] an affirmative re-fusal of white supremacy, anti-Blackness, the settler colonial state and a ra-cialized political economy of containment, displacement and violence" (Dai-gle and Ramírez 2019, 80). Our project also explores the tactics and reasons why some communities and their members may intentionally strive to veil their politics and/or cultivate positions of illegibility not just to hegemonic knowledge and politics but to other groups also calling for radical flights to the future.

These relational politics invite solidarities that begin from fighting against anti-Blackness in all communities. Related to this, they call white-identified people to take account of, and responsibility for, their role in benefiting from and bolstering a colonial state, a white-supremacist society, extractive, financialized capitalism, *and* forms of academic knowledge production that reproduce lethal liberalisms and normalize violence against racialized communities. One responsibility of white contributors and readers is not to appropriate the theory and politics imagined and fought for by racialized communities but rather to learn their own histories, to disrupt white supremacy through critiques of racial capitalism and settler colonialism and to build accountable relations to places and peoples with whom they work and live.

Abolishing Poverty: Engaging Pluriverse Politics and Futurities

The heart of this book explores the lessons arising from complex forms of resurgent/resistant politics to mount an argument for abolishing liberal poverty studies. Attempting to address pervasive inequality and endemic social suffering through liberal poverty studies is fundamentally flawed because poverty knowledge rests on logics of adverse incorporation and a racial ontology of difference that reproduces white supremacy in North America. Our book opens space for relational political thinking first by challenging the epistemological violence of liberal thought and action, specifically as expressed through poverty studies and white liberal mythologies of the American dream. In constructing discrete objects of social control, poverty studies sustain white supremacy by obscuring the poverty relation at the very heart of settler-colonial, racial capitalism. We argue that relational analysis is a condition of possibility both for uncovering the violences of the poverty relation and for knowing and being otherwise. Second, contributors disentangle the poverty relation itself in its material, political, and ontological dimensions, revealing the ways in which diverse social movements and communities struggle to construct dignified lives and forms of self-determination. Third, our chapters explore ongoing (or needed) conversations and practices of relational politics that can open space for building multiracial, intersectional, and intergenerational solidarities. As our book looks toward pluriverse politics beyond liberal poverty thought, contributors pose questions about how to respectfully and accountably participate in grounded relations of engagement that are simultaneously hopeful and fraught. They explore both possibilities and incommensurabilities arising from challenging anti-Blackness and Indigenous erasure in diverse communities, and they engage the persistent risk of white appropriation of radical thought and explore the very meanings of radicalism.

Challenging the epistemological violence of liberal thought and poverty studies, Ana Gutiérrez Garza and Jovan Scott Lewis trace how liberal poverty knowledge and action set up contradictions between communities of Mexican migrants and African Americans exposed to racialized impoverishment, even in social service provision by and for their communities. Through personal narratives and life stories gathered from within two communities in Tulsa, Oklahoma, they show how ideas of deservingness and merit produce ethics and imaginaries of personhood and community benchmarked to liberalism and state structures that ensure its reproduction. Their chapter demonstrates the difficulties and complexities of community formation as struggles to assert liberal personhood, demanded by liberal poverty governance, set racialized groups in opposition to each other as they struggle to assert social value and claim access to material assistance for their own communities.

In narratives of community uplift, the American dream, and poverty studies, whiteness is at once ontological and political, contributing in both registers to projects of lethal liberalisms. Victoria Lawson and Sarah Elwood's chapter, inspired by antiracist scholarship, traces the whiteness of liberal poverty studies. They argue that the historical racialized foundations of poverty studies, the social categories it reifies, and its complicity in liberal governance of settler-colonial, racial capitalism must all be exposed and dismantled. Lawson and Elwood trace the violent categorizations that sustain the poverty object, liberal governance, and white supremacy in the United States, arguing that these divert analysis from understanding and dismantling the poverty relation. They illustrate these arguments through reflection on their own roles in reproducing the whiteness of poverty studies through a narrowly conceived "relational poverty" project that is now actively being remade through collaborative learning. Their essay invites scholars to take up collective responsibility for disrupting (and eventually abolishing) white privilege and institutional/ structural racism in the academy, in poverty studies and far beyond.

Disorganizing poverty studies and its modes of thought and action lays bare the poverty relation as a site for political struggle. Foregrounding historical and ongoing material dispossession and racist projects of (de)legitimation, our collection interrupts and refuses the ontological object "poverty." In place of this static concept, several chapters explore the ways in which the poverty relation leads to banishment, erasure, denial of vital resources, or premature death. They illuminate the ways in which the poverty relation, sustained through liberal categorical frames, positions communities of color in opposition to each other in their struggles for self-determination, land, and life. Relational politics undertaken by diverse communities expose these relations of discipline and oppression and instead imagine into being forms of politics that refuse these separations and dispossessions. Yolanda González Mendoza exposes the workings of the poverty relation through her autobiographical account of her journey from Mexico to Seattle as well as through lifelong ethnography in her community in Mexico and the United States. Inspired by Black geographies' arguments that the oppressed, even as they are marginalized, produce space and live rich lives, her essay analyzes simultaneous geographies of oppression and un/thinkable resistance. She traces ways in which racial capitalism entrenches institutional racism to produce displacement, bordering, de-Indianization/mestizaje, and illegality. She shows how ideologies of modernity, racial capitalism, and bordering practices come together to produce the privileged individual, the "legal" liberal citizen, and its constituent Other, the "illegal." Her analysis traces how this production of "illegal" nonpersonhood authorizes forced mobility, labor exploitation, and family separation while making these harms appear to be logical and necessary. Yet her essay ultimately reveals ongoing practices of relational resistance from communities that are thriving in spite of oppressive norms. For instance, González Mendoza demonstrates that collective citizenship-sharing practices enable a reterritorialization of U.S. citizenship and disrupt and challenge the propertied, privileged constructions of person and citizen that stabilize liberal citizenship. Instead, collective citizenship ensures that cross-border and cross-generational relations of solidarity will endure.

Our collection explores creative reworkings of subjectivity and pluriverse politics that abolish propertied personhood and lethal liberalisms. Our contributors trace complex struggles and negotiations of community politics, forged by persons who have been rendered illegible and/or dispossessed within liberal racial capitalism, striving for solidarity and racial justice. Aaron Mallory writes about the overrepresentation of Black people within the ongoing HIV/AIDS epidemic, exploring the ways in which anti-Black racism is articulated through gender and sexual domination. At the same time, Mallory traces the ways in which race, gender, and sexuality become a basis for Black queer spatial agency to build advocacy. Juan Herrera explores multiracial solidarities and intergenerational struggles in the sixties Bay Area where the Chicano Movement worked in relation to Black Panther struggles against lack of educational access and police brutality. The chapter explores forms of community organizing that centralize care for people and communities as vital to building a politics of solidarity and liberation. Black, Indigenous, and Chicano activists' efforts to create health clinics, educational centers, arts organizations, and legal clinics and to fight police brutality all take aim at bodily harms of racial capitalism (hunger, ill health, injury, and death) and rest in large part on reclaiming (safe) spaces for a politics of care. Herrera argues that we need to reposition the care of people and impoverished communities as an important

form of politics advanced by social movement activism. Herrera grounds this
work in an ethics of collaborative research, partnering with activists to collectively frame research questions and guide the research project through
long-term partnerships.

Reworkings of political subjectivity and the politics of social change take
myriad forms. Priscilla McCutcheon and Ellen Kohl trace intersections of identity, spirituality, and social change among Black Christian men and women in
the U.S. South. They show how a Black church's emergency food program in-
tervenes in bodily hunger, claims land for sustainable farming, and carries forward food and environmental justice politics that originate in the Civil Rights
and Black Power movements. They trace how a social club's everyday rituals of care for grieving Black community members led them to connect the
pollution of lands to premature death. McCutcheon and Kohl theorize these
acts as politics of self-determination, resilience, and refusal that forge forms
of humanity and personhood denied under white supremacy. They explore
quotidian "quiet" politics that seek to create a "beloved community" through
everyday resistance that reclaims notions of Black respectability that are not
referential to white-supremacist liberal norms and that challenge institutionalized and intersectional oppressions of impoverishment, racism, and capitalism. Importantly, they also explore illegibilities within these relational politics. They trace how these quiet politics arising from Black religiosity are often
overlooked as activism and the ambivalent relationship that politics of self-
determination and uplift sometimes have to white-supremacist liberal frames.
They explore tensions that arise when Christian ethics of direct intervention
into material inequalities and recognition of the humanity of all people become enacted as "respectability politics" and blunt the call for other worlds
that lies at the heart of their vision of beloved community.

Relational politics, by definition, can arise only from accountable relations
to lands, histories, and present lives. Margaret Marietta Ramírez and Michelle
Daigle theorize radical relationality as an orientation, a praxis of decolonial
geographies. They explore traditions of resistance as a constellation of embodied understandings of liberation that are always grounded in, and fully accountable to, particular lands, places, and communities. Their essay explores
the ways in which places are shaped by traditions of resistance and resurgence
among Black, Latinx, and Indigenous communities as they discuss the possibilities for solidarity politics of self-determination and liberation. Ramírez and
Daigle explore how struggles for decolonial futures expose the interconnections of racial capitalism, colonialism, and white supremacy from one place
and community to the next, thus revealing commonalities in the parameters

of struggle. At the same time, they consider illegibilities and incommensurabilities that arise from "differential decolonial desires layered in one place" and how these play out in Black, Brown, and Indigenous peoples' interconnected struggles for land, space, self-determination, and freedom.

In closing, *Abolishing Poverty* disorganizes poverty studies as we know it by revealing the complicity of poverty thinking with projects of racial liberal governance. As COVID-19 lays bare yet again, liberal governance and racist dispossession are ongoing projects of social differentiation and material inequality. As the economy dives, inequality soars. As people rise up in protest against the inability of liberal governance to deliver, the criminal justice system fails to protect communities of color. This is a moment that lays bare the myth of liberal universal rights and protections, even as poverty studies doubles down on these projects by devaluing and disciplining racialized communities. Our collaboration breaks these claims by engaging diverse knowledges and staging critical conversations between antipoverty politics and Indigenous, Black, and Brown scholarship and activism. Relationality is the way that theory travels from one encounter to another, inviting reflection on how knowledge moves, how its meaning shifts, and how it might be challenged in different times and places. *Abolishing Poverty* argues for this project of relationality that abolishes poverty studies, reveals the material inequalities endemic to the U.S. system, and foregrounds political futures disavowed under liberal governance. Our book argues that disorganizing poverty thinking is a condition of possibility for joining conversations rooted in diverse frameworks for understanding the materialist bases for impoverishment and for articulating antiracist knowledges and political visions. These antiracist politics liberate people from individualized propertied personhood and instead build relational solidarities that reject racism that is corrosive to all people. In short, our book explores new infrastructures of possibilities and politics rooted in accountable relations to each other and from flights to the future that animate diverse communities.

NOTE

1. Poverty thinking refers to liberal, social-scientific, categorical thinking that constructs poverty as a noun or a characteristic and the poor as an object of discipline and control.

REFERENCES

Alexander, Michelle. 2010. *The New Jim Crow: Incarceration in the Age of Colorblindness.* New York: New Press.

Athena Co-Learning Collective. 2018. "A Hiquita for Teaching and Learning Radical Geography." *Antipode*, November 27. https://wp.me/p16RPC-1Rr.

Baldwin, Davarian L., and Emma S. Crane. 2020. "Cities, Racialized Poverty, and Infrastructures of Possibility." *Antipode* 52(2): 365–379.

Barnd, Natchee B. 2017. *Native Space: Geographic Strategies to Unsettle Settler Colonialism.* Corvallis: Oregon State University Press.

Bhandar, Brenna. 2018. *Colonial Lives of Property.* Durham, N.C.: Duke University Press.

Bledsoe, Adam, and Willie Jamaal Wright. 2019a. "The Pluralities of Black Geographies." *Antipode* 51(2): 419–437.

———. 2019b. "The Anti-Blackness of Global Capital." *Environment and Planning D: Society and Space* 37(1): 8–26.

Blomley, Nicholas. 2004. *Unsettling the City: Urban Land and the Politics of Property.* New York: Routledge.

Bonfil Batalla, Guillermo, and Philip A. Dennis. 1996. *México Profundo: Reclaiming a Civilization.* Austin: University of Texas Press.

Byrd, Jodi A., Alyosha Goldstein, Jodi Melamed, and Chandan Reddy. 2018. "Predatory Value: Economies of Dispossession and Disturbed Relationalities." *Social Text* 135(36.2): 1–18.

Cacho, Lisa M. 2012. *Social Death: Racialized Rightlessness and the Criminalization of the Unprotected.* New York: New York University Press.

Combahee River Collective. 1977. "Combahee River Collective Statement." http://circuitous.org/scraps/combahee.html.

Corntassel, Jeff. 2012. "Re-envisioning Resurgence: Indigenous Pathways to Decolonization and Sustainable Self-Determination." *Decolonization: Indigeneity, Education & Society* 1(1): 86–88.

Corntassel, Jeff, and Mick Scow. 2017. "Everyday Acts of Resurgence: Indigenous Approaches to Everydayness in Fatherhood." *New Diversities* 19(2): 55–68.

Coulthard, Glen. 2014. *Red Skin, White Masks.* Minneapolis: University of Minnesota Press.

Dahl-Bredine, Phil, and Stephen Hicken. 2008. *The Other Game: Lessons from How Life Is Played in Mexican Villages.* Maryknoll, N.Y.: Orbis.

Daigle, Michelle. 2016. "Awawanenitakik: The Spatial Politics of Recognition and Relational Geographies of Indigenous Self-Determination." *Canadian Geographer / Le Geographe Canadien* 60(2): 259–269.

Daigle, Michelle, and Margaret Marietta Ramírez. 2019. "Decolonial Geographies." In Antipode Editorial Collective (Ed.), *Keywords in Radical Geography: Antipode at 50,* 78–84. https://onlinelibrary.wiley.com/doi/10.1002/9781119558071.ch14.

De Genova, Nicholas, and Ananya Roy. 2020. "Practices of Illegalisation." *Antipode* 52(2): 352–364.

Espiritu, Yen Le. 2003. *Home Bound: Filipino American Lives across Cultures, Communities, and Countries.* Berkeley: University of California Press.

Gilmore, Ruth Wilson. 2002. "Fatal Couplings of Power and Difference: Notes on Racism and Geography." *Professional Geographer* 54(1): 15–24.

———. 2007. *Golden Gulag: Prisons, Surplus, Crisis, and Opposition in Globalizing California*. Berkeley: University of California Press.

———. 2017. "Abolition Geography and the Problem of Innocence." In Gaye Theresa Johnson and Alex Lubin (Eds.), *Futures of Black Radicalism*, 225–240. London: Verso.

Gilroy, Paul. 1993. *The Black Atlantic: Modernity and Double Consciousness*. Cambridge, Mass.: Harvard University Press.

Goeman, Mishuana. 2013. *Mark My Words: Native Women Mapping Our Nations*. Minneapolis: University of Minnesota Press.

Goldstein, Alyosha. 2012. *Poverty in Common: The Politics of Community Action during the American Century*. Durham, N.C.: Duke University Press.

Gutiérrez Garza, Ana. 2018. "The Temporality of 'Illegality': Experiences of Undocumented Latin American Migrants in London." *Focaal: Journal of Global and Historical Anthropology* 81(1): 86–98.

———. 2019. *Care for Sale: An Ethnography of Latin American Domestic and Sex Workers in London*. New York: Oxford University Press.

Herrera, Juan. 2012. "Unsettling the Geography of Oakland's War on Poverty: Mexican American Political Organizations and the Decoupling of Poverty and Blackness." *Du Bois Review* 9(2): 375–393.

Hunt, Sarah, and Cindy Holmes. 2015. "Everyday Decolonization: Living a Decolonizing Queer Politics." *Journal of Lesbian Studies* 19(2): 154–172.

Johnson, Gaye Theresa, and Alex Lubin (Eds.). 2017. *Futures of Black Radicalism*. London: Verso.

Kelley, Robin D. G. 2002. *Freedom Dreams: The Black Radical Imagination*. Boston: Beacon.

———. 2017. "Winston Whiteside and the Politics of the Possible." In Gaye Theresa Johnson and Alex Lubin (Eds.), *Futures of Black Radicalism*, 255–262. London: Verso.

Lawson, Victoria, and Sarah Elwood. 2018. *Relational Poverty Politics: Forms, Struggles, and Possibilities*. Athens: University of Georgia Press.

Lewis, Jovan S. 2018. "Structural Readjustment: Crime, Development, and Repair in the Jamaican Lottery Scam." *Anthropological Quarterly* 91(3): 1029–1048.

Lorde, Audre. 2007. *Sister Outsider*. New York: Ten Speed Press.

Luna, Jaime Martinez. 2015. "Comunalidad as the Axis of Oaxacan Thought in Mexico." *Upside Down World*, October 27. http://upsidedownworld.org/archives/hiqui/comunalidad-axis-of-oaxacan-thought/#123#.

Mahtani, Minelle. 2006. "Challenging the Ivory Tower: Proposing Anti-racist Geographies within the Academy." *Gender, Place & Culture* 13(1): 21–25.

Martineau, Jarrett. 2015. "Creative Combat: Indigenous Art, Resurgence, and Decolonization." PhD dissertation, University of Victoria.

Martineau, Jarrett, and Eric Ritskes. 2014. "Fugitive Indigeneity: Reclaiming the Terrain of Decolonial Struggle through Indigenous Art." *Decolonization: Indigeneity, Education & Society* 3(1): 1–12.

McCutcheon, Priscilla. 2016. "The 'Radical' Welcome Table." *Southeastern Geographer* 56(1): 16–21.

McCutcheon, Priscilla, and Ellen Kohl. 2019. "You're Not Welcome at My Table: Racial

Discourse, Conflict and Healing at the Kitchen Table." *Gender, Place & Culture* 26(2): 173–180.

McKittrick, Katherine. 2006. *Demonic Grounds: Black Women and the Cartographies of Struggle.* Minneapolis: University of Minnesota Press.

———. 2013. "Plantation Futures." *Small Axe* 17(3.42): 1–15.

McKittrick, Katherine, and Clyde Woods. 2007. *Black Geographies and the Politics of Place.* Bloomington: Indiana University Press.

Million, Dian. 2013. *Therapeutic Nations: Healing in an Age of Indigenous Human Rights.* Tucson: University of Arizona Press.

Moraga, Cherrie, and Gloria Anzaldúa. 1983. *This Bridge Called My Back: Writings by Radical Women of Color.* New York: Kitchen Table / Women of Color Press.

Moreton-Robinson, Aileen. 2015. *The White Possessive.* Minneapolis: University of Minnesota Press.

Mountz, Alison, Anne Bonds, Becky Mansfield, Jenna Loyd, Jennifer Hyndman, Margaret Walton-Roberts, Ranu Basu, Risa Whitson, Roberta Hawkins, Trina Hamilton, and Winifred Curran. 2015. "For Slow Scholarship: A Feminist Politics of Resistance through Collective Action in the Neoliberal University." *ACME* 15(4): 1235–1259.

Park, K-Sue. 2021. "Race, Innovation and Financial Growth: The Example of Foreclosure." In Justin Leroy and Destin Jenkins (Eds.), *Histories of Racial Capitalism,* 27–51. New York: Columbia University Press.

Pulido, Laura. 2018. "Geographies of Race and Ethnicity III: Settler Colonialism and Nonnative People of Color." *Progress in Human Geography* 42(2): 309–318.

Pulido, Laura, and Juan De Lara. 2018. "Reimagining 'Justice' in Environmental Justice: Radical Ecologies, Decolonial Thought, and the Black Radical Tradition." *Environment and Planning E: Nature and Space* 1(1–2): 76–98.

Ranganathan, Malini. 2016. "Thinking with Flint: Racial Liberalism and the Roots of an American Water Tragedy." *Capitalism Nature Socialism* 27(3): 17–33.

Robinson, Cedric. 1983. *Black Marxism: The Making of the Black Radical Tradition.* London: Zed Press.

Roy, Ananya. 2003. "Paradigms of Propertied Citizenship: Transnational Techniques of Analysis." *Urban Affairs Review* 38(4): 463–491.

———. 2017. "Dis/Possessive Collectivism: Property and Personhood at City's End." *Geoforum* 80: A1–A11.

Roy, Ananya, and Emma Shaw Crane. 2015. *Territories of Poverty.* Athens: University of Georgia Press.

Sangtin Writers and Richa Nagar. 2006. *Playing with Fire: Feminist Thought and Activism through Seven Lives in India.* Minneapolis: University of Minnesota Press.

Simpson, Audra. 2014. *Mohawk Interruptus.* Durham, N.C.: Duke University Press.

Simpson, Leanne Betasamosake. 2016. "Indigenous Resurgence and Co-resistance." *Critical Ethnic Studies* 2(2): 19–34.

———. 2017. *As We Have Always Done: Indigenous Freedom through Radical Resistance.* Minneapolis: University of Minnesota Press.

Spade, Dean. 2006. "Compliance Is Gendered: Struggling for Self-Determination in a Hostile Economy." In Paisley Currah, Richard Juang, and Shannon Minter (Eds.),

Transgender Rights: History, Politics and Law, 217–241. Minneapolis: University of Minnesota Press.

Trouillot, Michel-Rolph. 1991. "Anthropology and the Savage Slot: The Poetics and Politics of Otherness." In Richard Fox (Ed.), *Recapturing Anthropology: Working in the Present*, 17–44. Santa Fe, N. Mex.: School of American Research Press.

Tuck, Eve, and K. Wayne Yang. 2012. "Decolonization Is Not a Metaphor." *Indigeneity, Education & Society* 1(1): 1–40.

Valencia, Yolanda. 2019. "Inmigrante Indocumentado: Transnational Communities of Thriving in the Midst of Racial Structural Inequalities." PhD dissertation, University of Washington.

Walia, Harsha. 2013. "Transient Servitude: Migrant Labour in Canada and the Apartheid of Citizenship." *Race & Class* 52(1): 71–84.

West, Cornel. 2020. "Cornel West Explains the Protests." Video excerpt published by Bernie Sanders. www.youtube.com/watch?v=WTJLsAgOlko.

Woods, Clyde. 1998. *Development Arrested: The Blues and Plantation Power in the Mississippi Delta*. London: Verso.

Woods, Clyde, Jordan Camp, and Laura Pulido (Eds.) 2017. *Development Drowned and Reborn: The Blues and Bourbon Restorations in Post-Katrina New Orleans*. Athens: University of Georgia Press.

Wynter, Sylvia. 2003. "Unsettling the Coloniality of Being/Power/Truth/Freedom: Towards the Human, After Man, Its Overrepresentation—An Argument." *CR: The New Centennial Review* 3(3): 257–337.

Ybarra, Megan. 2017. *Green Wars: Conservation and Decolonization in the Maya Forest*. Oakland: University of California Press.

CHAPTER 1

Of Promise and Problem

The Poverty Politics of Recognition,
Race, and Community in Tulsa, Oklahoma

ANA P. GUTIÉRREZ GARZA AND JOVAN SCOTT LEWIS

I always tell my husband that we are an example of what can be achieved
through hard work and sacrifice. Things do not come easy.
—Rosa from Guanajuato

The hardship of racial poverty experienced by communities of Mexican migrants and poor African Americans in Tulsa, Oklahoma, is underwritten by
social relations, cultural practices, and political structures that make up an uneven and unequal economic topography. This chapter explores the quality of
that topography, which in Tulsa is marked by the increasing relinquishing of
state services to nonprofit organizations. Tulsa's unique social program landscape offers a detailed view of the ambivalences and contradictions inherent
in state social services scaling down. The result is the mobilization of politicized and institutionalized ideas of the community simultaneously organized
around ethical practices of care that include the simultaneous incorporation
and exclusion of people who seek help from nonprofit organizations. To understand the ambiguous and contradictory role of care, we join scholarship in
human geography and anthropology that questions the relevance of care in the
face of welfare and state entrenchment (Lawson 2007; White 2000; Milligan
and Wiles 2010; Staeheli and Lawson 2005; Gutiérrez Garza 2022; Wilde 2022;
Koch and James 2022). This framework allows us to contextualize the impact
that nonprofit organizations have in the lives of both communities. Moreover,
it enables us to understand how the imaginaries of the deserving and merited
community are configured through the values and practices of self-reliance.
Our case study establishes a dialogue with the book's aim to contest liberal
notions of poverty that rest on ontological and political claims of individualism, meritocracy, and white supremacy. In that vein, this chapter considers
the production of deserving neoliberal subjects and communities through the

production and control of racialized difference. We show how the focus on self-reliance echoes the state's notions of liberal subjects responsible for their poverty. Therefore, we must find resources and engage in self-fashioning practices to change the subjects' own social and economic circumstances (Harvey 2005; Larner 2003; Gilbert 2002; Wacquant 2012).[1]

This chapter offers a comparative examination of the constricted economic and social articulations of the historical and everyday assemblages of race, gender, and inequality, which are the intersectional lived inequalities and disparities these communities navigate, as embedded in the economic experiences of these communities. This comparative and critical ethnic study examines the state's politics and policies as the background against which interethnic relations are set, measured, and framed. Set within racialized forms of personhood that maintain these communities, we examine communities' subordination to various forms of social control and dispossession. Furthermore, the relationship between African American and Latin American communities demonstrates a complex negotiation of solidarity and discord and generally of the politics of mutual mis/recognition. This chapter presents the difficulties and complications of community formation and relations. It focuses on how these poor communities generate coping strategies through respective displays of value to secure their engagement with the interventions of nonstate organizations and other aid programs concerned with alleviating poverty.

We explore how racialized and impoverished subjects deal with the denial of social personhood. We do so through the comparative analysis of personal narratives and life stories from the respective vantage point of Mexican migrants and African American people in Tulsa through social valuations of care regimes toward family and children. Our analytical framework considers the question of whether these two groups navigate and engage with different institutions/programs, with a particular interest in their experience with and perceptions of early education programs. In examining these experiences and practices, we show how aspirational paradigms that emerge from both the personal and community narratives of progress and within the policy discourses of the organizations complicate these communities' perceptions of themselves and each other. Ultimately these discourses and paradigms, we argue, qualify these communities as sites of possibilities to become the right type of parent or citizen or become a problem for the state within a neoliberal logic.

Our discussion presents differentially racialized poverty and its resulting hardships as mediated through these spaces and their concomitant ideologies, rules, and expectations, constructing concrete ideas and imaginaries of both communities. Understanding the quality of that experience and the positionalities that it produced takes an analysis of the assemblages of economic hardship. For each community, this assemblage comprises the histories of their emplacement in Tulsa, alongside the city's history, the formation and function of their respective senses of community, and their incorporation into the local political economy. Taken together, these qualify as notions of race and ethnicity that operate, struggle even, within the constricted economic and social structures of everyday life in Tulsa. Therefore, this discussion presents the challenges of navigating the conditions of poverty within and against the interventions of state agencies and other aid programs concerned with alleviating poverty.

Our research is based on fieldwork in Tulsa among Mexican and African American women who participated in the early education program Educare. We collected the life stories of fifty women and used semistructured interviews to gather data on care arrangements and forms of cooperation around child care. Our interviews investigated emic notions of care and well-being of children, good parenthood, and notions of success (social and economic). We developed the analysis by comparing the data gathered through the interviews and our personal experiences in the field. We both worked with and interviewed women actively participating in these early education programs and hence were involved in the various programs that the state and nonprofits have to alleviate poverty and create self-reliant individuals. Most of our interlocutors worked as community lay advisors, called Promotoras, at the Center for Family Resilience in the Department of Human Development and Family Science at Oklahoma State University, a center funded by the George Kaiser Foundation (founders of Educare).[2]

During our conversations, it became clear that despite the differences between these two communities women had similar ideas about their roles as mothers and, more importantly, what they had to do to fit the model of the deserving liberal subjects. At the same time, during our conversations, it became evident that regardless of women's efforts to become a particular type of mother (typified by the white American middle class), their racialized and gendered subjectivities deeply marked their successes or failures. Furthermore, our own racial (Black and Mexican) and gendered positionalities informed how our fieldwork analyses developed. The narratives and quotes we selected for our chapter are from the interviews; therefore, the reader will find sections written in the first person and the third. This chapter discusses two distinct stories of two communities that have been subjected to forms of social control that correspond to their racial and class identities. These identities, however, do not exist in isolation; they play a fundamental role in the much-needed imaginary of the American poor.

Historical Incorporation

Oklahoma gained statehood in 1907 after acquiring Indian Territory land through agreements that reversed the already-compromised terms of sovereignty arising from Indian Removal in the 1830s. The first African Americans arrived in what would become Oklahoma as Freedmen members and the slaves of the Five Civilized Tribes that made their way west along the Trail of Tears. In the 1890s, a second wave followed the short-lived promise of a land free of Jim Crow. By the time Mexicans began migrating to Oklahoma in 1910, the state had a crop of all-Black towns and the Greenwood District of Tulsa, home to a thriving commercial community of Blacks, had earned the moniker of Negro Wall Street. The Mexicans arrived via the Bracero Program to fulfill the great demand for labor in burgeoning industries in the Southwest (coal mines, cotton fields, meatpacking plants, oil fields and quarries, and railroads). The 1920s saw challenges that impacted both communities.

In 1921 the African American community suffered the Tulsa Race Massacre, which saw white mobs raze Greenwood. Despite negligence on the part of local authorities and the National Guard to protect Greenwood's residents or to stem the violence on the part of its white citizens, the millions of dollars in property damage, and the hundreds of lives lost, these residents were never compensated, leaving the burden to rebuild to the decimated community. In 1929, with the onset of the Depression, the government implemented campaigns to deport, intimidate, and "voluntarily repatriate" Mexican migrants. The intent of this repatriation, according to Balderrama and Rodriguez, was threefold: "to return indigent nationals to their own country, in this case, Mexico; to save welfare agencies money; and to create jobs for real Americans" (2006, 104), narratives that still resonate in current immigration policies throughout the country. During labor shortages resulting from World War II, Mexican migrants were brought back to Oklahoma to work on the railroads, in cotton fields, and in other industries under the Bracero Program. However, the continuing demand for agricultural and unskilled labor continued to pull many unauthorized workers.

The 1960s witnessed the arrival of Mexican Americans who moved to Oklahoma from agricultural jobs in the valley of Texas in search of more stable, year-round employment. The numbers of Mexican-born residents of Oklahoma grew by 1980, even when the economic crisis pushed many native-born Oklahomans out of the state. By 1986 more than twenty thousand unauthorized residents of Oklahoma legalized their status following the Immigration Reform and Control Act (IRCA). Although IRCA succeeded in legalizing and bringing out of the shadows thousands of immigrants, the Hispanic population in Oklahoma remained relatively invisible since they were interspersed throughout neighborhoods in various cities and remained isolated from the native population by language barriers. From midcentury through the early 1990s, the now predominantly Black area of North Tulsa, with Greenwood serving as the southern border, saw a series of devaluations and dispossessions through urban renewal. The construction of Tulsa's highway system bifurcated neighborhoods, causing social and economic destabilization and starting a pattern of deepening impoverishment that continues today.

After 9/11, state senators established tighter border controls, bringing more U.S. Immigration and Customs Enforcement agents to the state, and allowed local law enforcement agencies to get involved and have authority to enforce federal immigration laws. New regulations were put in place, and the passage of HB 1804 barred unauthorized migrants from receiving public assistance. Although HB 1804 mirrored existing federal law provisions, it created a sense of heightened vigilance, suspicion, and intolerance among private citizens, public employees, business owners, and officers.

These histories of dispossession and exploitation show how racialized communities, when factored into the calculation of neoliberal capitalism facilitated by policies at all levels, are produced as "kinds" of people. In this case, the "illegal" Mexican migrants and "poor" African Americans become signifiers or various forms of deviance. As De Genova and Roy have argued, Mexican migrants "have been rendered effectively synonymous with migrant 'illegality,' to the point that this dubious distinction has become a constitutive feature of the racialization of Mexicanness within the U.S. racial order" (2020, 353). This notion of illegality creates a need, an unabated desire, to become incorporated. The result is these communities subscribing to external qualifications of deservingness and value that resonate within neoliberal models of white middle-class Americanness. When thinking comparatively between Tulsa's African American and Mexican communities, these ideas are complicated and sometimes contradictory but follow the same desire to move past their structurally relegated positions.

A Cycle of Hurt

This structural displacement is illustrated by the story of Shantel, an African American single mother of three young children. She worked hard to support them alongside paying her way through Tulsa Community College. She feared that the challenges her mother faced, and her mother before her, had already fallen to her. It was only a matter of time before her children, especially her two daughters, would see the same fate. This intergenerational anxiety was colored by the fear that one could not outrun their past. While Shantel fought to stave off what she thought was inevitable, Keisha had already fallen victim to it. Keisha's mother had been imprisoned, which is unsurprising given that Oklahoma has the second highest state percentage of incarcerated women. At twenty-one, Keisha, the mother of two toddlers, now found herself faced with the prospect of also caring for her two younger sisters. After several months of looking after four children on her own—her father and her daughter's father were also serving time in prison—Keisha had a mental breakdown. Less than a year later, she suffered another. As a result, Keisha spent six months in a mental health facility. Thankfully, a friend was willing to take in her daughters but could not care for her younger sisters, whom Keisha had no choice but to give to foster care. In one of our conversations, Keisha shared the difficulty of the decision: "It really hit me. Because I had my little sisters for over a year, and foster care told me I either need to adopt them or put them in the system, the pressure was on, and I didn't have anybody to call, and I was like 'I don't know what to do!'"

Keisha's mental break and Shantel's fear of the same or worse directly result from how poverty and the inequalities that induce it impact the lives of so many women of color. These are adversities that cause the extreme stress of their circumstances. Anxieties like these can be seen as the unfortunate symptoms of intergenerational poverty—the reproduction of overall systemic, but primarily economic, vulnerability and instability. The markers of this intergenerational and systemic condemnation show up in premature births, lower quality education, and health care. Education and employment then pose complex propositions: how does one do better when one literally cannot afford to do so?

Stories of dispossession and structural inequality back in Mexico mark the migrant personhood of Hispanics and their eventual racial locations in Tulsa. For instance, Claudia arrived in Oklahoma twenty years ago with a suitcase and her six-year-old child. "I came to the U.S. because I needed to get away from my violent husband. After years of being abused, I decided that if I wanted to live, I needed to escape. I owe it to myself, but mostly to my daughter." She did not know anyone but found people at the local Catholic church who helped her find a cleaning job, housing, and schooling for her child. Her daughter grew up in Tulsa, and although she did not have any documents, she had become part of the DREAMers movement and was planning to go to college. However, at sixteen she became pregnant by a man who turned out to be a violent drug dealer. The story, according to Claudia, was repeating itself. "It was like starting all over again." This time, however, she needed to protect her daughter and her grandchild from the father. With minimal resources due to their undocumented status, Claudia found a second cleaning job at night and helped her daughter care for the baby. Her main concern at this point in her life was to remain invisible to avoid *la migra* and get deported. "Getting separated from my family would really be the end of this American dream that I am still dreaming," she told me while we sat at her kitchen table and drank coffee.

For forty-three-year-old Carmen, who lived in the rural area of Zacatecas, Mexico, and struggled to live off the land, migrating to California with her husband and four children in the late 1990s was the solution to their economic problems. The lack of support from the state and the structural poverty in which rural families, like Carmen's, live in Mexico have pushed thousands of migrants to search for better opportunities in the United States. They crossed the border through the hills with the help of a coyote and started their new lives in California. After ten years of living there and realizing that the family was fractured due to the two sons' involvement in gangs and drug dealing, Carmen and her husband decided to move to Tulsa, where they had family and where jobs were vast and housing affordable and, most importantly, where her sons could have a second chance. She told me the story of her journey to the United States while sitting in her house eating quesadillas and drinking Coca-Cola. She has just returned from her cleaning job at a hotel, and although she was tired, she enjoyed sharing her life story with me.

> Moving to Oklahoma represented the hope that I needed to save my sons from prison and drug addictions. We believed that starting all over again would help them recovering and would help us as a family. Unfortunately, it did not work; they both ended up in prison for a few years in Oklahoma before they were deported back to Mexico. It was my fault; I left them alone when they were kids back in California because I had to work all day and sometimes nights as well. I did not pay enough attention to them; I had no choice; it was either support them and bring food to the table or like in Mexico, die of hunger.

What do these stories tell us about structural poverty? What do these women have in common? The stories presented here illustrate the cycle of hurt in which poor women from Mexico and African American women from Tulsa find themselves trapped. Generational suffering and the experience of the stigma of failure reveal the conditions of structural poverty. Failure is compounded by perceptions of motherhood that are intimately linked to social reproductive roles. Within their families, these women are the primary carers and are responsible for the social outcomes for their children. When they desire for their kids to "turn out right," they seek more than their children simply becoming good people. However, these women's poverty, intertwined with their racial and class identities and their position vis-à-vis whiteness, meaningfully impact their chances to secure ideal futures for their children. These conditions of structural discrimination and an overall permanent precarity inevitably create a sense of an almost cultural ineptitude and incapacity to improve despite their efforts. In this regard, it is through the figure of the mother as the bearer of moral values and the person who holds the key to the family's success, particularly the children, that we must understand the cycles of poverty and dispossession. Poverty circumscribes these women's lives at economic, social, and emotional levels, and as a result, it becomes impossible to surmount.

Aspiration and Deservingness

How do people living in a constant state of dispossession and precarity manage to navigate a system that pigeonholed them as being unfit? In this section, we illustrate what the subscription to external notions of value and deservingness looks like in the lives of Mexican migrants and African Americans. The first time I visited Jennifer's house, I realized how extremely clean and nicely decorated it was. There were framed studio family photos in the living room, two big sofas, a dining table for eight people, a huge television, and a piece of furniture with shelves where the family keeps the crockery and other family photos. She was twenty-four years old and migrated to California with her parents and two brothers eighteen years before. Originally from the State of Mexico, the family followed the grandfather and the father, who had crossed the border more than twenty years ago. Rosalia, the mother, crossed the border with her sister Amelia and six children between them. After paying thousands of dollars to a coyote, they successfully crossed the border through the desert in two days. Like other migrants, they came to Tulsa ten years earlier after struggling in California with unaffordable and dreadful housing and unemployment. Oklahoma was a second migration destination that offered good opportunities in terms of jobs (construction, roofing, factory work, and service-sector jobs) and, more importantly, affordable housing.

Migrant families in Tulsa, in contrast to California, could afford to rent or even buy two- to three-bedroom houses where they could live without sharing rooms with strangers. For most, purchasing a home represents the American dream and the possibility to break the cycle of poverty—structured along racial lines—in which they grew up back in Mexico. The American dream is also shaped by the possibility of speaking English, having a car, getting a free education for children, and consuming goods they cannot get back home (Mahler 1995; De Genova 2002, 2005; Menjívar 2000, 2006).

The view for people like Jennifer is that Mexico hinders people's opportunities to improve despite their efforts and hard work (particularly for Brown people), while the United States offers opportunities to those self-made subjects who are willing to work hard, to make the right sacrifices, and, in a self-fashioning type of way, to become new (neoliberal) subjects. "I always tell my husband that we are an example of what can be achieved through hard work and sacrifice. Things do not come easy, so when you see people who have a nice car or a house, it is probably because they are hard workers," Rosa, from Guanajuato, told me during our interview while pointing at the *troika* (the pickup truck) that her husband recently bought.

These notions resonate with liberal ideas that frame poverty as an individual failure based on an almost intrinsic weakness of character that gets in the way and disallows certain people to achieve their dreams and overcome dispossession and inequality. Though migrants are aware of the structural social and economic conditions that restrict people's progress in Mexico, the way they talk about poverty reflects those liberal notions of personal failure. This ideology is supported by the figures that they embody in the United States. On the one hand, they are perceived as hardworking people capable of sustaining forms of manual labor unwanted by most and as people who are willing to make enormous sacrifices for their families. Even among the most conservative circles, their recognized and added value is erected upon their labor, upon their capacity to be docile and malleable subjects. This image has become part of their self-identity and becomes relevant when migrants compare themselves to other racialized communities in Tulsa. For instance, according to Mexican migrants, the poverty that characterizes African Americans and Native Americans has to do with their reliance on welfare versus developing an ethic of hard work and their inability to release their painful pasts marked by colonialism and the violence of slavery. "Ana, these *morenos* [referring to African Americans] have suffered, I know, but they need to get over it and stop being so comfortable with the help that they get from the government, otherwise they will never succeed," Rosa explained to me. As Lisa Marie Cacho notes, "Claiming deservingness through demonstrating respectability assumes that we can make a clear distinction between people of color who are criminal and people of color who are respectable, but this distinction is far from being fixed or stable" (2012, 119).

In this regard, some Mexicans aspire toward this notion of respectability as economic success through an "ethic" of hard labor. Still, hard work has paid small dividends in respectability or opportunities for many African American working poor in North Tulsa, whose landscape is surprisingly vacant of public life. The best chance to see public social life in the Black community of North Tulsa is on a Sunday after church. "Everyone goes to church, and I mean everybody," shared Shameca Brown, who works as a community lay advisor at the Center for Family Resilience at OSU–Tulsa. At Metropolitan Baptist, Shameca's claim seems substantiated. The people whom I meet seemed "respectable" in every sense. Speaking with members of the congregation and many other residents in North Tulsa, it became clear that the issue of deserving was no longer a question that they asked themselves. Instead, they were fixed upon the recognition of their denial.

So while there is a notion that depicts the migrant person as an usurper who deprives citizens of their fundamental rights and resources, it leaves open the question of what kind of figure the working poor African American represents. Regardless of the achievements and efforts of either community to make themselves into deserving subjects, they remain a marginalized community and, in their respective ways, disposable or deportable, but fundamentally disposable. Such figuration has its origins in the intersections of history with the political economy of the U.S. nation-state and its need for cheap and disposable labor across time. Despite the multiple changes to immigration law and the welfare system's modifications, a deep-rooted and immutable condition embodies the figure of the Mexican migrant and the poor African American constructed through a draconian production of laws and regulations. These regulations allow or deny access and processes of equal incorporation that can be exploited while simultaneously extending the promise of opportunity.

Landscape of Help

Within the circumstances of precarious emplacement, the poverty experienced by each group has come to define their very existence. Despite existing in Oklahoma for over a century, mobility out of this position is difficult because the economies in which these groups navigate and seek opportunities are at times tenuously constructed. That construction is defined by casual, often illegal, and sometimes even dangerous work. The framework of inequality that secures these opportunities limits expectations of success. In the case of Mexican migrants, this mobility is also underpinned by the lived experience of "illegality" and, for African Americans, "criminality." Where the economy fails these groups, an arrangement of agencies and organizations organized around the state, church, and nonprofit sector seeks not only to mitigate the poverty endemic to these communities but also to control, manage, and turn people into respectable neoliberal subjects. These subjectivities exist in parallel because of the criminalization that both communities regularly experience. Criminalization defines some as "deviant" and in doing so separates them from those normalized as "needy" in these communities. These interventions articulate the notions of deserving and merit and work to propagate the idea people must "work" to earn their support. Additionally, these institutions, rather than fully recognizing the structural issues of neglect and exploitation that have caused these communities' circumstances, instead locate their challenges in their failure to succeed in the spheres of education and parenting. Others, particularly church organizations, identify their specialisms around health care issues for the poorest and least able.

Many of these projects and programs are funded by organizations that, with vast wealth originating from oil and banking industries in Tulsa, can produce societal outcomes based on their ideations and the personally held philosophies and principles of foundation benefactors. Tulsa's billionaires, like George Kaiser, whose wealth derives from oil and banking, and the Schusterman and Zarrow families, both from Tulsa, have dedicated much of their fortunes to philanthropic projects intended to fill the gaps created by long-standing state budget cuts. According to funders, philanthropy in Oklahoma is used as a resource to alleviate poverty and inequality. Still, that alleviation structures the frameworks of success and progress rooted in their inherently white, upper-middle-class, and often liberal philosophical backgrounds. These families' philanthropic foundations have covered services ranging from education to health care and public parks. Hundreds of millions of dollars stream from private donors to fill the service gaps but do not manage to replace equitable service distribution provided by the state.

For instance, the Charles and Lynn Schusterman Family Philanthropies focuses on preventing, intervening, and treating child abuse and neglect in Israel and Tulsa. They are involved in reforming Tulsa's public education system and provide development opportunities for teens and professional development for teachers through various coaching and mentoring programs. Similarly, the Anne & Henry Zarrow Foundation targets poverty by supporting housing and shelter resources, social services, and mental health and indigent health care initiatives. The initiatives of the George Kaiser Family Foundation include criminal justice reform, programs for women in recovery after incarceration, community health projects, and Tulsa Educare, a pre-K program partly subsidized with federal Head Start grants. Our research worked with families who were recipients of the Educare program funded by the Kaiser Foundation. According to the foundation, Educare is a "research-based program with a foundation in the best of early childhood practices that ensure school readiness of children most at risk for school failure." The program involves a partnership between private philanthropists, Head Start /Early Head Start, Tulsa Public School officials, and community partners dedicated to narrowing children's achievement gap in their communities. These organizations form a social welfare system that resembles a practice of aid that recalls the efforts of foreign actors in developing countries.

One entry point into this matter is our work with poor mothers who have enrolled their children in early childhood intervention school programs. Through partnerships between philanthropists and the local Tulsa government, these programs, modeled on Head Start / Early Head Start, seek to narrow the achievement gap for children in their communities. They do it through a curriculum that develops school readiness to prepare students to learn on par with their middle-class peers when they start kindergarten. Opportunities like these early childhood intervention programs do much to secure as great a chance as any for eventual mobility for their students (Gormley et al. 2011; Lowenstein 2009). However, the problem that we began to address is that despite those demands and limited resources, these programs often insist upon intense family engagement due to their design based on middle-class models of intensive forms of parenthood. Here is where a disconnect occurred for the mothers who worked with us. One of the requirements under this family engagement regime is the Parent as Teacher (PAT) program. This program is a voluntary parent education and family support program for families who have children from birth to three years of age. Parents are supported by PAT-certified parent educators who know about child development and early learning. The program aims to "capture teachable moments in everyday life to enhance their child's language development, intellectual growth, social development, and motor skills."[3] Most importantly, this program is inspired by philanthropy's tackling poverty strategies characterized by participatory approaches in the interests of helping people to help themselves and by managerialism inspired by the "will to improve" (Li 2007).

For the Mexican community, the help offered by these programs represents the only gateway to, first, justify their dangerous and complicated journeys to America and, second, achieve respectability despite their collective identifications as racialized and disposable migrants. Participation in these projects is inextricably linked to the migration goal of *ser alguien en la vida* ("to become someone in life"), a dream that can be achieved only in the United States. Becoming someone in life, or what can be put as turning out well, was explained to us as a combination of a good education at home and school and self-reliance. Within this triad, mothers are at the center of making moral persons of their children by providing care at home and by transmitting good moral values such as respect for others, honesty, and becoming good people free of vices. These, according to Mexican mothers in Tulsa, are aspects that will help their children becoming self-reliant individuals who will achieve their personal best. Turning out well entails finding better opportunities through hard work and good education in the United States.[4] When asking about the expectations for the future of their children, Elena looked at her six-year-old girl who was playing with a stuffed animal on the floor of the caravan house and told me, "I see her [daughter] graduating from university with a good job and money. I do not see her as a millionaire but earning enough money to live a comfortable life. I see her breaking the poverty chain (*romper la cadena*) that has circumscribed the lives of my ancestors and my own back in Mexico. I want her to think that the priority is not to work but to study so she can earn a title and then work." Prioritizing education over money entails the acquisition of social and cultural capital that these Mexican migrants have never had within their families back in Mexico. A lack of education is seen to lead to poverty and the possibility of making harmful choices, like marrying too young, getting pregnant, or becoming friends with the wrong people. The rationale behind breaking the poverty chain is much more social than economic, much more racialized along the lines of a middle-class white lifestyle that could provide stability, success, and security.

For the Black community in North Tulsa, given the particularly complicated history inherited from the demise of Greenwood's famed Black Wall Street, the question is if these programs are developing a community on its own terms. Unlike members of the Mexican community, who recognize the complicated process of *becoming* American, African Americans have a particular challenge. As such, they have too long been beholden to narratives not of their own making. Instead, they have worked according to the schemata developed by others seeking to dictate the terms of their existence. And so with these programs they fall yet again into the discursive bind of Blackness where suffering and struggle predominate. These terms are the definitive bases upon which Blackness in North Tulsa is formed and must operate. In this context, Black communities are condemned to the qualification of needing improvement. This qualification, in turn, reifies the notion of Blackness as a deviant mode of existence. Thinking back to Shantel, we see her anxiety rooted in a desire to escape this very fact. With the two antecedent generations before her having lived the stigma of failure, with her odds increasingly long, she aspired to break the cycle of her poverty becoming an intergenerational inheritance. Still, she found it impossible to free herself from the stigma and the drawbacks attached to her racialized subjectivity.

There are several practices that these social programs require from these communities, such as training, empowerment, and capacity building. These are perceived as unquestionably "good," in terms of both their assumed effectiveness and the moralities they imply. However, perhaps unsurprisingly, the values and practices of self-reliance, especially at the community level, can often be at odds with development projects that despite their best intentions seem to never fail at relaying a message of ineptness or deficiency to those they seek to help. There are multiple ambivalences and contradictions inherent in such development initiatives. This point is made evident by the fact that very few provide any of the structures or services used or engaged by the middle class, many of whom serve as the workers in, and even models for, these initiatives. These initiatives reinforce the neoliberal scaling down of social services that are the state's responsibility (Staeheli and Brown 2003; Peck 2004; Katz 2001; Cope 2001).

The Challenge of Progress

For African American mothers, the basis of the PAT program and others like it is identifying a deficiency. The deficiency is first located in the child. As in the case of the word gap model by which lower-class children are identified as having significantly limited vocabulary compared to their middle-class peers, this deficiency is seen not only as an issue with their abilities but effectively as a function of the parents' incapacity to adequately teach, to parent, to *mother*. As a result, parents are given teaching tools and are encouraged to model "good" behavior. The training is usually done in visitation sessions, carried out by a group of mothers previously trained at the Center for Family Resilience at OSU. The center organized program facilitators into two groups, one dedicated to working with African American women and the other focused on Mexican/Hispanic migrants.[5] These women, called Promoters or Promotoras, visited women from both communities weekly, offering training in children's health, development, and early education. They were also in charge of monitoring and screening mothers' work with their children and disciplining them when necessary. Shameca explained that one of the lessons included parenting suggestions such as "labeling your own feelings in difficult situations," which was done by telling the child, "I feel so mad. I am going to go take some deep breaths in the other room to get myself under control." And even when waiting in lines, parents should not cut, to teach the child how they would want them to respond in a similar situation. For the African American mothers, prescriptions like these were laughable at best and outright patronizing at worst. While the ability to take part in a variety of social programs and to reap their benefits meant accommodating these prescriptions and being "trained" accordingly, the ideas of progress, aid, and development as incorporated and circulated by these programs did not sync up with the ideals and expectations of the African American mothers in the program. These programs, rather than taking the ideas of these women's intersectional positions seriously, flattened them to one-dimensional adjectival qualifications of poor, Black, mother.

Instead of fully appreciating "how profoundly race and racism shape the modern idea of the human," these programs resist both the complexity but also histories of what have created their circumstances, overlooking the "essential role that racialized and racializing assemblages play in the construction of modern selfhood" (Weheliye 2014, 4). Moreover, these organizations and agencies ignoring these histories fail to recognize that any intervention into poverty must hold them at the core of their programs' conceptualization, inception, and application.

For Mexican mothers, these prescriptions were necessary prerequisites to gain membership into a social group and a society that will enhance their children's opportunities in the future. For instance, among the Mexican Promotoras who oversaw training, it was essential to convince mothers that children needed to be sent to Educare (or other early education programs) from an early age, even though most mothers believed that babies and toddlers should remain under the care of their mothers or other family members (like siblings or grandmothers). "No one will love and take care of my baby as I do. It breaks my heart to think about sending my baby to school at an early age," Susana from Mexico comments.

Similarly, Sara explains that "Promotoras say that if I want my child to have better opportunities in this country, I have to send him to Educare as soon as possible because they will teach him and will teach me how to exploit his full potential. I came to this country to provide a better future for my children. I know I have to adapt and change for them; it is just very different from the way we were raised and the way we raise our kids in Mexico." For Mexican women, becoming a mother isolated from kinship networks that help raise children is not the ideal way to care for children. The presence of a community of care is considered pivotal in making up good people. When the opposite happens, and mothers are isolated from such networks of care, it is seen as a negative consequence of migration due to a lack of a network in the new place. For these mothers, being told by these programs that children need to be sent to school at an early age *and* that mothers must also become teachers at home seems contradictory. Nevertheless, women's ideas and imaginations of these programs advertise ideals related to the American dream and becoming American. This category is imagined and explained as becoming closer to a family model, which implies white and middle class.

Again, for the African American participants, theirs is not a narrative of becoming American and therefore incorporated into the normative sense of citizenship, articulated as their community being full of promise for Mexican immigrants. No, for African Americans, their existence is an aberrant form of incorporation, and so rather than the promise of incorporation, they are presented as a problem. This framework is unsurprising given that Mexican culture valorizes whiteness as intertwined with assumptions of upward mobility, cultural refinement, and an accomplishment.[6] This is a consequence of a national racial order in Mexico that has historically pushed for a nation built on an idea of mixture (*mestizaje*) in which whiteness is at the top of the racial pyramid and has been preserved as a symbol of distinction and social improvement (Wade 2001, 2005, 2010; Goldberg 2009; Moreno Figueroa 2010; Moreno Figueroa and Tanaka 2016). However, not everyone can self-fashion themselves into these ideal middle-class "white" Americans. In this regard, some Mexican mothers would talk about and emphasize the difference between them and other Mexicans and Hispanics. Poor Brown Mexicans who have been incorporated into Mexico's liberal order as racialized and impoverished subjects, once in Tulsa, reproduce differences and forms of subordination between them and other poor subjects as part of their strategies to achieve full personhood. The attempts to define boundaries prove futile as the liberal order in the United States relies on this community's exclusion and subordination. Still, efforts to become American, to "civilize" themselves and get rid of the *Indito* (Indigenous), hence the Brownness, become part of the new habitus they need to construct and secure belonging in the United States. "As you have seen, most of the people here are from Mexico, but they come from rural Mexico, so they do not have education, they don't speak English, and more importantly, they do not even speak proper Spanish. It is very difficult to convince them that their children need proper time and education. It is hard to get them involved and educate them. Culture gets in the way," Sara said during the interview.

According to some mothers, "culture" gets in the way by creating obstacles for migrants to become more American, whiten themselves, and become "better" people. The so-called culture has important ethnic, racial, and class implications that reflect the racial and class structure that subsists in Mexico (and various countries of Latin America), where white middle-class identifications and aspirations are given primacy at the top of the racial pyramid. Regardless of people's efforts to become less Mexican, to perform being American, their racial indexes and identifications maintain them in constricted economic and social spaces embedded in a structural inequality characterized by racial systems of social control crosscut by the legal production of illegality (Boehm 2012; Chavez 2008; Coutin 2005; Menjívar and Kanstroom 2014; Gutiérrez Garza 2018). Some of the strategies that Mexican communities use to fight against such valuations arise from their active participation in early education programs like Educare. Because migrants' aspirations revolve around the future success of their children or their possibilities to succeed, programs that promise the alleviation of poverty through the teaching of strategies of liberal self-fashioning are quite successful. More importantly, considering that the Mexican women interviewed had staggeringly low levels of education (the average being primary school), the prospects of improvement through schooling in the United States were regarded as crucial to their children's futures.

We could argue that the early education programs in Tulsa offer much-needed help for those mothers who, regardless of being employed full-time, are interested in improving their children's success rates from an early age. One fundamental feature of such programs is that their goals are to educate children and, as women explained, help them get ready for school and educate parents. Parents (particularly mothers) and children are in unison learning how to learn and how to teach; becoming a teacher is regarded as an ingredient for good parenting. The women who attend these programs must constantly reflect on their roles as mothers and as teachers to improve the lives and prospects of their children. Through these programs, children can learn how to be American, advance, and prepare for school. The process also involves monitoring the continuous efforts that parents must make to self-fashion new subjectivities as parents. The monitoring is done not only by the institutions and teachers but also by children who surveil and correct their parents. These modes of surveillance and control are necessary for the programs' social and financial success; however, at the same time, these programs reproduce the structural conditions that keep migrants' personhood invisible and understood as an inferior other.

It is essential to note the early role of caregiver that many impoverished people played as children, especially girls, to younger siblings. During fieldwork, we both encountered several cases in which the oldest daughters were in charge of their siblings' caring and education while mothers were at work. Structural conditions of inequality and poverty and the lack of state resources to help families in need challenge the educational and developmental model pushed by early education programs like Educare. In that model, the presence of mothers is fundamental in the making up of "good children." The practical reality of women who had to work part- or full-time to support the household constantly got in the way of achieving the personhood demanded by the programs, creating feelings of ineptitude and guilt. They find themselves trapped in the responsibility of not being the caring mothers they should be for their children and the guilt of not being good teachers helping in the development of their children. Particularly for African American parents with children at these schools, many felt the required practices were condescending and too similar to something they would encounter with the Department of Children and Family Services. These contradictions and incongruences might be assessed as being a problem of cultural relativity, but we think such a conclusion does not go far enough. Instead, work needs to be done in revealing the complex ethical-moral terrains in which such programs and policies are played out. Doing so will show how such programs are at odds with historically and culturally produced ethics of the raced poor by understanding their agency, rationalities, and moral orders of the factors that keep them poor.

The one-size-fits-all logic proves to be similarly problematic when working with racialized impoverished communities. When working within these contexts of poverty, such programs must strive to go beyond received notions of what is and is not "good," especially when that idea of good is coupled with the problematic preposition "for." Such programs must alter their logic from this abstract question: "How can we bring about the end of poverty?" This question grants an unending capacity and license to reproduce an ever-increasing scope and cycle of need, by continuing to ignore the deeper root causes of poverty (Scherz 2014, 140). This change cannot be made by simply critiquing the work of organizations and programs seeking to alleviate disparities as a middle-class imposition or explaining why such projects fail to work. Because in fact many of them *do* work, or at least inasmuch as they can provide metrics of impact (see Gormley 2008; Gormley et al. 2005; Garces, Thomas, and Currie 2002). To be sure, the reliance on statistical modeling obscures the intimate and daily challenges and traumas many programs' participants experience. Therefore, the issue is not qualifying the success that these programs have but assessing and questioning how the lack of an in-depth assessment of the needs, realities, and wants of the people they aim to assist reproduces a liberal order that depends upon the existence of those same poor people.

The Paradoxes of Liberal Incorporation

Envisaging how to better the lives of poor women requires enabling them to identify their challenges on their terms, creating sustainable change, and providing a collective partnership for social mobility rather than reproducing impermeable senses of immobility. Understanding the navigation of poverty at both the individual and community levels requires thinking about the hope and aspirations that drive the poor's lives. In Tulsa, the history of Black enfranchisement and self-determination during the era of Black Wall Street continues to shape the ideals and expectations for the quality of an aspired for life while simultaneously making painfully evident how the raced poor continue to face disenfranchisement and external dependency. Mexican migrants' aspirations of becoming successful and achieving the American dream are shaped by their racialized presence, targeted through legal regimes of deportation and thus erasure from the social landscape. Through attempting to better their lives, either through enrolling their children in programs like Educare or hustling to make a living by working several jobs, both communities have engaged in social practices and performances of deservingness to help them to insert themselves into educational programs that will break the poverty cycle and allow their children to attain full personhood. This chapter has provided a nuanced account of various structural positions in Tulsan society by examining the structuring notions of history, citizenship, and race. We see that the experience of poverty as a historically generated framing of community runs against this liberal order, here represented by the development frameworks of philanthropic organizations and nonprofits. The paradox is that this racialized and impoverished subject cannot be fully incorporated into the liberal order because the liberal order depends on subordination, control, and racialized difference.

NOTES

1. We understand this self-reliant subject in a Foucauldian sense by which an individual engages in "technologies of the self which permit individuals to effect their own means or with the help of others a certain number of operations on their own bodies and souls, thoughts, conduct, a way of being, so as to transform themselves in order to attain a certain state of happiness, purity, wisdom perfection or immortality" (Foucault 1988, 18).

2. The program was led by Dr. Joseph G. Grzywacz, the Kaiser Family Foundation Professor of Family Resilience.

3. The program is coordinated by various partners, including Head Start, the Community Action Project, Union Public Schools, and YMCA. Besides offering parents training, PAT also helps families link with other community services and providers as needed.

4. Considering that all of the Mexican women interviewed had staggeringly low levels of education (the average being primary school), the prospects of improving through schooling in the United States were regarded as a crucial factor in their children's futures.

5. Both of us worked in close relation with these women; they were the ones who gave us access to other women of both communities.

6. This racial identification with whiteness originates from a colonial history in which mestizaje, as a whitening process, became the foundation of the Mexican state. Mestizaje is not necessarily an ideology of mixed race but a mixture that entails a racial hierarchy whereby Indigenous and Black people would eventually disappear through the process of *blanqueamiento* (whitening) (Wade 2005, 2010; Goldberg 2009).

REFERENCES

Balderrama, Francisco E., and Raymond Rodriguez. 2006. *Decade of Betrayal: Mexican Repatriation in the 1930s.* Albuquerque: University of New Mexico Press.

Boehm, Deborah A. 2012. *Intimate Migrations: Gender, Family, and Illegality among Transnational Mexicans.* New York: New York University Press.

Cacho, Lisa Marie. 2012. *Social Death: Racialized Rightlessness and the Criminalization of the Unprotected.* New York: New York University Press.

Chavez, Leo R. 2008. *The Latino Threat: Constructing Immigrants, Citizens, and the Nation.* 2nd ed. Stanford, Calif.: Stanford University Press.

Cope, Meghan. 2001. "Between Welfare and Work: The Roles of Social Service Organizations in the Social Regulation of Labor Markets and the Regulation of the Poor." *Urban Geography* 22(5): 391–406.

Coutin, Susan Bibler. 2005. "Contesting Criminality Illegal Immigration and the Spatialization of Legality." *Theoretical Criminology* 9(1): 5–33.

De Genova, Nicolas. 2002. "Migrant 'Illegality' and Deportability in Everyday Life." *Annual Review of Anthropology* 31: 419–447.

———. 2005. *Working the Boundaries: Race, Space, and "Illegality" in Mexican Chicago.* Durham, N.C.: Duke University Press.

De Genova, Nicholas, and Ananya Roy. 2020. "Practices of Illegalization." *Antipode* 52 (2): 352–364.

Foucault, Michel. 1988. *Technologies of the Self: A Seminar with Michel Foucault.* London: Tavistock.

Garces, Eliana, Duncan Thomas, and Janet Currie. 2002. "Longer-Term Effects of Head Start." *American Economic Review* 92(4): 999–1012.

Gilbert, Neil. 2002. *The Transformation of the Welfare State.* Oxford: Oxford University Press.

Goldberg, Theo. 2009. *The Threat of Race: Reflections on Racial Neoliberalism.* Oxford: Wiley-Blackwell.

Gormley, William T. 2008. "The Effects of Oklahoma's Pre-K Program on Hispanic Children." *Social Science Quarterly* 89(4): 916–936.

Gormley, William T., Ted Gayer, Deborah Phillips, and Brittany Dawson. 2005. "The Effects of Universal Pre-K on Cognitive Development." *Developmental Psychology* 41(6): 872–884.

Gormley, William T., Jr., Deborah A. Phillips, Katie Newmark, Kate Welti, and Shirley Adelstein. 2011. "Social-Emotional Effects of Early Childhood Education Programs in Tulsa." *Child Development* 82(6): 2095–2109.

Gutiérrez Garza, Ana P. 2018. "The Temporality of Illegality: Experiences of Undocumented Latin American Migrants in London." *Focaal* 81: 86–98.

———. 2022. "'Te Lo Tienes Que Currar': Enacting an Ethics of Care in Times of Austerity." *Ethnos* 87(1): 116–132.

Harvey, David. 2005. *A Brief History of Neoliberalism.* Oxford: Oxford University Press.

Katz, Michael B. 2001. *The Price of Citizenship: Redefining the American Welfare State.* New York: Metropolitan Books.

Koch, Insa, and Deborah James. 2022. "The State of the Welfare State: Advice, Governance and Care in Settings of Austerity." *Ethnos* 87(1): 1–21.

Larner, Wendy. 2003. "Neoliberalism?" *Environment and Planning D: Society and Space* 21(5): 509–512.

Lawson, Victoria. 2007. "Geographies of Care and Responsibility." *Annals of the Association of American Geographers* 97(1): 1–11.

Li, Tania Murray. 2007. *The Will to Improve: Governmentality, Development, and the Practice of Politics.* Durham, N.C.: Duke University Press.

Lowenstein, Amy E. 2009. "Fostering the Socio-emotional Adjustment of Low-Income Children: The Effects of Universal Pre-Kindergarten and Head Start in Oklahoma." PhD dissertation, Georgetown University.

Mahler, Sarah J. 1995. *American Dreaming: Immigrant Life on the Margins.* Princeton, N.J.: Princeton University Press.

Menjívar, Cecilia. 2000. *Fragmented Ties: Salvadoran Immigrant Networks in America.* Berkeley: University of California Press.

———. 2006. "Liminal Legality: Salvadoran and Guatemalan Immigrants' Lives in the United States." *American Journal of Sociology* 111(4): 999–1037.

Menjívar, Cecilia, and Daniel Kanstroom. 2014. *Constructing Immigrant "Illegality": Critiques, Experiences, and Responses.* Cambridge: Cambridge University Press.

Milligan, Christine, and Janine Wiles. 2010. "Landscapes of Care." *Progress in Human Geography* 34(6): 736–754.

Moreno Figueroa, Mónica G. 2010. "Distributed Intensities: Whiteness, Mestizaje and the Logics of Mexican Racism." *Ethnicities* 10(3): 387–401.

Moreno Figueroa, Mónica G., and Emiko Saldívar Tanaka. 2016. "'We Are Not Racists, We Are Mexicans': Privilege, Nationalism and Post-Race Ideology in Mexico." *Critical Sociology* 42(4–5): 515–533.

Peck, Jamie. 2004. "Geography and Public Policy: Constructions of Neoliberalism." *Progress in Human Geography* 28(3): 392–405.

Scherz, China. 2014. *Having People, Having Heart: Charity, Sustainable Development, and Problems of Dependence in Central Uganda.* Chicago: University of Chicago Press.

Staeheli, Lynn A., and Michael Brown. 2003. "Where Has Welfare Gone? Introductory Remarks on the Geographies of Care and Welfare." *Environment and Planning A: Economy and Space* 35(5): 771–777.

Staeheli, Lynn A., and Victoria Lawson. 2005. "Geographies of Care, Justice and Responsibility: Thinking beyond Neo-liberal 'Truths.'" Miller Lecture, Pennsylvania State University, December 9.

Wacquant, Loïc. 2012. "Three Steps to a Historical Anthropology of Actually Existing Neoliberalism." *Social Anthropology* 20(1): 66–79.

Wade, Peter. 2001. "Racial Identity and Nationalism: A Theoretical View from Latin America." *Ethnic and Racial Studies* 24(5): 845–865.

———. 2005. "Rethinking Mestizaje: Ideology and Lived Experience." *Journal of Latin American Studies* 37(2): 239–257.

———. 2010. "The Presence and Absence of Race." *Patterns of Prejudice* 44(1): 43–60.

Weheliye, Alexander G. 2014. *Habeas Viscus: Racializing Assemblages, Biopolitics, and Black Feminist Theories of the Human.* Durham, N.C.: Duke University Press.

White, Julie A. 2000. *Democracy, Justice and the Welfare State: Reconstructing Public Care.* University Park: Penn State University Press.

Wilde, Matt. 2022. "Eviction, Gatekeeping and Militant Care: Moral Economies of Housing in Austerity London." *Ethnos* 87(1): 22–41.

CHAPTER 2

The Whiteness of Poverty Studies

Abolishing Poverty and Engaging Relational Politics

VICTORIA LAWSON AND SARAH ELWOOD

> We have this notion that somehow if you are poor you cannot do it.
> Poor kids are just as bright and just as talented as white kids.
> —Joe Biden (in Willies 2019)

> White opposition to public assistance programs has increased since 2008—
> the year that Barack Obama was elected. The researchers [Wetts and Willer]
> also found that "showing white Americans data suggesting that white privilege
> is diminishing—that the U.S. is becoming majority nonwhite, or that the gap
> between white and black/Latino incomes is closing—led them to express more
> opposition to welfare spending," with white respondents supporting cuts to
> food stamps despite the programs largely benefitting white Americans.
> —P. R. Lockhart (2018)

Derogatory, racialized representations of those experiencing impoverishment permeate U.S. popular culture, research findings, and policy debates. These representations are powerful drivers of ongoing public resentment, disgust, and even hatred toward those constructed as poor. While President Biden caught himself and followed up with an accounting of difference among those who experience impoverishment, this (mis)statement reflects widely held presumptions in popular culture about whiteness and success in the United States. Research on public assistance further demonstrates that white people are reluctant to support welfare funding, despite majority usage of benefits by white people, because they imagine those constructed as racial others as primary recipients—people they understand as undeserving or threatening. These quotes are the tip of the proverbial iceberg of the ways in which toxic ideas about "poor people" and "poverty" circulate in popular culture and broadly held social imaginaries in North America. We argue that liberal, social-science poverty studies reproduce hegemonic white-supremacist arguments about inequality and injustice, and as such, this form of poverty knowledge and practice must be disorganized and abolished.

Liberal poverty studies refers to ontological, material, and governance projects that rely on the construction of a poverty object: constructed variously as a measure, a social category, and/or a state of being (Dean 1991). This poverty object is rendered abundantly in the "poverty industry," which includes academic and policy work on poverty in the United States (and other North Atlantic states), a flourishing of expertise and activism addressing constructions of global poverty, as well as popular culture and political discourse (Roy et al. 2016). In the United States, the problem of poverty is "solved" through incorporation into racial-capitalist economies for subjects who conform to universalized norms of Eurocentric whiteness, individual responsibility, and meritorious behavior (Schram 2000; Gustafson 2011). These logics of incorporation are rationalized through discourses of individual freedom, meritocracy, and choice, and people experiencing impoverishment are represented as in need of reform, threatening, and/or criminal and therefore utterly removable (O'Connor 2001; Hancock 2004). In this move to either reform or exclude racialized and dispossessed people, the question of poverty is rendered technical and apolitical through ontological moves that categorize people in terms of degrees of self-improvement, property ownership, personal responsibility, morality, and comportment (Gustafson 2011; Bhandar 2018). Poverty then, as a concept, trope, and social category, judges, demeans, and does violence to persons framed as "less than" by adversely incorporating them into racial capitalism. In these ways, poverty studies validates the imaginary of a liberal state and society made up of rational subjects with "free choice" to participate and succeed.

In the United States, this poverty object has historically been a condition of possibility for the construction of a universal whitened liberal subject. Within Western democracies this subject is argued to hold equal rights for participation in public and political life (Elwood, Lawson, and Sheppard et al. 2017; Rancière 2004; Balibar 1991; Read 2007). However, this idealized citizen is universalized through norms of whiteness and middle classness that construct an imaginary of equal opportunity when in actuality white power is constructed on a logic of racialized difference and devaluation that is essential to the operation of racial capitalism (Goldstein 2012; Million, personal communication, 2018). In this way, poverty studies reinscribes the paradox of liberal governance (here traced through U.S. welfare state practices), resting on the claim of a "universal subject" who upholds the seeming morality of (exclusionary) property and citizenship rights while simultaneously U.S. racial capitalism rests on loss, disposability, and the differentiation of human value, rooted in claims of white superiority. Racial capitalism rests on the expropriation of labor, land, and resources, but equally fundamentally capitalism requires social separateness—the delegitimation and deactivation of collective relations between people and lands/places—in order to make dispossession, exploitation, and premature death justifiable (Gilmore 2002; Reddy 2011). As Melamed (2015, 77) argues, "Most obviously, [capitalism] does this by displacing the uneven life chances that are inescapably part of capitalist social relations onto fictions of differing human capacities, historically race." Settler colonialism relies on a violent redefinition of land as property, as a commodity that can be individually held/titled and separated from Indigenous communities (Goldstein 2017; Coulthard 2014). The U.S. settler-colonial project denationalizes tribes and minoritizes Indigenous people within the liberal settler nation-state, breaking relations of collectivity and relationality with the more-than-human world. As such, settler-colonial relations produce loss of sovereignty and lands, continually reproducing inequality and social devaluation by deploying individualizing ideologies of propertied personhood as a basis for liberal (differential) inclusion and exclusion.

Central to our argument here, U.S. liberal poverty knowledge contributes to the sustenance of white supremacy through twinned emphases on seeming inadequacies and needs for reform of racialized persons. This ontological move to categorize those experiencing impoverishment as "the problem," and hence socially devalued, reinscribes a white-supremacist racial hierarchy that posits the "inherent superiority of white Europeans over non-white people, an ideology that was used to justify the crimes against indigenous people and Africans that created the nation" (Jensen 2005, 3–4). In framing the supposed solution to poverty as aspiring to become idealized, whitened, middle-class citizen-subjects, poverty knowledge perpetuates white supremacy in the United States. Centering this poverty concept is an ontological-political move that justifies white supremacy by obscuring the operations of racial capitalism—rooted in the historical and ongoing dispossessions of stolen lands and stolen labor that are foundational causes of racialized differentiation and impoverishment. We argue that the "whiteness of poverty studies" encompasses both foundational ontological-political moves in liberal poverty theory *and* epistemological moves that continue to center and reproduce them in poverty knowledge making. We argue that the whiteness of poverty studies is produced and sustained in interconnected registers of theory and practice and, in so doing, upholds white supremacy.

We illustrate this argument in two ways. In the second section we show

how the ontologies of liberal poverty knowledge inflect poverty policies in the contemporary United States and reinscribe white supremacy by securing political and cultural systems that support material advantages of whiteness and class privilege. In the third section we trace how the whiteness of liberal poverty studies is secured through epistemological relations of poverty knowledge making that remain tethered to the racial limits of liberal poverty knowledge. Critiquing our long-term relational poverty research agenda, we show how our theoretical-political project of shifting poverty analysis toward relational thinking remained tethered to white liberal poverty ontologies and modes of incorporation because we failed to apprehend the racial limits to the concept of poverty. Our theoretical origins in Marxist feminist structural relationality did not go far enough, failing to center racialization as a (violent) ontological foundation of settler-colonial personhood in the United States. We show how our epistemological reflexes—conditioned by the enduring white supremacy of U.S. academia, our own structural privilege, and our efforts to reform the poverty concept—ensured that we continued to not recognize (or be challenged for) the ways in which our work reproduced the whiteness of poverty studies.

Finally, the fourth section outlines an urgent politics of building knowledge otherwise to challenge disciplining and white-supremacist frames. We argue for accountable relationality as a sustained practice of critique that apprehends the whiteness of theorizing and abolishes the poverty concept to instead center racial capitalism as a violent foundation of material-social inequalities. In so doing, accountable relationality interrupts the everyday workings of structural/institutional racism in academia that perpetuates enactments of white supremacy. Dismantling the whiteness of poverty studies requires theorizing and interrogating our own participation in modes of thought that make and remake the ontological objects and ways of knowing that sustain white supremacy in the academy and society writ large. We humbly offer this essay as an example of our own ongoing work, even as we are also aware that we make clueless oversights and ask wrongheaded questions. Sustained critique of our own knowledge project is one way of being in accountable relation with colleagues who have prompted us repeatedly to recognize the limits of the poverty concepts and to theorize the ways in which the whiteness of poverty studies upholds racial capitalism and white supremacy. Yet this approach is fraught with wicked tensions. Critical analysis of our own limits and learning is a crucial part of dismantling the whiteness of poverty studies, yet inevitably runs the risk of seeming to celebrate our growth. However, interrogating our journey allows us to trace the possibilities of unlearning poverty in accountable

relation. Most fundamentally, our chapter argues that disrupting our investments in white supremacy starts by understanding that our apparatuses for
knowing inequality and social justice are actually drivers of racial capitalism.

White Supremacy Advanced through Liberal Poverty Studies

The whiteness of liberal, social-scientific poverty studies stems from what this
knowledge project both avows and simultaneously disavows. Liberal poverty
knowledge diagnoses poverty as failure to self-actualize, failure to achieve the
propertied personhood of the idealized citizen-subject (Bhandar 2018; Roy
2017). The remedy avowed by this diagnosis is reform and differential incorporation of those named as poor. This partial incorporation and management
of impoverished subjects is central to the stability of the U.S. ideological project of liberalism built on meritocracy, individualism, property ownership, and
white supremacy. White supremacy refers to a system of taken-for-granted,
unremarked, and hegemonic societal domination through claims of the normative superiority of whiteness that produces material benefits for white
people in sites such as the law, property ownership, political power, claims
for rights, and more (Harris 1993; Lipsitz 1995). Within this system, white-
supremacist norms, values, and beliefs are framed as if universal but are actually enjoined to white people in particular times and places (Jensen 2016;
Gillborn 2005; Bonds and Inwood 2016). Our usage of "white supremacy" de-
parts from the contemporary harnessing of the term to white-nationalist violence manifest in mass shootings and explicit visibility of white-nationalist
racism in U.S. popular culture (see Gilroy 1993 on the vital importance of this
distinction). "Supremacy" is significant because it directs attention to the sustained historical project of racial capitalism that, in the U.S. context, accrues
value to whiteness.

We argue that liberal poverty theory, and the interventions it authorizes,
perpetuates whiteness to resolve the inherent tension between the liberal claim
of universal rights to property as the basis of social life and the imperatives of
racial capitalism in the United States. In making this argument, we do not center whiteness as identity, nor do we see whiteness as an ahistorical, stable ontological object. Rather, U.S. white supremacy is a historically specific resolu-
tion of the paradox of liberal governance. Namely, that liberal governance rests
on the claim of "universal propertied personhood," while simultaneously U.S.
racial capitalism rests on loss, disposability, and the differentiation of human
value. We argue here that liberal poverty studies solidifies projects of differential social valuation and contributes to the stabilization of a racial caste system

of social control in the United States, produced, historically and today, through the distinct but intertwined projects of racial capitalism and settler colonialism (Cacho 2012; Byrd et al. 2018; Simpson 2017; Coulthard 2014; Gilmore 2002; Alexander 2010).

Differential social valuation operates through modes of government that establish which subjects have the right to claim rights, full personhood, and political voice/power. Impoverishment arises from racial-capitalist social relations that must differentiate owners from workers and, simultaneously, workers from indigents. Historical and ongoing dispossessions transform impoverished, racialized persons into a binary of wage laborer or indigent, while poverty governance frames moral social life through personal responsibility to provide for a patriarchal family (Dean 1991). This historical binary of wage laborer/indigent manifests today in framings of deserving/undeserving, law abiding/criminal, legal/illegal, decent/disgusting, each of which assigns social value through a distinction between subjects who are in a position to have made the "free choice" to sell their labor and those who are not, or cannot be, in waged work. The idea of poverty rests on assumptions that social value (full personhood) is conferred by being a wage worker and/or recognition by the state as a property owner with rights to hold or profit from property (Roy 2017). Precisely because of the liberal ideology that all people hold "free choice" to be a wage worker or to own property, chronically unemployed or vulnerably employed persons, who are disproportionately poor people of color, are unable to establish the root causes of their impoverishment in racial discrimination (Cacho 2012; Jensen 2016). That is, within U.S. liberal conceptions of impoverishment, modes of propertied personhood that have been historically limited to white people are framed as universal. Social value came to be defined in white middle-class terms that construct racialized, impoverished persons as "the problem" in need of reform, while simultaneously defining legitimate personhood through their very exclusion.

The whiteness of contemporary U.S. poverty studies rests on its commitment to these conceptions of propertied personhood and racialized social value that ensure that whiteness confers material advantages and is protected as a form of property. That is, whiteness is not an ontology but the effect of repeatedly enacted commitments to the ideological and institutional forms that enable racialized devaluation and dispossession. The benefits of whiteness are secured through the mundane workings of institutions *and* through normative tenets of liberal poverty studies (competitive individualism, meritocracy, fairness, "equal" opportunity, and so on) that protect whiteness and white people, while simultaneously seeming to appear detached from processes of racialized dispossession. Countless U.S. policies and institutional practices operate social safety net programs; the law / criminal justice, housing, taxation, banking, and employment systems operate in ways that protect white people (and further deny and remove material benefits from people of color). The material advantages of whiteness accrue through the impoverishment of BIPOC people: Black unemployment is twice the rate for white people (Wilson 2019); Black people in the United States have a poverty rate 15 percentage points higher than the rate for white people, and for Native Americans this rate is 16.5 percentage points higher (Hymowitz 2019); the wage gap between white and Black people has grown significantly since 2000 (Gould 2019), and rates of Black home-ownership have dropped dramatically since 2001 (Goodman, McCargo, and Zhu 2018). These racialized experiences of life in the United States result from structures, processes, and institutions organized around a "possessive logic" of whiteness that reproduces white domination, entitlement, ownership, and control (Moreton-Robinson 2015; Alcoff 1998; Sleeter 1996; Jensen 2016).

Liberal poverty studies and policies/programs rest on racialized dispossession, and this violent ontology of racialized social value judges and demeans racialized dispossessed persons who are constructed as "poor and deficient." This in turn sustains the liberal poverty discourse of "fairness" and "deserving-ness," measured by the successes of white society. There are innumerable examples of racialized social devaluation within poverty policy and poverty theory. For instance, reforms to the social safety net over the past four decades have focused on reducing access to assistance rather than addressing the root causes of the need for assistance. Reducing access for those in need requires justification, typically delivered through racist and gendered judgments about who is impoverished and why. One striking example of social devaluation lives in toxic renditions of the "welfare queen" trope that dominated public debates around the Personal Responsibility and Work Opportunity Reconciliation Act of 1996 (PRWORA) and constructed welfare recipients as Black, morally bankrupt, disgusting women (Schram 2000). The persistence of this trope is rooted in discourses about Black women developed during slavery and still pervasive within the U.S. white-supremacist racial hierarchy. Hancock (2004, 26) argues that the "stereotype of Black women as bad mothers dates to slavery, when the terms 'Jezebel' and 'Mammy' represented oversexed and asexual women respectively . . . who shared in common neglect of their own children, in favor of having sex (the 'Jezebel') or tending the master's children (the 'Mammy')." Constructing Black women in need of social assistance as "welfare queens" continues this theme of "bad parenting" and delegitimizes them as interlocutors with rights and voice. As Sparks (2003, 172) argues, "Welfare recipients who opposed any part of the reforms . . . were portrayed as trouble-makers, not as citizens who might have important insights into public policy." This toxic rhetoric ensured that women of color receiving welfare could not be respected interlocutors in the debate because they had been judged against white, middle-class norms and found deficient (see also Schram 2000).

These forms of racialized social devaluation are produced and sustained by social-scientific poverty studies research. Researchers reinforce the rationales for punitive and restrictive welfare policies, rarely challenging their theoretical foundation: that the idealized liberal citizen-subject rests on the normalization of whitened, middle-class, propertied personhood. A classic example is the Chicago School, which located impoverishment in (deficient, immoral, racialized) bodies and behaviors, a theoretical assertion of the supposedly lesser social value of racialized persons that misapprehends residential segregation and forced mobilities as "natural succession" rather than as modes of racialized (dis)possessions (Park and Burgess 1925; for a critique, see Baldwin and Crane 2020). Daniel Moynihan, a sociologist by training, commissioned the groundbreaking report titled "The Negro Family: The Case for National Action" while assistant secretary of labor. This report was pivotal in shaping poverty policy while framing "the problem of poverty" as destructive "ghetto" culture and family "dysfunction" rather than structural oppressions (Moynihan 1965). Subsequent social-scientific poverty work perpetuates related theoretical claims, such as connecting impoverishment, racialization, and criminality (Wilson 1987; Murray 1985) or evaluating the effectiveness of "deconcentration of poverty" and "social mix" programs (Cisneros and Engdahl 2009; Levy, McDade, and Bertumen 2011). These studies represent a vast body of work that reinscribes the unremarked individualized, white, middle-class, propertied subject as the norm. Liberal poverty theory has long understood impoverished, racialized people as flawed and in need of reform while obscuring the basis of "poverty" itself in racialized understandings of who has rights to hold property.

These theorizations directly animate U.S. poverty policy. For instance, the passage of PRWORA further solidified the white-supremacist racial hierarchy through dramatic restrictions on social assistance and requirements that poor parents work outside the home, while doubling down on the narrative that impoverished persons are racialized, oversexed, and criminal. Pittman (2015) analyzes how access to social assistance is framed around white middle-class nuclear family norms of parenting that, in turn, devalue Black family life. These policies ignore the mass incarceration of African American men (who are made to be absent parents), the disproportionate removal of Black children by the child welfare system, and the deep poverty experienced by African American families. This social milieu leads many Black grandmothers to assume primary parental roles for their grandchildren, even as they remain unrecognized as legitimate beneficiaries of social assistance. Cash assistance from the Temporary Assistance for Needy Families program, child care subsidies, and housing vouchers all exclude grandmothers from benefits that recognize their parental roles. This is justified on the basis of white, middle-class, nuclear family norms that intensify racialized intergenerational poverty for Black families while simultaneously framing these families as deficient and irresponsible. Liberal poverty knowledge constructs racialized persons as deficient for not conforming, while the social, political, and economic context makes this impossible. Then, having constructed their lesser social value on white, middle-class criteria, liberal actors and policies punish racialized persons for not meeting these norms. The ongoing making of this kind of poverty knowledge and policy is a direct outcome of the social devaluation of racialized persons (Elwood, Lawson, and Nowak 2015).

These forms of social devaluation reproduce and justify a racial caste system in the United States (Cacho 2012; Alexander 2010). This racial caste system secures white power through such institutions as the criminal justice, social safety net, banking/finance, and education systems, which exclude racialized persons from voting rights and access to work, food, housing assistance property, education, and career opportunities. Alexander (2010) shows how the criminal justice system reproduces racial discrimination through racial profiling, disproportionate police violence, extreme sentencing laws, and the exclusionary treatment of persons with criminal and felony convictions. One in three African Americans born today will be incarcerated during their lives (Wilson 2019), and incarceration stretches well beyond literal imprisonment, including systems of surveillance, control, and marginalization through parole, future ineligibility for social safety net benefits, and social stigma. Liberal poverty discourse and practice reproduces this racial caste system by regulating and criminalizing the sexual, family, working, and civic lives of people experiencing impoverishment. For instance, the 1996 passage of PRWORA explicitly created a racial undercaste to appeal to white swing voters. In the midst of a punitive war on drugs targeting communities of color, the new law instituted a lifetime ban on eligibility for welfare cash assistance, food stamps, and public housing "for anyone convicted of a felony drug offense, including simple possession of marijuana" (Alexander 2010, 57). The very possibility of these ongoing intimate connections between criminal justice systems and liberal poverty policies arises from discursive equivalences between poverty and criminality. Gustafson (2011) elaborates on the ongoing complementary operations of the welfare and criminal justice systems. Liberal poverty policy criminalizes people in need of social assistance through programs such as Operation Talon, which requires welfare recipients' personal data to be released to law enforcement upon request. Welfare offices are sites for law enforcement sting operations targeting persons with outstanding warrants, and biometric data are shared between welfare and criminal justice systems.[1] In all these ways the welfare system, supposedly created to support people in need, has become an extension of the criminal justice system, and poverty policy continues to punish people of color (Gustafson 2011; Eubanks 2018).

Twinned projects of social devaluation and racialized social control are at work not just in liberal poverty policies and governance but also in persistent reinscriptions of white supremacy in institutions of research and education. Poverty knowledge is forged in what Ybarra (2019) terms "historically white colleges and universities (HWCUs)," at research conferences that require knowledge to be performed through Western/colonial norms to be recognized as legitimate (Hunt 2013; Rodriguez 2017), and by academic societies that do not recognize or intervene in racist structures of exclusion (Moser, Hendricks, and Vives 2017). In all these sites of knowledge making, white supremacy is reproduced through projects of differential incorporation of racialized persons (Peake and Kobayashi 2002; Pulido 2002; Baldwin and Crane 2020). For instance, Arday (2018) traces experiences of anti-Blackness within the academy, showing how normative whiteness is perpetuated in curricula, reading lists, hiring and promotion decisions, and microaggressions that devalue his presence as a Black man and subject him to frequent violence. Patton and Jordan (2017) and Gusa (2010) demonstrate ways in which scholars of color are delegitimized and silenced by the white-supremacist logics, norms, and practices of universities, recognized only if they conform to white institutional norms and rules.

These institutional conditions ensure that liberal poverty knowledge is made and enacted in brutally white spaces created by systemic racialized removals. In universities and research centers, academics, policy makers, and program administrators are inscribed in—*and often personally advantaged by*—systems that routinely devalue the voices and experiences of racialized, impoverished people. The whiteness of poverty studies and policies is continuously (re)produced not just by theoretical concepts but also by their enactment in laws, policies, and actions that demean, disadvantage, and dispossess racialized persons. There is an intimate relationship between the making of poverty knowledge in racialized institutions and racialized dispossession resulting from the knowledge they disseminate.

The Whiteness of Theorizing: Reproducing
Possessive Investments in Whiteness

We set out the *whiteness of theory*—the concepts that obscure the origins of "poverty" in racialized dispossession and propertied personhood, and the ways these are enacted through laws, policies, and institutional workings that reproduce white supremacy. As Rinaldo Walcott (2016) notes, "Questions coming from Whiteness carry with them the intimate seeds of the brutalities of their very asking. . . . There is a long history of whiteness framing questions . . . in ways that seek to replicate the brutalities of White imposition." Here, we turn to the *whiteness of theorizing*. That is, whiteness is always also epistemological—a way of knowing embedded in relations that are calibrated for white supremacy. Walcott points to relations of white imposition and violence enacted through knowledge-making practices as mundane as posing clueless questions. We take up this thread, arguing that the whiteness of liberal poverty studies is secured through epistemological relations in everyday knowledge making that allow the racial limits of liberal poverty studies to remain unseen and unchallenged (by some). We trace these operations of whiteness through our own theorizing, drawing examples from the conceptual evolution and transformation of our relational poverty research. We tell this story to demonstrate our own efforts to move toward more accountable relations of knowledge making. We revisit our research questions and analyses that allowed status quo white supremacy at the heart of liberal poverty theory to remain untroubled. We argue that this is not only a problem of theory (though it certainly is that as well) but a consequence of the relentless workings of whiteness in the making of poverty knowledge. This analysis does not resituate us as "good white people" (Griffin 1998; Applebaum 2010) nor suggest that the racial limits of poverty thought can be addressed through individual white self-criticality. Rather, by exposing how the whiteness of theorizing allows the racial toxicity of the poverty concept to remain unchallenged, we show that dismantling the whiteness of poverty studies requires reorienting not only our theoretical claims but also the epistemological relations of our theorizing.

Feminist and antiracist scholars argue that systemic and structural positions within white supremacy not only enable material advantage, possession, and taking but produce whiteness as a "site of opacity" (Yancy 2014). That is, conferred domination, self-segregation, and assumptions of superiority perpetually reenlist white-identified people in affirming white norms and practices, while also allowing them to refuse to recognize how these norms and practices perpetuate white supremacy (Mills 2007; Sullivan and Tuana 2007; Gusa 2010; DiAngelo 2011; Teel 2014; Yancy 2014). Variably named as white cluelessness (Teel 2014), white racial ignorance (Mills 2007), white fragility (DiAngelo 2011), or epistemological ignorance (Sullivan and Tuana 2007), this work focuses on whiteness as an epistemological orientation that is continuously made and remade through persistent refusal to recognize white supremacy and myriad forms of racialized exclusion. That is, white epistemological ignorance generates everyday practices of denying racial oppression and re-centering white power. Other scholars connect these epistemological reflexes directly to propertied personhood, noting how "white logics of possession" include routine habits of thought in which white-identified people engage everything as ours/theirs to consume, with little to no awareness of having done so (Lipsitz 1995; Bonds 2019). We use these propositions to illuminate how U.S. poverty knowledge making functions as a racializing apparatus—continually reinforcing the whiteness of liberal poverty studies, even in research that adopts a critical orientation to it. Through analysis of our own relational poverty research agenda, we trace the whiteness of our theorizing—epistemological reflexes that continuously overlook the foundation of the poverty concept in white supremacy and racialized dispossession. These reflexes are maintained through white institutional dominance, and for white-identified scholars aiming to critique poverty studies, this continual reinscription of epistemological ignorance poses a persistent tension: whiteness is simultaneously a focus of critical inquiry and the obstacle to that criticality.

As white-identified middle-class women, we are subjects and beneficiaries of propertied personhood and white supremacy, in the academy and in society at large. Our middle-classness rests on parents' uneven but generally upward mobilities in the United States and the United Kingdom. They and we benefit from structures calibrated to ensure white supremacy—the GI Bill, mortgage lending, labor protections and benefits in white-dominated sectors of employment and education, and much more. Our trajectories as scholars are marked by access to elite schooling through "merit"-based subsidies whose markers of "merit" rested upon mechanisms of racialized differentiation and removal (for instance, scholarships based on standardized testing that advantages white students, disproportionate exclusion of students of color from financial aid for higher education). These same systems mark our careers as academics: rapid trajectories through graduate education into secure tenure-track positions, quick promotion to greater job security and higher pay, and consistent access to stable housing. We have learned, researched, and taught in white-dominated universities produced through removals of people of color via the school-to-prison pipeline, racial disproportionality in student debt, institutional racism in hiring, promotion, and tenure, the ill health consequences that accrue from everyday aggressions, and more (Smith 2009; Scott-Clayton and Li 2016; Lee and Hicken 2016; Arday 2018; Johnson 2018). We have experienced precarity and (micro)aggressions as women, and one of us as a lesbian, but at the intersection of middle-classness and whiteness, these experiences have been episodic and mitigated by powerful allies. In short, our lives and scholarly work are thoroughly inscribed in the very structures and institutions of liberalism that conceal white supremacy and racial dispossession behind false promises of equal access and individual merit, in liberal poverty studies and poverty policy. As we show below, our theorizing and its institutional contexts have reflected and sustained these dynamics: even as we critiqued liberal tenets of poverty governance, we failed to theorize the racial limits of "poverty" as a concept, even when directly asked to do so.

Much of our scholarship over the past decade has centered on articulating relational theorizations of impoverishment, framing a field of "geographical relational poverty studies," and coalescing a community of critical scholars through the Relational Poverty Network. Our research has, for example, explored the poverty politics enacted by middle-class people, asking when, where, and why they apprehend structural processes of impoverishment and forge pro-poor politics, work toward inclusive social policy, and fight against poverty governance and the divisive narratives that legitimize it (Elwood, Lawson, and Nowak 2015; Lawson and Elwood 2014). We proposed geographical relationality as an analytical framework for revealing the limits to liberal poverty studies, arguing that relational sociospatial ontologies, antiessentialist modes of explanation, and boundary-crossing dialogic processes as modes of thought and action offer a basis for repoliticizing poverty beyond these limits (Elwood, Lawson, and Sheppard 2017). Most recently, we have theorized relations between "thinkable" poverty politics of governance and differential incorporation and "unthinkable" poverty politics: restless, unruly tactics, meanings, and claims that refuse the terms of prevailing racial-capitalist social and economic orders (Lawson and Elwood 2018).

Throughout, our concept of relational poverty animated a limited form of relational analysis that emphasizes Marxian feminist structural analysis and simultaneously elides the centrality of racialization (Hickey 2009; Mosse 2010; O'Connor 2001; St. Clair and Lawson 2013). From this conceptual vantage point we focused on material exploitation to understand impoverishment, but without sufficient attention to the ways in which the human differentiations necessary to capitalism rely on racialization. Our analyses have been ori-ented around theoretical claims that perpetuated (or at best left unchallenged) the persistent whiteness of theory in poverty studies. At the broadest level, our relational poverty theorizing has been a knowledge project oriented to-ward "reforming" poverty studies through relational analysis—without rec-ognizing, as we argued above, that the poverty concept originates in racial vi-olence. We continued to center "poverty," in effect leaving unquestioned the whiteness of liberal poverty studies. We theorized systems of racial differenti-ation and control as simply one of many intersecting processes producing im-poverishment (along with class relations, gendering, and so on). Paradoxically, even as we critiqued poverty studies, we reproduced its liberal erasures, for in-stance in our analysis of middle-class poverty politics. This work began from the proposition that middle-class people's attitudes and responses to impov-erishment could be key sites for disrupting divisive cultural politics and forg-ing cross-class coalitions fighting for inclusive social policy (Elwood, Lawson, and Nowak 2015; Lawson et al. 2015). This assumption is replete with episte-mological reflexes that persistently fail to see white supremacy at work in the U.S. liberal regime: theorizing liberal antipoverty policies as inclusive requires overlooking their systemic racial limits, such as the exclusion of (largely Black) agricultural and domestic workers from the 1935 Social Security Act and de facto state investments in securing material advantages of whiteness. Related to this, our hopeful orientation to cross-class alliance politics rests on epis-temological ignorance of the racial limits of incorporation politics. Theoriz-ing cross-class alliance as a site of transformative poverty politics is possible only by leaving untheorized the role of the liberal state in racial violence and the state's continued role in facilitating middle-class people's possessive invest-ments in whiteness. Even as we sought to critique liberal poverty studies, our relational poverty theorizing continued to reinscribe whiteness, relying upon theoretical assumptions and omissions that ensure the reproduction of white supremacy, even as it is held out of view (for some).

These theoretical exclusions are reinforced in everyday encounters of pov-erty knowledge making (reviewer comments, presentation Q&As, invitations to collaborative projects) within institutions that have systematically removed people of color and persistently devalued them as less legitimate interlocu-tors in academic knowledge production (Arday 2018; Johnson 2018). Reviews of our National Science Foundation proposal that built the Relational Pov-erty Network critiqued the proposed network for having no sociologists rep-resented when in fact sociologists of color from Argentina and South Africa were listed. They were not seen as adequately representing the discipline. Only when white sociologists from the United States were added to the proposal was this work funded. At the time, we read this critique as national chauvinism, but we now consider it also as an example of seeing people of color as invisible or illegitimate knowledge makers in the U.S. academy. Peer reviews of our theorization of relational poverty urged us to double down on the poverty concept rather than interrogating its normative liberal foundations in whiteness and class privilege (Elwood, Lawson, and Sheppard 2017). Specifically, one reviewer asked, "Is there something though about 'poverty' . . . that makes relationality more thinkable," urging us to more boldly elaborate this linkage. This question reinforces the whiteness of poverty studies: it urged us to double down on centering "poverty" rather than asking us to (as colleague Dian Million later did) call out the racial violence of that very concept. In academic knowledge-making practices such as grant seeking and publishing, possessive investments in whiteness are reinscribed by prioritizing white scholars and reproducing the normative power of a liberal, whitened poverty concept.

The whiteness of academic knowledge production and white institutional dominance also leads to certain questions being left unasked or inadequately answered. For instance, we have rarely been asked questions that built a racialized critique of our relational poverty framing. When such questions were posed, not only did we not recognize what was being asked, we responded in ways that recentered the whiteness of poverty theory. For instance, when presenting our middle-class poverty politics work on racialized place making in a HOPE VI development, we were asked a question that invited us to recognize the foundational anti-Blackness on which socially engineered mixed-income neighborhood projects rest. We responded with a class analysis that did not recognize the always already racialized workings of class politics (Elwood, Lawson, and Nowak 2015). In this moment, we failed to grasp the centrality of racialization to the conception of who is constructed as poor and excluded within that neighborhood. In another example of questions ignored, as we invited colleagues to join our book theorizing relational poverty politics, those who study radical politics of racialized dispossessed groups consistently told us that their work wasn't about "poverty." We reiterated our structural analyses of class and inequality and theorized their work as unthinkable poverty politics—essentially recentering a white liberal framing of poverty. Rereading these quotidian encounters illustrates some forms that white logics of possession take in everyday theorizing and how the whiteness of poverty studies is sustained. When colleagues of color directly refused the concept of poverty, our practical and intellectual response was to inscribe them into our whitened theorization of relationality, an epistemological reflex that stabilizes the whiteness of poverty studies.

We trace how the whiteness of our theorizing was expressed as a set of theoretical silences that critiqued, but nonetheless upheld, liberal poverty theory ultimately reinscribing white supremacy. Scholars like us are the legible and materially advantaged subjects of the racial ontologies of liberal personhood and the systems of governance, violence, and removal that uphold them. This institutionalization of white supremacy in the academy enables white epistemological ignorance that is reproduced and rewarded in the everyday relations of poverty theorizing. We expose how the whiteness of liberal poverty theory is ensured through epistemological regimes of poverty knowledge making, the inscription of scholars like us into them, and institutional conditions that allow the whiteness of theorizing to remain unchallenged (or refused and unrecognized). This apparatus makes and remakes the enduring whiteness of poverty studies. Our analysis underscores the urgency of not only reorienting our theoretical objects/claims but also fundamentally transforming the relations of knowledge making toward accountable relations that set the conditions of possibility for theorizing otherwise.

Toward Accountable Relationality and Building Knowledge Otherwise

Liberal poverty studies sustain white supremacy in the U.S. academy and society. This leads us to two claims. First, the liberal poverty concept must be abolished, as we have argued throughout this chapter. Second, knowledge must instead be made through practices of *accountable relationality*. This concept arises from Black queer ethics—an ontological-political project of forging subjects and relations outside of white-supremacist and heteropatriarchal structures of life and personhood (Young 2016). Accountable relationality involves sustained critique of one's own "theoretical and personal connections" to these violent structures/relations, as a basis for being and knowing otherwise (Young and Miller 2015, 292). For white scholars and liberal poverty studies, the ontological-political work of accountable relationality means naming and challenging white-supremacist, settler-colonial, racial-capitalist, and heteropatriarchal formations that produce social injustice and impoverishment *and* interrogating how these formations shape our own theoretical and structural embeddedness in these very systems. In this essay, a critical examination of our relational poverty work has revealed how we refused to recognize the racial limits to our white Marxian and feminist analyses and the ways that our possessive investments in whiteness secured our positions in white-supremacist institutions and knowledge production. Accountable relational theorizing insists on the centrality of racialized difference to histories and presents of capitalist and settler-colonial oppressions.

Accountable relationality is also an epistemological orientation to building knowledge otherwise that entails scholars becoming agents of change and engaging in forms of immanent critique that undo white privilege. Creating transformative educational spaces begins from posing, hearing, and responding to critical questions about our relations to white supremacy, racial capitalism, and propertied personhood. But it goes far beyond: transforming academic spaces through accountable relationality is an ethics, a politics, and an ongoing practice of analyzing embodied present histories of racialized social life and building knowledge with scholars of color and racialized, dispossessed communities (Byrd et al. 2018). For scholars like us, accountable relationality means learning how to think and act in sustained critical tension with white supremacy because this establishes conditions for reflexive, critical, care-full questioning that builds "the intimacies of being and being-together from which new worlds arise" (McTighe 2018).

These intimacies of being together have involved critical, generous, and sustained engagements from antiracist thinkers that have pushed us to transform our theoretical-political trajectory. Black-, Latinx-, and Indigenous-identified colleagues have insistently posed questions from outside the liberal limits of poverty studies, with a commitment to both rupture the whiteness of our theory and challenge us to recognize our own possessive investments in it. Students in our graduate seminars have noted the racial limits to our theoretical affinities, identifying our enthusiasm for "alliance politics" as calibrated to liberal, thinkable structures of inclusion that rest upon racial unthinkability. They have called out our political optimism as rooted in liberal presumptions of incorporation into norms of morality, middle classness, and individual responsibility that ultimately uphold white supremacy. One discussant of *Relational Poverty Politics* pointed out that our theorization of "unthinkable poverty politics" ignored long histories of Black radical thought and social movements (Miller 2018). Another colleague noted that by centering "poverty," even critically, we foreclose theorizations of inequality arising from Indigenous ontologies and do violence to community and life-land interconnections that are fundamental to living well (Million, personal communication, 2018). We learn the theoretical and political limits of our prior conceptualizations of relationality through these repeated care-full critiques by colleagues who challenge us to disrupt our white frames of knowing.

Accountable relationality is the generative space where engaged critique and epistemological humility come together. The critique of our omission of Black radicalism is also an invitation to apprehend the possessive whiteness of our theoretical claims about relational poverty politics. By seeming to "discover" what was there all along, as a basis for claiming our own theoretical innovations, we were sustaining white supremacy in the academy. Our colleagues' supportive rebukes and pointed invitations to other theoretical-political trajectories emerge from conversations sustained over many years. Relations of care, trust, humility, and interconnectedness are conditions of possibility for posing questions across racialized difference and for giving voice to, and taking responsibility for, our complicity with the violences of white supremacy. For us as white feminist thinkers with considerable investment in "reforming" liberal poverty studies through relational poverty theory, being accountable to these relations has meant arguing for abolishing "poverty" as a concept; for learning from relational politics at the intersections of Black, feminist, Latinx, and Indigenous thought-life-action; and for remaking concepts and institutions against white supremacy through new forms of engagement, new forms of action, and new knowledges.

Disrupting, disorganizing liberal poverty studies is one example of the transformations of the academy and its practices of knowledge production that deconstructs white-supremacist modes of knowing. Collaborators in this volume argue that the work going forward is for scholars to be agents of change who fight for relationality as a project of generative disruption, not inclusion. The role of this chapter in that larger work has been to critique poverty studies and the academic spaces/research that sustain them, to ensure that this immanent critique can happen and is heard. We argue for transformations of academic space and practice that are led by diverse scholars, epistemologies, and analyses and that reduce the barriers that separate disciplines in ways that disconnect studies of identity from those focused on materiality. Indeed, our central argument in this essay rests on this insight: that by separating identity from capitalist oppression, it becomes possible to legitimate white supremacy *and* racialized dispossession through construction of poor, racialized subjects. Ultimately, this chapter argues that disorganizing liberal poverty studies creates space for the urgent work subsequent chapters in this volume do: building diverse analyses of impoverishment, rooted in multivalent ways of knowing and pluriverse politics.

NOTE

1. These systems of racial control operate through data and capture whose antecedents stretch to back to slavery and beyond (Benjamin 2019; Browne 2015).

REFERENCES

Alcoff, Linda. 1998. "What Should White People Do?" *Hypatia* 13(3): 6–26.

Alexander, Michelle. 2010. *The New Jim Crow: Incarceration in the Age of Colorblindness.* New York: New Press.

Applebaum, Barbara. 2010. *Being White, Being Good: White Complicity, White Moral Responsibility, and Social Justice Pedagogy.* Lanham, Md.: Lexington Books.

Arday, Jason. 2018. "Understanding White Racism in the Academy." In Azeezat Johnson, Remi Joseph-Salisbury, and Beth Kamunge (Eds.), *The Fire Now: Anti-racist Scholarship in Times of Explicit Racial Violence,* 26–37. London: Zed.

Baldwin, Davarian, and Emma S. Crane. 2020. "Cities, Racialized Poverty, and Infrastructures of Possibility." *Antipode* 52(2): 365–379.

Balibar, Etienne. 1991. "Racism and Nationalism." In Etienne Balibar and Immanuel Wallerstein (Eds.), *Race, Nation, Class: Ambiguous Identities,* 37–67. London: Verso.

Benjamin, Ruha (Ed.). 2019. *Captivating Technology: Race, Carceral Technoscience, and Liberatory Imagination in Everyday Life.* Durham, N.C.: Duke University Press.

Bhandar, Brenna. 2018. *Colonial Lives of Property.* Durham, N.C.: Duke University Press.

Bonds, Anne. 2019. "Race and Ethnicity II: White Women and the Possessive Geographies of White Supremacy." *Progress in Human Geography* 44(4): 778–788. https://doi.org/10.1177/0309132519863479.

Bonds, Anne, and Joshua Inwood. 2016. "Beyond White Privilege: Geographies of White Supremacy and Settler Colonialism." *Progress in Human Geography* 40(6): 715–733.

Browne, Simone. 2015. *Dark Matters: On the Surveillance of Blackness.* Durham, N.C.: Duke University Press.

Byrd, Jodi, Alyosha Goldstein, Jodi Melamed, and Chandan Reddy. 2018. "Predatory Value: Economies of Dispossession and Disturbed Relationalities." *Social Text* 135(36.2): 1–18.

Cacho, Lisa M. 2012. *Social Death: Racialized Rightlessness and the Criminalization of the Unprotected.* New York: New York University Press.

Cisneros, Henry, and Lora Engdahl. 2009. *From Despair to Hope: HOPE VI and the New Promise of Public Housing in America's Cities.* Washington, D.C.: Brookings Institution Press.

Coulthard, Glen. 2014. *Red Skin, White Masks.* Minneapolis: University of Minnesota Press.

Dean, Hartley. 1991. *Social Security and Social Control.* London: Routledge.

DiAngelo, Robin. 2011. "White Fragility." *International Journal of Critical Pedagogy* 3(3): 54–70.

Elwood, Sara, Victoria Lawson, and Samuel Nowak. 2015. "Middle Class Poverty Politics: Making Place, Making People." *Annals of the Association of American Geographers* 105(1): 123–143.

Elwood, Sarah, Victoria Lawson, and Eric Sheppard. 2017. "Geographical Relational Poverty Studies." *Progress in Human Geography* 41(6): 745–765.

Eubanks, Virginia. 2018. *Automating Inequality: How High-Tech Tools Profile, Police, and Punish the Poor.* New York: St. Martin's.

Gillborn, David. 2005. "Education Policy as an Act of White Supremacy: Whiteness, Critical Race Theory and Education Reform." *Journal of Education Policy* 20(4): 485–505.

Gilmore, Ruth Wilson. 2002. "Fatal Couplings of Power and Difference: Notes on Racism and Geography." *Professional Geographer* 54(1): 15–24.

Gilroy, Paul. 1993. *The Black Atlantic: Modernity and Double Consciousness*. Cambridge, Mass.: Harvard University Press.

Goldstein, Alyosha. 2012. *Poverty in Common: The Politics of Community Action during the American Century*. Durham, N.C.: Duke University Press.

———. 2017. "On the Reproduction of Race, Capitalism and Settler Colonialism." Paper, Symposium on Race and Capitalism: Global Territories, Transnational Histories, University of California, Los Angeles, Luskin Institute on Inequality and Democracy.

Goodman, Laurie, Alanna McCargo, and Jun Zhu. 2018. "A Closer Look at the Fifteen-Year Drop in Black Homeownership." Urban Institute. https://www.urban.org/urban-wire/closer-look-fifteen-year-drop-black-homeownership.

Gould, Elise. 2019. "Stark Black-Wide Divide in Wages Is Widening Further." Economic Policy Institute. https://www.epi.org/blog/stark-black-white-divide-in-wages-is-widening-further/.

Griffin, Gail. 1998. "Speaking of Whiteness: Disrupting White Innocence." *Journal of the Midwest Modern Language Association* 31(3): 3–14.

Gusa, Diane. 2010. "White Institutional Presence: The Impact of Whiteness on Campus Climate." *Harvard Educational Review* 80(4): 464–489.

Gustafson, Kaaryn. 2011. *Cheating Welfare*. New York: New York University Press.

Hancock, Ange-Marie. 2004. *The Politics of Disgust: The Public Identity of the Welfare Queen*. New York: New York University Press.

Harris, Cheryl. 1993. "Whiteness as Property." *Harvard Law Review* 106(8): 1707–1791.

Hickey, Samuel. 2009. "Rethinking Poverty Analysis from the Margins: Insights from Northern Uganda." *Afriche e Orienti* 11(2): 119–136.

Hunt, Sarah. 2013. "Ontologies of Indigeneity: The Politics of Embodying a Concept." *Cultural Geographies* 21(1): 27–32.

Hymowitz, Kay. 2019. "New Insights into the Poverty and Affluence Gap between Major Racial and Ethnic Groups." Institute for Family Studies. https://ifstudies.org/blog/new-insights-into-the-poverty-and-affluence-gap-among-major-racial-and-ethnic-groups.

Jensen, Robert. 2005. *The Heart of Whiteness: Confronting Race, Racism and White Privilege*. San Francisco: City Lights.

———. 2016. "White Privilege/White Supremacy." In Paula Rothenberg (Ed.), *White Privilege: Essential Readings on the Other Side of Racism*, 157–162. New York: Worth.

Johnson, Azeezat. 2018. "An Academic Witness: White Supremacy Within and Beyond the Academy." In Azeezat Johnson, Remi Joseph-Salisbury, and Beth Kamunge (Eds.), *The Fire Now: Anti-racist Scholarship in Times of Explicit Racial Violence*, 15–25. London: Zed.

Lawson, Victoria, and Sarah Elwood. 2014. "Encountering Poverty: Space, Class and Poverty Politics." *Antipode* 46(1): 209–228.

———. 2018. *Relational Poverty Politics: Forms, Struggles, and Possibilities*. Athens: University of Georgia Press.

Lawson, Victoria, Sarah Elwood, Santiago Canevaro, and Nicolas Viotti. 2015. "'The Poor Are Us': Middle Class Poverty Politics in Buenos Aires and Seattle." *Environment and Planning A* 47(9): 1873–1891.

Lee, Hedwig, and Margaret Hicken. 2016. "Death by a Thousand Cuts: An Examination of the Health Implications of Black Respectability Politics." *Souls* 18(2–4): 421–445.

Levy, Diane, Zach McDade, and Kassie Bertumen. 2011. *Effects from Living in Mixed-Income Communities for Low-Income Families*. Washington, D.C.: Urban Institute.

Lipsitz, George. 1995. "The Possessive Investments in Whiteness: Racialized Social Democracy and the 'White' Problem in American Studies." *American Quarterly* 47(3): 369–387.

Lockhart, P. R. 2018. "Republicans Say Race Isn't a Factor in the Food Stamp Debate: Research Suggests Otherwise." *Vox*, June 13. https://www.vox.com/policy-and -politics/2018/6/13/17460362/race-food-stamps-snap-farm-bill-2018-republicans -welfare.

McTighe, Laura. 2018. "Many Hands Make Light Work." In Courtney Bender and Nancy Levine (Eds.), *Is This All There Is? The Immanent Frame: Secularism, Religion, and the Public Sphere*, March 9. http://tif.ssrc.org/2018/03/09/many-hands-make -light-work/.#123#.

Melamed, Jodi. 2015. "Racial Capitalism." *Critical Ethic Studies* 1(1): 76–85.

Miller, Maegan. 2018. "Untitled Panelist Remarks, 'Relational Poverty Politics: Forms, Struggles, Possibilities.'" Panel sessions, Association of American Geographers, New Orleans, April 2018.

Mills, Charles. 2007. "White ignorance." In Shannon Sullivan and Nancy Tuana (Eds.), *Race and Epistemologies of Ignorance*, 11–38. Albany: State University of New York Press.

Moreton-Robinson, Aileen. 2015. *The White Possessive*. Minneapolis: University of Minnesota Press.

Moser, Sarah, Michael Hendricks, and Luna Vives. 2017. "Academia's Moral Entanglements in the Face of a Racist Regime." *ACME: An International Journal for Critical Geographies* 16(2): 1–10.

Mosse, David. 2010. "A Relational Approach to Durable Poverty, Inequality and Power." *Journal of Development Studies* 46(7): 1156–1178.

Moynihan, Daniel. 1965. "The Negro Family: The Case for National Action." Washington, D.C.: U.S. Department of Labor, Office of Policy Planning and Research.

Murray, Charles. 1985. "Have the Poor Been Losing Ground?" *Political Science Quarterly* 100(3): 427–445.

O'Connor, Alice. 2001. *Poverty Knowledge: Social Science, Social Policy and the Poor in 20th Century U.S. History*. Princeton, N.J.: Princeton University Press.

Park, Robert, and Ernest Burgess. 1925. *The City*. Chicago: University of Chicago Press.

Patton, Lori, and Jodi Jordan. 2017. "It's Not about You, It's about Us: A Black Administrator's Efforts to Disrupt White Fragility in an Urban School." *Journal of Cases in Educational Leadership* 20(1): 80–91.

Peake, Linda, and Audrey Kobayashi. 2002. "Policies and Practices for an Anti-racist Geography." *Professional Geographer* 54(1): 50–61.

Pittman, LaShawnDa. 2015. "How Well Does the 'Safety Net' Work for Family Safety

Nets? Economic Survival Strategies among Grandmother Caregivers in Severe Deprivation." *Russell Sage Foundation Journal of the Social Sciences* 1(1): 78–97.

Pulido, Laura. 2002. "Reflections on a White Discipline." *Professional Geographer* 54(1): 42–49.

Rancière, Jacques. 2004. *The Philosopher and His Poor*. Durham, N.C.: Duke University Press.

Read, Jason. 2007. "Politics as Subjectification: Rethinking the Figure of the Worker in the Thought of Badiou and Rancière." *Philosophy Today* 51(suppl.): 125–132.

Reddy, Chandan. 2011. *Freedom with Violence: Race, Sexuality and the U.S. State*. Durham, N.C.: Duke University Press.

Rodriguez, Clelia. 2017. "How Academia Uses Poverty, Oppression, and Pain for Intellectual Masturbation." *Race Baitr*, April 6. https://racebaitr.com/2017/04/06/how-academia-uses-poverty-oppression/.

Roy, Ananya. 2017. "Dis/Possessive Collectivism: Property and Personhood at City's End." *Geoforum* 80: A1–A11.

Roy, Ananya, Genevieve Negrón-Gonzales, Kweku Opoku-Agyemang, and Clare Talwalker. 2016. *Encountering Poverty: Thinking and Acting in an Unequal World*. Berkeley: University of California Press.

Schram, Sanford. 2000. *After Welfare: The Culture of Postindustrial Social Policy*. New York: New York University Press.

Scott-Clayton, Judith, and Jing Li. 2016. "Black-White Disparity in Student Loan Debt More Than Triples after Graduation." *Evidence Speaks Reports* 2(3). https://www.brookings.edu/wp-content/uploads/2016/10/es_20161020_scott-clayton_evidence_speaks.pdf.

Simpson, Leanne Betasamosake. 2017. *As We Have Always Done: Indigenous Freedom through Radical Resistance*. Minneapolis: University of Minnesota Press.

Sleeter, Christine. 1996. "White Silence, White Solidarity." In Noel Ignatiev and John Garvey (Eds.), *Race Traitor*, 257–265. New York: Routledge.

Smith, Chauncee. 2009. "Deconstructing the Pipeline: Evaluating School-to-Prison Pipeline Equal Protection Cases through a Structural Racism Framework." *Fordham Urban Law Journal* 36(5): 1009–1049. https://ir.lawnet.fordham.edu/ulj/vol36/iss5/5.

Sparks, Holloway. 2003. "Queens, Teens and Model Mothers: Race, Gender and the Discourse of Welfare Reform." In Sanford F. Schram, Joe Brian Soss, and Richard Carl Fording (Eds.), *Race and the Politics of Welfare Reform*, 171–195. Ann Arbor: University of Michigan Press.

St. Clair, Asun Lera, and Victoria Lawson. 2013. "From Poverty to Prosperity: Addressing Growth, Equity and Ethics in a Changing Environment." In Linda Sygna, Karen O'Brien, and Johanna Wolf (Eds.), *A Changing Environment for Human Security: New Agendas for Research, Policy and Action*, 203–215. London: Earthscan.

Sullivan, Shannon, and Nancy Tuana (Eds.). 2007. *Race and Epistemologies of Ignorance*. Albany: State University of New York Press.

Teel, Karen. 2014. "Feeling White, Feeling Good: 'Anti-racist' White Sensibilities." In George Yancy (Ed.), *White Self-Criticality beyond Anti-racism: How Does It Feel to Be a White Problem?*, 21–36. Lanham, Md.: Lexington Books.

Walcott, Rinaldo. 2016. "Episode #7: 'I Don't Want to Ask You a F'ed Up Question' with

Rinaldo Walcott." In Eve Tuck, *The Henceforward* (podcast), November 27. http://
www.thehenceforward.com/episodes/2016/11/27/i-I-want-to-ask-you-a-fd-up
-question-with-rinaldo-walcott.

Willies, Egberto. 2019. "Her 'Poor Kid, Not White' Story Shows the Gravity of His
Freudian Slip." August 11. https://egbertowillies.com/2019/08/11/joe-biden-freudian
-slip-2/.

Wilson, Valerie. 2019. "Black Unemployment Is at Least Twice as High as White
Unemployment at the National Level and in 14 States and the District of Columbia."
Economic Policy Institute. https://www.epi.org/publication/valerie-figures-state
-unemployment-by-race/.

Wilson, William Julius. 1987. *The Truly Disadvantaged: The Inner City, the Underclass,
and Public Policy*. Chicago: University of Chicago Press.

Yancy, George. 2014. "Introduction." In George Yancy (Ed.), *White Self-Criticality beyond Anti-racism: How Does It Feel to Be a White Problem?*, xi–xxvii. Lanham, Md.:
Lexington Books.

Ybarra, Megan. 2019. "On Becoming a Latinx Geographies Killjoy." *Society & Space*,
January 23. http://societyandspace.org/2019/01/23/on-becoming-a-latinx
-geographies-killjoy/.

Young, Thelathia Nikki. 2016. *Black Queer Ethics, Family, and Philosophical Imagination*.
New York: Palgrave Macmillan.

Young, Thelathia Nikki, and Shannon Miller. 2015. "Asé and Amen, Sister! Black Feminist Scholars Engage in Interdisciplinary, Dialogical, Transformative Ethical Praxis."
Journal of Religious Ethics 43(2): 289–316.

CHAPTER 3

Relationality as Resistance

Dismantling Colonialism and Racial Capitalism

YOLANDA GONZÁLEZ MENDOZA

> [The] tendency of European civilization through capitalism was thus
> not to homogenize but to differentiate—to exaggerate regional,
> subcultural, and dialectical differences into "racial" ones.
> —Cedric J. Robinson (2000)

In this chapter I expose workings of racial capitalism through autoethnographical accounts of my migration journey from Mexico to the United States as well as through detailed lifelong ethnography and testimonials from my extended Mexican immigrant community in Washington State. I center our story as Mexicans of Indigenous descent who have been displaced from our history (via modern nationalistic projects of subject formation) and from our community and land in Mexico (via colonial and neocolonial practices that produce simultaneous displacement and immobility) and in turn have been legally criminalized and trapped in exploitative jobs in what is now the United States. As I tell our story, I embed a racial political-economic analysis of displacement within an investigation of subject formations. This structural analysis of displacement, inequality, and impoverishment through racial-capitalist processes and iterations of liberal governance and its identity projects disorganizes liberal poverty knowledge that focuses on individual actions and blurs structures of power—past and present. While previous work on racial capitalism has focused on anti-Blackness (Bledsoe and Wright 2019; Robinson 2000; Reese 2018; Sharpe 2016), my analysis shows how practices of de-Indianization work alongside anti-Blackness to further entrench institutional racism, producing displacement, bordering, and illegality. More specifically, our story as displaced Mexicans of Indigenous descent demonstrates how the national project of *mestizaje*, ideologies of development following Western models, and multiple bordering practices come together to produce and reproduce the privileged individual, the "legal" liberal citizen (whitened colonizers), and its constituent Other, the "illegal alien" (displaced Indigenous-descended peoples).[1] In turn this production of "illegal" nonpersonhood authorizes forced and illegalized mobility, further distancing us from our land, family, and communities, and traps immigrant communities into labor exploitation, while making these harms appear to be logical and necessary. More than the deportability threat in our everyday life (De Genova 2002), illegality produces detrimental intergenerational and relational harms. These vital insights, resulting from structures of power that produce impoverishment and inequality, uncover the profound limitations (and misinformation) of liberal poverty knowledge that focuses on individual action and assumes that all people have freedom of choice. Overall, our grounded story reveals how logics of white supremacy justify geographies of oppression along the Mexico-to-U.S. migration journey and facilitate conditions for racial capitalism and ongoing expansion of the settler-colonial empire.

Simultaneously, Mexican Indigenous descent communities, including mine, continue to enact relational ways of being and knowing—which are passed from generation to generation, adapted and readapted—to produce meaningful, dignified, and humane life in the midst of state-sponsored violence across space. My structural critique writes history from the perspective of Indigenous-descent and displaced peoples as a way to produce something meaningful for us (Smith 2013; Valencia 2019a; Wilson 2008). I bring together political-economic processes with embodied experiences of displacement from our land, our history, and ourselves. While disorganizing liberal knowledge is important, my larger goal here is to strengthen our collective consciousness through a deeper understanding about where our condition (of displacement) comes from and how we might move toward decolonial futures.

The stories I share offer an example of resistance by displaced Indigenous descent communities through enacting communal relationality across space and generations. Indeed, such relational communality performs a level of disengagement from the harms of racial state oppressions that insist on using their power, policies, and laws to harm people both in Mexico and in the United States (Valencia 2019a).

Through this chapter, I tell my story, my family's, and that of my community, of living with forced im/mobilities, political economies, and ideological projects (e.g., of having been made to learn the fictions of history of nation and subjecthood making) that racial capitalism, white supremacy, and settler colonialism depend upon. I also offer an example of ongoing everyday life resistance from Mexican immigrant communities that are thriving under state oppression in the United States. My work draws on and contributes to Critical Latinx Indigeneities, which is rooted in the relation between displacement of Indigenous communities from Latin America, mass incarceration of immigrants (many of whom are Indigenous) in the United States, and ongoing settler-colonial imperial expansion on Indigenous lands made "empty" via displacement in Latin America (Saldaña-Portillo 2017). I offer our story as an example of how settler imperial expansion also operates in rural communities of Mexico. Our community has been made mestiza and reveals how the processes of mestizaje and legal bordering are important factors that facilitate further land dispossession and intergenerational separation.

As I narrate our story, theory explains our life and our life becomes theory. Considering that ours is one of thousands of similar (but not identical) experiences, I begin with autoethnography to narrate in detail our story of experiences and struggles across borders. First, our story includes displacement in places of origin in the context of racial political economy resultant from U.S. imperialism and internal colonialism—ongoing racism that began over five hundred years ago (Cusicanqui 2010; Gonzalez Casanova 1965)—subject formation that centers white supremacy, reinforces Spanish colonial racialized social orders, and enables U.S. imperial expansion. Second, our story includes the ways in which the legal border and U.S. immigration law trap people as exploitative labor in the United States, separating them and future generations from our lands (and community), making land "empty" for future foreign investment. Overall, my essay reveals ongoing state violence against Indigenous descent communities as it constitutes legally exploitative labor and empty lands for ongoing settler-colonial expansion. Nevertheless, such communities continually resist colonial and imperial violence. Since the focus of this chapter is on migration, I conclude with an empirical and theoretical example of everyday practices of disruption from communities that are thriving in spite of oppressive norms in the United States.

These practices demonstrate that resistance to racial capitalism is partly accomplished through communal politics of solidarity that transform citizenship from an individualized private property—as an expression of personhood as per liberal normalized logics (Harris 1993; Macpherson and Cunningham 2011; Porter 2014; Roy 2017)—into a community tool that enables connections of families across space, colonizing borders and generations. Such connections reinforce community relations and trans-spatial belonging, enabling more relational, meaningful, humane, and social life—a kind of personhood that exceeds (and contradicts) the limits of white propertied personhood within racial capitalism. In this vein, my work contributes to Chicana feminists' call for women of color to write our own stories in ways that empower our communities and also unveil the workings of state violence (Alarcón 1990; Aldama 2001; Blackwell 2011). I am also in conversation with Black scholars who indicate that the oppressed, even as they are marginalized, produce and experience spaces of thriving (McKittrick 2006; McKittrick and Woods 2007). In addition, I engage with Indigenous theorization of relationality, codependence, and networks of care (Daigle and Ramírez 2019; Martínez Luna 2015; Simpson 2017; Smith 2013; Wilson 2008). Overall, this chapter contributes to this collection in two ways: it (1) interrupts and challenges liberal poverty knowledge and (2) highlights a form of everyday resistance from Indigenous-descent immigrant communities. This resistance is informed by knowledge rooted in collective ways of being and knowing that contradict liberal forms of propertied personhood. Drawing on Indigenous, decolonial methods (Smith 2013; Wilson 2008), my goal is to write stories (and histories) from our perspective as Indigenous descent dis/placed peoples and also to shift the gaze toward seeing ourselves as people with agency whose ways of being and knowing are powerful and crucial to our resistance from the dehumanizing harms of racial capitalism.

Racial Political Economy of Displacement

These were my mother's repeated painful words as my father would make rushed plans to come to El Norte again: "Por qué te tienes que ir otra vez? Llevanos contigo! Yo quiero conocer El Norte—Ese lugar que nos ha robado a ti" (Why do you have to leave again? Take us with you! I want to get to see El Norte—That place that has stolen you from us). His journey was due in large part to constant decreases in the value of corn (which our extended family cultivates in our rural community) and a shortage of jobs in Mexico, especially after the debt crisis of 1986 and increasing neoliberal policies initiated, encouraged, and enforced by the United States through the International Monetary Fund and other powerful Washington-based institutions (Clapp 2012; Lawson 2010; Sparke 2013). In the middle of the argument my father would remind my mother that he would never take us to the United States without papers because crossing *por el cerro* (through the mountains) was extremely dangerous. However, he was undocumented and thus risked his own life every time (Andreas 2012; Nevins 2007; Urrea 2004; Valencia 2017). Getting a visa was (and is) almost impossible and overly expensive. At the time of writing, a nonrefundable fee of about two hundred dollars is required as part of the application package (see https://mx.usembassy.gov). Nevertheless, in Mexico over half of the population lives in poverty (Gonzalez 2019), and such poverty as well as increased violence—resulting in large part from colonialism and U.S. imperial power over Mexico—are precisely the conditions people are often forced to run away from (Bacon 2008; Barajas 2009; Boehm 2011; Nevins 2007; Valencia 2017; Wright 2011). The relative instability of Mexico (and Central America) with the United States ensures that people almost exclusively seek migration to El Norte. And yet the people who need visas the most cannot afford to even apply. In addition, such visas are mostly denied because the U.S. consulate requires proof of wealth to qualify. Yet impoverishment, illegalization, increased violence, denial of documentation, and the dangers impoverished people encounter in the migration journey are all direct consequences of government policy. However, most of these conditions often seem to be disconnected and normalized and get framed as consequences of individual action(s) through mainstream discourses of self-help, deservingness, and irrational decision making.

Soon after marrying my mother, my father migrated to the United States, always promising that it would be the last time. However, that last time never materialized. A few months after returning from his two-year-long trip to the United States, plans to migrate would repeat due to extremely low wages, ongoing lack of employment, and constant devaluation of agrarian crops in relation to other essential goods. This condition is rooted, in large part, in the search for Western modernity. Increased poverty and violence have been ongoing challenges and struggles, especially for *campesinos*, since Mexico's independence because structures of power and racial logics stayed the same (Menchaca 2001). In the latter period, Mexico formally began its race toward industrialized "development" following the model of the West. This mode frames household farming, and thus rural mestiza and Indigenous communities, as backward and as impeding progress and modernity (Bonfil Batalla and Dennis 1996; Stetson 2012; Villalba 2013). Sylvia Wynter's letters reveal how soon after our political independence—especially since the 1950s—we

> fell into the mimetic trap . . . because the West is now going to *reincorporate* us as neocolonialists, and thereby mimetically, by telling us that the problem with us *wasn't* that we'd been imperially subordinated, *wasn't* that we'd been both socioculturally dominated and economically exploited, but that we were *underdeveloped*. The West said: "Oh, well, no longer be a native but come and be Man like us! Become homo economicus!" While the only way we could, they further told us, become *un-undeveloped*, was by following the plans of both their and our economists. The catch was that our economists, like the

distinguished Caribbean economist Sr. Arthur Lewis, had been educated in British imperial universities, like many of us. (Wynter, quoted in McKittrick 2015, 20–21)

While Wynter was writing about the Caribbean, she was making a broader argument about colonial structures that reveals ways in which ahistorical and depoliticized Western-centric discourses of the problem (undevelopment) and solution (development) become dominant and normalized not only in the Caribbean but also in Mexico and the so-called developing world in general.

Mexico (as the entire "developing world") is blamed for their *own* lack of "development" and thus poverty (Escobar 1995). Mexico also fell into the mimetic trap and continues its determination (originally imposed by Spain) to no longer be native in order to achieve development. This meant focusing on supporting industrialization and urbanization while disregarding household farming, which was seen as representing a "backward" way of life (Bonfil Batalla and Dennis 1996; Stetson 2012). Such is the power of Western development discourse that the Mexican government encouraged campesinos—those more linked to Indigenous way of life (Alanís Enciso 2017; Bonfil Batalla and Dennis 1996; Rubin 2014)—to migrate to the United States during the Bracero Program (between 1942 and 1964).[2] A goal of Bracero was for campesinos to learn industrial and "modern" farming methods and then bring these skills back to Mexico in support of development and modernity (Alanís Enciso 2017). This way of thinking reinforces Western superiority while also producing the idea that rural communities' knowledge is backward and irrelevant. Indeed, *bracero* derives from the Spanish word *brazo* (arm), meaning that the program targeted arms for physical, "unskilled," and thus cheap labor. In the twenty-two years of the program's existence, five million people, mostly from rural communities, worked as braceros (Calavita 1992). In this case, people were (and are) encouraged to move across borders to fulfill seasonal demands for cheap and disposable labor.[3] Seasonal visas, currently granted under the H-2A visa program, afford power for employers to choose their workers according to their productivity levels. Once the worker's youthfulness is extracted, they can easily be discarded, not hired again, and prevented from entering the United States. They grow older back in their rural communities without retirement or medical benefits from the United States. This form of laboring reproduces impoverishment. It legally constrains people from demanding fair wages or better working conditions or obtaining social benefits—although contributions toward social benefits are automatically deducted from their paychecks. This form of laboring is possible due to ongoing neoliberal trade agreements and austerity programs of dispossession and organized abandonment across colonizing borders. As such, neocolonial controls over labor, mobility, identity, and nationality work to reproduce and sustain a racial political economy of exploitation. This form of laboring is *not* due to individual decisions.

The Mexican government constantly reduces social spending to comply with U.S.-imposed austerity programs (Clapp 2012; Cupples 2013). One consequence is the lack of educational investment, especially in rural communities. The highest education level in El Rancho (rural community in Mexico where I resided through age seventeen) is tele-secundaria (middle school via televised lectures), with one teacher for three grades. As a consequence, children don't receive a strong foundation to move onto high school or higher education, making it impossible for youth to compete for the few available stable jobs. Also, with NAFTA in 1994, the Mexican market was inundated with highly subsidized products including corn, while austerity programs prevented the government from subsidizing its farmers. As a result, rural communities like El Rancho that rely on this crop for consumption and sale could no longer compete with the artificially low prices from the United States and Canada (Clapp 2012; Bacon 2008). It's cheaper to buy than to grow corn, beans, tomatoes, and other basic foods that rural communities grow. The price of agrarian products keeps decreasing in relation to the prices of gas, clothes, shoes, soap, and other essential and industrialized goods. As Bonfil Batalla and Dennis (1996) indicate, Mexico, which invented corn, now has to buy it! At the time of writing this essay, and after about seventy years of Western development projects, over eleven million people earn a minimum wage of Mex$123.22 per day (US$6.36). These wages reflect an increase of 20 percent in January 2020; however, with most groceries and essential products being comparable to U.S. prices, these wages aren't nearly enough to survive. For example, a kilo of beef currently costs around Mex$200.00, equivalent to approximately US$11.00 (almost twice the daily minimum wage!); a jar of VapoRub (a topical medicine popular in my community) is currently about Mex$90.00, or US$5.00 (almost the entire day's earnings); gas is often more expensive in Mexico than in the United States; and the list goes on and on. These are examples of everyday scarcities produced through unequal trade and power relations.

These unequal trade and power relations across national borders, coupled with austerity program, make places unlivable, forcing people to move, to embark on the journey to El Norte in search of their lost jobs (Nevins 2007), a journey that has been made dangerous through legal criminalization of (and legal barriers to) mobility. Government policy produces both the conditions and need to move but also legally prevents people from moving. Thus, impoverished people are simultaneously pushed to, and legally prevented from, moving (Walia 2021). Those who survive crossing the deadly buffer zone we call the U.S.-Mexico border become criminalized and captive labor for the benefit of the already rich in the United States (De Genova 2004). Indeed, a criminalized life is often the only future for impoverished people. Either their presence in the United States is criminalized through the immigration law (Cacho 2012), or they're criminalized in Mexico through the war on drugs—a war encouraged and supported by the United States through programs such as the Merida Initiative, which depicts them as drug dealers (Corva 2008; Mercille 2011; Paley 2014; Wright 2011). This way, the murdering of thousands of impoverished people continues with impunity as they're linked to this illicit business and thus framed as deserving to die, or as unlawful noncitizens, nonpersons who broke the law when crossing the U.S.-Mexico border (Valencia 2019b). As noncitizens under the racialized migration law, they're labeled as already criminals in the United States (Cacho 2012). Such conditions restrict movement (both physical and social), trapping people in exploitative jobs in the United States, and determine who is and who isn't deserving of protection by white-supremacist laws made by and for whites.

As my father was forced to engage in the deadly journey to the North and became a criminalized noncitizen whose deportable labor enriched the already rich, my mother, who never attended school, was essentially a single mom working in the informal economy, selling food in the streets. My four older siblings and I would help her from a very young age. Mine was (and is) hardly the only case. Thousands of children in Mexico and Central America must help from a very young age by working in the informal economy (Aufseeser 2015). Also, similar to my case, it is common for children to grow up without one or both parents because they're forced to migrate to the United States in search for jobs lost to the negative effects of ongoing economic, political, and social-imperial processes that create unlivable conditions. In the meantime, public schools—as part of the apparatus of the state—continue to play a significant role in the pursuit of Western development and liberal personhood by erasing/negating the Indian in us.

"No Longer Be a Native but Come and Be Man Like Us!"

Through public education we learned that our Indigenous languages are "dialects," not languages, that our Indigenous knowledges are "myths"—unreal, unscientific, subjective—because Indigenous peoples had a different and supposedly irrational cosmology and way of seeing the world. At elementary school I was taught that Christopher Columbus was a hero who "discovered" us when he arrived in the Americas by accident. Little did I know that we lived not in America but by Tzintzuntzan, in Purépecha territory, beside the Anáhuac or Tenochtitlán (Aztec Empire); more broadly, we lived in what Kuna people currently refer to as the continent of Abya Yala (Valle Escalante 2014). As Mignolo (2005) indicates, for the people in this land, America didn't exist. It was not a place on the map waiting to be "discovered." Rather, America was invented by the colonizers who gave it that name. I learned that our Indigenous ancestors are all gone/dead and now we are all a new race of *mestizos*, thanks to Columbus who "rescued" us. Now we supposedly have Spanish blood and are closer to Western in modernity and civilization. Consequently, we learned to celebrate our buried past and to detach ourselves from "them," framed as "Indigenous backward," that is, us. October 12, the day that Columbus arrived, has been declared El Día de la Raza, a national holiday in celebration of his arrival, which enabled the possibility of a new and "better" race—the mestizo. I used to participate unquestioningly in parades organized as part of such celebrations by our public schools and government.

At age of seventeen, I along with my mother and one of my sisters finally migrated to the United States and reunited with our father and extended community in Pasco, Washington, a city where over 70 percent of the population identifies as Hispanic (Latinx), mostly Mexicans. While my three older siblings would've loved to join us, they couldn't because they were already over the age of eighteen, which disqualified them by the time our application for documents, submitted by my father years earlier, was processed. This example illustrates how racist immigration laws and bordering practices produce legalized separation of families and communities. Making the journey to the United States converted us into immigrants of color. As Mexican mestizas of Indigenous descent, we became marked the "other," again! Saldaña-Portillo (2017) asks, "When does an Indian stop being Indian?" Inspired by this question I wonder, is that through miscegenation with whites? Through mestizaje as an imposed identity? When one learns a distorted history and is forced to forget our Indigenous languages? Or when one moves across the colonizer's national borders? In effect, our mobility is framed as migrating, unlike the mobility of white Europeans and their descendants (Rana 2010; Walia 2014). We are othered in Mexico as "backward" campesinos by the Mexican elites and the oligarchy who have bought into and/or are mandated through U.S. imperial policies to adopt a mimetic development model. We are also legally criminalized and discriminated against in the United States by white settlers and liberal governance (Camacho 2008; Corva 2008; De Genova 2004; Cacho 2012; Ngai 2004; Spade 2011). Being Mexican in the United States is a derogatory identity (Cacho 2012). This identity is attached not only to a country but also to a racialized category. After the invasion of Mexico, the United States denied most Mexicans citizenship due to our hypervisible Indigeneity and thus our nonwhiteness (Menchaca 1993). This continues currently as our presence—our hypervisible Indigenous presence—in the United States is synonymous with the "illegal alien" (De Genova 2004). In turn, such othering and bordering across space ensures our distancing and displacement from our land and some forms of life.

The racist political-economic relations laid out in the preceding section are enabled by historical projects of racial formation and ideologies of the nation. This section briefly traces how these racial projects secure white supremacy in the formation of the Mexican nation and continue to be reproduced through institutions of liberal governance (e.g., public schools). La Secretaría de Educación Pública (SEP, the Secretariat of Public Education), created in 1921 by Mexican president Álvaro Obregón, controls teaching materials in public schools. José Vasconcelos—a creole born in Oaxaca from French and Spanish parents—was named head of the SEP. While Vasconcelos was not of mixed race, he believed that the ongoing mixing of races would produce a superior race, the cosmic race (Vasconcelos 1997). He considered Indigenous as inferior and backward and the Spanish as superior and rescuers through their white race and religion. Nevertheless, he warned against imitating the Western model of material modernity. During his leadership in the SEP, art flourished, murals narrating the story of Mexico were painted, and education reached rural communities. However, the knowledge disseminated was (and continues to be) distorted and told through the European eye because Vasconcelos deemed Indigenous as inferior.

As a result, most people in Mexico know very little about ourselves (Bonfil Batalla and Dennis 1996). Most have learned a limited history written by and for the West, where the West is the expert and hero who saves the "backward" other (Said 1979). Often, kids are bullied for looking Indigenous or for speaking a native language. And so the modern and mestizo national *identity*, which conceals ongoing racism, has been successfully imposed and normalized. Just the mere fact of learning Spanish qualifies people as mestizos because supposedly they've "mixed" their culture by adopting the Spanish language. However, not knowing Spanish represents a barrier for accessing higher education and the few stable and better-paid jobs that might become available.

As such, the majority of Mexicans, including my rural campesina community, have adopted this "modern" identity and buried part of our Indigenous "past" (Bonfil Batalla and Dennis 1996). Indeed, Mestizaje is a national state project of denial as it obscures Indigenous ways of life and their/our presence (Cusicanqui 2010). This national Mestizo identity also conceals white supremacy, settler colonialism, and ongoing neocolonial processes. In other words, through mestizaje, everyone is supposed to be the same, including white descendants who continue to inhabit white-supremacist power. This invalidates challenges to settler colonialism as now, supposedly, we are *all* equal and therefore are *all* both colonizer and colonized. Indeed, through teaching this distorted history in schools the state can deny colonization and its erasure of Afro-Mexican populations, thus seeking to negate Indigenous life by "purifying" our blood through whiteness (Martínez 2008; Smith 2013).

These racist political-economic processes that explain contemporary displacement are rooted in colonial social organizing that draws from (and sustains) white supremacy for the past 530 years. The quest to eradicate the Indian in Mexico has been an ongoing white supremacy project since colonization from Spain, and it's now combined with settler colonialism and imperialism from the United States. As such, mimicking Western development is part of the ongoing white supremacy pursuit to "save" the nonwhite from our supposed lack of humanity by eradicating the "nonhuman" part of us, our Indian and our Blackness. Mexican migrants to the United States then experience the related, but distinct, white-supremacist U.S. racial formation, as seen in histories of racial exclusion and bordering, as I discuss below.

Becoming the "Other" in El Norte

Soon after the arrival of our family in the United States, in order to help pay for the cost of our trip, my sister and I applied to work in restaurants and stores. But ability with English and previous experience were requirements, so we were told. We had no choice but to work in the agricultural industry: planting, picking, and sorting trees for one company; then planting onions for another; then sorting asparagus for yet another. Within six months we moved through many different jobs. Given their seasonal nature and the need to pay off the loan that funded our trip, while also contributing to living expenses, we had no choice but to work at IBP, now Tyson's Wallula beef plant (a fancy name for the slaughterhouse). This was by far the worst job I've ever done, but nevertheless it was full-time, stable employment. This slaughterhouse employs about fourteen hundred people—many of whom are Mexican immigrants or of Mexican descent. Women are often placed in lower-level, lower-paid jobs—supposedly lighter work but requiring faster movement of hands—and are rarely promoted. There are clear hierarchies in this corporation where the dirty job of killing the cow for the privileged consumer takes place (see Pachirat 2011). The few top managerial jobs are occupied by white males. Middle management positions are mostly granted to men and some white women; jobs of lower ranks are generally performed by women of color. I was placed in a lower-level and low-paid but high-velocity job. Some women from my community have performed this job for over twenty years. Instead of being promoted, they tend to get demoted as their hands and bodies are permanently worn out through the years and thus are stuck in the same position or given even lower-rank jobs. Similar to the women who work in *maquiladoras* in the northern Mexican border (Wright 2001), the lives of women of color are extracted as they add value to the meat being processed in the slaughterhouse. This work is out of sight and out of mind for consumers. As Pachirat (2011) indicates, invisibility justifies much violence toward the animals and the workers behind the gray walls of the slaughterhouse.

I was able to run away from these backbreaking jobs by attending upper-level education classes, after overcoming a series of barriers and with the support from my community and beyond. Sadly, the majority of Mexican people, many of whom are de-Indianized mestiza/os/es, cannot do this because of racist white-supremacist laws that work to legally keep some people under vulnerable and impoverished conditions. Inability to escape exploitative work is also due to structurally violent conditions suffered in places of origin, which forced many to migrate with few resources.

Since its foundation, the United States has depicted various populations, including poor whites, Africans, Indigenous, Chinese, Japanese, Southeast Asians, and Mexicans, as perfect for physical "unskilled" labor through racial othering discourses (Calavita 1992; Robinson 2000; Gilmore 2002; Nevins 2002).[4] Such depictions enable legal criminalization, discrimination, and exploitation of targeted racialized populations. For the past century—especially since the Bracero Program in 1942—Mexican (and broadly Latinx) communities have been the targeted group. Soon after the Bracero Program ended in 1964, this same population became illegalized through immigration laws (De Genova 2004). Over 50 percent of the eleven million undocumented immigrants in the United States are Mexicans. As Cacho (2012) argues, legally, they have no rights to have rights. They've been excluded from protection but not from punishment under the rule of law (Cacho 2012; De Genova 2004).

However, lack of legal documentation forces many into exploitative jobs that reproduce impoverishment.

My story so far has illustrated that global colonial violence is justified by racial logics imposed by Western societies across Mexico and what is currently known as the United States.[5] Racial state violence in Mexico and in the United States prepares many to become cheap labor and become trapped in exploitative jobs.

Trapped: The Pain of Immobility

While my father was able to see his family by engaging in circular migration as an undocumented immigrant from the 1970s to the 1990s, increasing criminalization and punishment of the presence and mobility of people of color have made circular migration almost impossible. For instance, at the time of my writing, the Trump administration's proposed funding for a border wall amounted to $18.4 billion, for additional construction of 882 miles of wall along the 2,000-mile border (Miroff 2020). While deterrents like this will not completely stop people from trying to cross because conditions of displacement have not been addressed (Ramos 2002), such barriers, in combination with increased technological intelligence, militarization, and organized crime, do increase both the danger and the costs of crossing.

As such, legal separation of families continues to be intensified across space. As Nita explains, "La razón principal para tener papeles, es nada mas para ir a ver a mi familia!" (The most important reason to have papers, is only to be able to go see my family) (personal interview, 2016). The pain that comes with the inability to go back to Mexico to see family and community there is palpable in my mixed-status Mexican immigrant community in the United States.

For most of the women who participated in my research, the primary reason they yearn to obtain legal status isn't necessarily to obtain employment (this can somehow be obtained anyway, they say) or to draw social benefits or to be able to vote, but rather to be able to travel back to Mexico. They yearn to connect with their roots and see the families they've not seen for a very long time. This is what is most valuable to them and what they've lost in *seeking* the American dream. As Chinita, who has not been able to see her parents, extended family, or community for over twenty years, said,

> Me gustaría tener papeles para viajar. Quiero regresar de donde yo soy. Es algo que anhelas: regresar a tus raíces, ver a tu familia que hace mucho no has visto. Por buscar el sueño americano, avece pierdes algo tan valioso, que es la

familia. . . . Es lo que mas anhelas—eso sería la razón numero uno de querer papeles; porque trabajas de una forma, pero la parte mas valiosa [es] volver.

I would like to have papers to travel. I want to go back to where I am from. This is something that one yearns: return to your roots, see your family that for a long time you have not seen. For seeking the American dream, sometimes one loses something so valuable, that is the family. . . . That is what one yearns the most—that would be the number-one reason to want papers because you work one way or another, but the most valuable part, is to return. (Chinita, personal interview, 2016).

Family separation is a high price to pay for *seeking* a dream that has not been made for us, people of color; on the contrary, such a dream might be true for only selected white privileged people who continue to benefit from accumulation of wealth and status generated from the ongoing privatization of stolen lands and labor from Indigenous and Black populations in the United States, Mexico, and around the world. Many in my community have lost what is more valuable to them—the ability to go back to their roots and family. White-supremacist laws, policies, and interventions contribute to the making of disadvantageous conditions at places of origin, forcing many to leave their home and land as they embark on a journey that has been made dangerous. But then such laws also criminalize and deny mobilities. Forced, criminalized, and denied mobilities are central to the workings of white-supremacist bordering and othering, which entrench anti-Blackness and de-Indianization logics enabling (and normalizing) extraction of resources, labor, land dispossession, and denial of life chances.

Nita explains that the *only* reason why she would like to have papers is to go see her family. She says, "La razón principal para tener papeles, es nada mas para ir a ver a mi familia" (The most important reason to have papers, is only to be able to go see my family). Nita has not been able to see her mother and siblings for over twenty years, and lately she's been suffering from anxiety and depression. She mentioned that she deeply misses her family in El Rancho and that in the meantime her body is giving up due to a lack of sleep from getting up as early as two o'clock, often seven mornings a week, to work on the farm. During the warmer season—for over half of the year—Nita (as most farm workers) has to be at the job site at around four o'clock in the morning and works for over twelve hours, earning minimum wage.

Further, for Lola, her primary reason for wanting papers is to go back to her barrio in El Rancho and scream. Lola said that she would like to obtain papers para poder ir pa México. Porque de que tengo ganas de ir, si, tengo ganas de ir. Pero me hago a la idea que no [puedo]. El hermano de Pedro que se vino hace dos años con su esposa, pagaron US$7,000 por cada uno [para cruzar la frontera]. Lo primero que haría si yo pudiera ir seria . . . echarme unos gritos ahí en el barrio. Aquí no grito porque aquí no voy a sentir igual de bonito. [Es que] Yo allá me echaba los gritos desde chiquita.

to be able to go to Mexico. Because that I want to go, yes, I want to go. But I realize that I can't. The brother of Pedro who came two years ago with his wife, paid US$7,000 for each [to cross the frontier]. The first thing I would do if I could go would be . . . to scream there in the neighborhood. I don't scream here because I'm not going to get the same beautiful feeling. [The reason is that] I used to scream there since I was little. (Lola, personal interview, 2016)

Here, Lola wasn't just referring to simply screaming. This is what we call *güaipear*; it's a specific kind of sound that can be interpreted as masculinist, but some women in my community in Mexico, including Lola, would often also güaipear since childhood. Not everyone can do this, as it requires certain skill. Güaipear often takes place in fiestas when ranchera music is playing, or in the case of El Rancho, it is also done in the *cerros* (mountains) or just in the open. It expresses happiness and produces a feeling of relief, freedom, empowerment, and belonging; but also the sound makes the space feel happy in general. It is a complicated but amazing feeling that is linked to place, community, people, sound, and belonging. This is why for Lola, as can be the case for others, güaipear in the United States wouldn't generate the same amazing feeling. Lola would like to scream (to güaipear), but only in her barrio, located in El Rancho, the place she used to scream as kid—the place where her roots are—and so the only place where she would feel amazing to güaipear. However, in 2014, it cost U.S.$7,000 to cross the U.S.-Mexico deadly buffer zone. By 2021 the price had doubled. For Lola, who has not been able to return to her community for over fifteen years, as for all undocumented immigrants, the possibility of going in order to güaipear there, and to see family and reconnect with roots, continues to worsen as both cost and risks have exponentially increased. This example reflects how people in El Rancho connect/relate to place, sound, and each other. As Wilson (2008) indicates, we are our relations, and our relations are knowledges. This also reveals some losses produced by forced/denied mobilities and why the ability to return is so utterly crucial—only in El Rancho can the full structure of feeling, of specific relations, be experienced and passed from generation to generation.

This awareness and the yearning to share these feelings and relational ways of being and knowing with their children have led my immigrant community to support each other in order to reconnect the community across generations and colonizing borders. Their organizing and politics draw from ways of being and knowing that center relational communality, have been passed from generation to generation, and have been adapted and readapted in order to confront ongoing and new state-led racial violence in Mexico and in the United States.[6] I conclude with an example that illustrates how resistance to racial capitalism is partly accomplished through communal politics of sharing that transform citizenship from individualized private property—as an expression of personhood per liberal normalized logics (Harris 1993; Roy 2017)—into a community and reterritorialized tool that enables connections of families across space, colonizing borders, and generations. Such connections reinforce intercommunity relations and trans-spatial belonging for new generations, contributing to the production of meaningful humane and social life—a kind of personhood that exceeds the limits of white propertied personhood within racial capitalism.

Relational Communality as Resistance

While in theory the majority of Mexicans, including my own community, have adopted the de-Indianized non-Black identity of mestizo, in practice Indigenous and Indigenous-descent (mestizo) communities continue to enact ways of being and knowing that challenge ongoing colonial and imperial racial-capitalist oppressions. Such resistance emerges from relational ways of being and knowing and draws from communality as a way of life. Zapotec Indigenous scholar Jaime Martínez Luna (2015) refers to communality as Indigenous forms of life that center the community. Communality means that everything is by and for the community, including the land, work, and fiestas (Martínez Luna 2015). Communality also informs how life is organized and experienced in rural mestizo communities. These ways of being and knowing, which require practices of respect, solidarity, and reciprocity, have been passed from generation to generation and have been adapted and readapted in order to confront ongoing and new forms of racial state violence both in Mexico and, in the case of migrants, also in the United States (Valencia 2019a).

Logics of communality—as a way of being in and knowing the world— enable the ongoing support and sharing of resources that tend to be framed and practiced as individual property by liberal logics in the United States. These resources include housing, food, money, time, and celebrations. While the specific examples vary, I share how my immigrant community has transformed U.S. citizenship (a private and protected "property" afforded those deemed "worthy" by white-supremacist law; Cacho 2012; Spade 2011) into a reterritorialized communal tool that enhances transborder and intergenerational community connection. Such practices are rooted in ways of being and knowing that draw from Indigenous values of respect, solidarity, and reciprocity that continue to be practiced in both Indigenous and de-Indigenized communities in Mexico. These ways of being and knowing are then brought to the United States as a form of border thinking (Mignolo 2000), adapted and re-adapted to confront legal structural discrimination and barriers enabled by (and sustained through) logics of racial capitalism.

In El Rancho, a mestiza (de-Indianized) community where I lived until 1995, connections to place and to each other are centered on the production of meaningful and dignified life. The majority of my participants and community in Washington migrated from this place. El Rancho is located in Michoacán, one of the poorest states in Mexico. We have a large and inclusive community and multiple relations in this little town of about eight hundred residents. We also have networks with other, smaller surrounding communities. Whenever there was a celebration, we were all invited. We could just go visit anyone anytime, and we were welcome to sit and eat. In fact, we cleaned our home thoroughly every day just in case someone would come to visit us. In the evenings we sat outside, by the sidewalk, and talked with whoever was passing by, who would often sit and join the conversation.

Apart from having a large network of close family members, my mother would always relate us to everyone, pulling connections from multiple generations back, making all adults my aunts and uncles and younger kids my cousins. I remember one day I told her, "Okay, I guess I'll never be able to date anyone as everyone is my cousin!" That made my mom happy. Whenever we met someone new, my mom or family members would ask, "Where are you from? What is your last name? Are you from this or that family?" And then boom! They would find our connections, either through blood, or through having lived in the same place at one time, or through knowing the same families, or through *compadrasgo*. Finding our connections and putting people in context to place and multiple relations are ongoing Indigenous practices around the world (Wilson 2008).

Besides living in relation, people in El Rancho continue to enact communality through the land, work, and fiestas that are by and for the community (Martínez Luna 2015). Despite the Mexican government's efforts to weaken the *ejido* (communal) system, the land in El Rancho continues to be communal; fiestas are organized by the people and for the people; and for community projects, everyone is expected to contribute work, food, or another type of support. In the context of local and transnational state-led racial capitalism, relational communality matters because it enables the ongoing production of meaningful and humane life. As Wilson (2008) states, our relations define who we are and what we know. The state does not have full power to give or take away personhood and humanity; our multiple relations across space and generations sustain them.

Such ways of relating continue to inform how life is organized in El Rancho and also inform communal logics of relating in the United States, where our mere presence is criminalized through white-supremacist laws, such as the immigration law. While immigrants in my U.S. community practice a version of relational communality, many recognize that ways of living like El Rancho cannot be fully replicated in the United States, as in the case of Lola, who cannot reproduce the same feeling and connections experienced through güaipear. These embodied ways of being, knowing, doing, and feeling are at risk of being lost in a society where these relations are ignored, devalued, and disrupted due to forced and denied mobilities. As such, many in my community yearn to send their kids to Mexico, to El Rancho, so they can experience and learn from other ways of living there. Also, families back in Mexico constantly express a desire to see them again and/or to meet their grandkids. My teenaged daughters (who recently were able to visit El Rancho for the first time) have told me it is not the same to learn about this way of life through stories from parents and/or family members in the United States. Rather, powerful learning and connections come from actually being there and experiencing how people treat each other as family, as relatives, even if they are not family by blood. The experiences of walking everywhere and being able to talk to everyone; being invited into people's homes, kitchens, and celebrations at any time; and feeling at home, allowed them to feel welcomed, safe, and included. As Smith states, "To be connected is to be whole" (2013, 148). Such experiences of interconnection, belonging, and wholeness in turn can continue to influence how community relations are practiced by Mexican immigrants in the United States across generations. While I was able to finally take my own kids back to El Rancho, many in my community are legally denied this possibility.

In response to this yearning and drawing on logics of relational communality—where relations determine who we are, our personhood, and our humanity, and where sharing practices are centered—some Mexicans with U.S. citizenship in our immigrant community arrange to bring U.S.-born children of undocumented community members back to El Rancho. As such, some community members use the privilege and right of mobility granted through citizenship to become bridges and interconnectors of the community across legal physical barriers and across generations.[7] Rather than keeping these privileges to themselves as individualistic private property as per liberal understandings of citizenship, they instead build a way of life that centers relationality and solidarity. They convert their privileges into community tools that then strengthen relations of solidarity and trust between undocumented parents, Mexican U.S. citizens, and the community in El Rancho. Once there, grandparents and/or family introduce the U.S.-born children to everyone in the community. The children are placed in relation as members of specific families, who already relate to everyone. This way, the children are able to ontologically connect with the community in Mexico at the same time as they experience other ways of being, knowing, relating—and thus humanity.

This is a powerful way in which relational communality enables the making of U.S. citizenship into a community tool to enhance community relations, and thus humanity, across colonizing borders. My community demonstrates that sharing privileges granted from privatized framings of citizenship strengthens community relations between undocumented parents and the Mexican U.S. citizens who use their privilege to move across the physical buffer zone known as the U.S.-Mexico border and to act as a bridge in solidarity across space and generations. This is an expression of humanity and full personhood and radical politics of disruption and refusal that emerge from logics of relational communality as ways of being and knowing. This relational communality illustrates relational reworkings of liberal formations, refuses liberal projects of citizenship and exclusion, connects with ongoing (and opens up new) terrains and practices of struggle in Mexico and across Abya Yala—the Indigenous name for the entire continent we inhabit (Valle Escalante 2014).

T/here, for over five hundred years, Indigenous communities have resisted not only de-Indianization as an identity but also, most importantly, detrimental material consequences that emerge from a de-Indianized (liberal) way of life that centers capitalism, which requires constant displacement. A few of many powerful examples of Indigenous resistance include the Mexican Revolution of 1910 led by Indigenous communities in defense of communal (non-privatization) ownership of lands, the Zapatistas (Indigenous groups from Chiapas) in opposition to neoliberal economic policies of extraction and war since the early 1990s (Khasnabish 2013), and Indigenous and de-Indianized (mestiza) communities who practice relational communality in their everyday. Examples include preserving land as communally held ejidos in contrast to capitalist privatization (Martínez Luna 2015; Valencia 2019a; Villalba 2013) and Berta Cáceres's (an Indigenous Lenca woman) opposition to neoliberal projects that violate the rights of rivers to flow freely. For her, as for many Indigenous communities, rivers are sacred and alive, holding memories, spirits, and deep interconnections with all kinds of life that are denied in liberal, racial-capitalist ontologies. These struggles resist de-Indianization, fight for relational communal ways of life, and resist ongoing colonialism informed by liberal poverty knowledge and liberal logics of humanity. I join these calls for a world where all forms of life and ways of being and knowing are respected and where radical relations of care among humans and nonhuman life, lands, and waters are restored.

NOTES

1. Indigenous peoples from Latin American continue to face land dispossession, displacement, racism, and criminalization (Menchaca 2001; Saldaña-Portillo 2017; Ybarra 2017), but mestizaje matters because it facilitates our de-Indianization, internalized racism, and distancing from our roots and land, which in combination with (im)mobilities enable expansion of settler-colonial imperialism.

2. The Bracero Program, a wartime emergency initiative, was implemented in 1942 to ease a shortage of agricultural labor in the United States. This program proved a dream for U.S. growers as it provided an uninterrupted, cheap, and captive labor supply. Braceros were expected to work exclusively for the specific grower-contractor regardless of working conditions and to return soon after the season ended, and they were prohibited from organizing (Calavita 1992).

3. Today workers move across the border through seasonal labor programs such as the H-2A and H-2B visas, meant to recruit seasonal workers, mostly from Mexico, to fulfil the demands for cheap labor by the agriculture and food industry.

4. According to Ruth W. Gilmore, racial capitalism didn't originate with Black slaves; poor whites had been converted into cheap labor before then (Card 2020).

5. Racial logics are imposed across the Americas.

6. As Valencia (2019a) demonstrates, there have been multiple practices rooted in Indigenous relational communality across time and space, but here I focus on how such practices—which enable community relations across space and generations—challenge liberal, individualistic propertied personhood and humanity.

7. To clarify, this is often the case for people who have family and a large community back in El Rancho. However, for those who were most deeply affected by the wave of violence, due in large part to the war on drugs waged and encouraged by the United States, it has not been easy to send their kids back to El Rancho. Even for those who have documents, returning or bringing their kids can be unsafe.

REFERENCES

Alanís Enciso, Fernando Saúl. 2017. *They Should Stay There*. Russ Davidson (Trans.). Chapel Hill: University of North Carolina Press.

Alarcón, Norma. 1990. "Chicana Feminism." *Cultural Studies* 4(3): 248–256. https://doi .org/10.1080/09502389000490201.

Aldama, Arturo J. 2001. *Disrupting Savagism*. Durham, N.C.: Duke University Press. http://public.eblib.com/choice/publicfullrecord.aspx?p=1167484.

Andreas, Peter. 2012. *Border Games*. Ithaca, N.Y.: Cornell University Press.

Aufseeser, Dena. 2015. "The Problems of Child Labor and Education in Peru." In Peter Kelly and Annelies Kamp (Eds.), *A Critical Youth Studies for the 21st Century*, 181–195. Leiden: Brill. https://doi.org/10.1163/9789004284036_014.

Bacon, David. 2008. *Illegal People*. Boston: Beacon.

Barajas, Manuel. 2009. *The Xaripu Community across Borders*. Notre Dame, Ind.: University of Notre Dame Press.

Blackwell, Maylei. 2011. *Chicana Power!* Austin: University of Texas Press.

Bledsoe, Adam, and Illie Jamaal Wright. 2019. "The Anti-Blackness of Global Capital." *Environment and Planning D: Society and Space* 37(1): 8–26.

Boehm, Deborah A. 2011. "U.S.-Mexico Mixed Migration in an Age of Deportation." *Refugee Survey Quarterly* 30(1): 1–21. https://doi.org/10.1093/rsq/hdq042.

Bonfil Batalla, Guillermo, and Philip Adams Dennis. 1996. *México Profundo*. Austin: University of Texas Press.

Briy, A. 2020. "Zapatistas: Lessons in Community Self-Organisation in Mexico." *Open Democracy*, June 25. https://www.opendemocracy.net/en/democraciaabierta /zapatistas-lecciones-de-auto-organizaci%C3%B3n-comunitaria-en/.

Cacho, Lisa Marie. 2012. *Social Death*. New York: New York University Press.

Calavita, Kitty. 1992. *Inside the State*. New York: Routledge.

Camacho, Alicia Schmidt. 2008. *Nation of Nations*. New York: New York University Press.

Card, Kenton. 2020. "Geographies of Racial Capitalism with Ruth Wilson Gilmore." *Antipode Online*, 2022. https://antipodeonline.org/geographies-of-racial-capitalism/.

Clapp, Jennifer. 2012. *Food*. Cambridge: Polity.

Corva, Dominic. 2008. "Neoliberal Globalization and the War on Drugs." *Political Geography* 27(2): 176–193. https://doi.org/10.1016/j.polgeo.2007.07.008.

Cotera, María Eugenia, and María Josefina Saldaña-Portillo. 2015. "Indigenous but Not Indian? Chicana/os and the Politics of Indigeneity." In Robert Warrior (Ed.), *The World of Indigenous North America*, 575–594. New York: Routledge.

Cupples, Julie. 2013. *Latin American Development*. New York: Routledge.

Cusicanqui, Silvia Rivera. 2010. *Ch'ixinakax Utxiwa*. Translated by Molly Geidel. Cambridge: Polity.

Daigle, Michelle, and Margaret Marietta Ramírez. 2019. "Decolonial Geographies." In *Keywords in Radical Geography: Antipode*, 78–84. Hoboken, N.J.: John Wiley. https:// doi.org/10.1002/9781119558071.ch14.

De Genova, Nicholas. 2002. "Migrant 'Illegality' and Deportability in Everyday Life." *Annual Review of Anthropology* 31(1): 419–447. https://doi.org/10.1146/annurev .anthro.31.040402.085432.

———. 2004. "The Legal Production of Mexican/Migrant 'Illegality.'" *Latino Studies* 2(2): 160–185.

Escobar, Arturo. 1995. *Encountering Development*. Princeton, N.J.: Princeton University Press.

Gilmore, Ruth Wilson. 2002. "Fatal Couplings of Power and Difference." *Professional Geographer* 54(1): 15–24. https://doi.org/10.1111/0033-0124.00310.#123#.

Gonzalez, Abraham. 2019. "Mexico to Hike Daily Minimum Wage." *Reuters*, December 17. https://www.reuters.com/article/us-mexico-wages-idUSKBN1YL051.

Gonzalez Casanova, Pablo. 1965. "Internal Colonialism and National Development." *Studies in Comparative International Development* 1(4): 27–37.

Harris, Cheryl I. 1993. "Whiteness as Property." *Harvard Law Review* 106(8): 1707–1791. https://doi.org/10.2307/1341787.

Khasnabish, Alex. 2013. *Zapatistas*. London: Zed Books.

Lawson, Victoria. 2010. "Reshaping Economic Geography?" *Economic Geography* 86(4): 351–360. https://doi.org/10.1111/j.1944-8287.2010.001092.x.

Macpherson, C. B., and Frank Cunningham. 2011. *The Political Theory of Possessive Individualism : Hobbes to Locke*. Wynford ed. Oxford: Oxford University Press.

Martínez, Maria Elena. 2008. *Genealogical Fictions*. Stanford, Calif.: Stanford University Press.

Martínez Luna, Jaime. 2015. "Comunalidad as the Axis of Oaxacan Thought in Mexico." *Upside Down World* (blog), October 27. http://upsidedownworld.org/archives /mexico/comunalidad-axis-of-oaxacan-thought/.

McKittrick, Katherine. 2006. *Demonic Grounds*. Minneapolis: University of Minnesota Press.

———, ed. 2015. *Sylvia Wynter: On Being Human as Praxis*. Durham, N.C.: Duke University Press.

McKittrick, Katherine, and Clyde Adrian Woods. 2007. *Black Geographies and the Politics of Place*. Chico, Calif.: AK Press.

Menchaca, Martha. 1993. "Chicano Indianism." *American Ethnologist* 20(3): 583–603. https://doi.org/10.1525/ae.1993.20.3.02a00070.

———. 2001. *Recovering History, Constructing Race*. Austin: University of Texas Press.

Mercille, Julien. 2011. "Violent Narco-Cartels or U.S. Hegemony?" *Third World Quarterly* 32(9): 1637–1653. https://doi.org/10.1080/01436597.2011.619881.

Mignolo, Walter. 2000. "The Many Faces of Cosmo-Polis: Border Thinking and Critical Cosmopolitanism." *Public Culture* 12(3): 721–748.

———. 2005. *The Idea of Latin America*. Malden, Mass.: Blackwell.

Miroff, Nick. 2020. "Trump Planning to Divert Additional $7.2 Billion in Pentagon Funds for Border Wall." *Washington Post*, January 13. https://www.washingtonpost .com/immigration/trump-planning-to-divert-additional-72-billion-in-pentagon -funds-for-border-wall/2020/01/13/59080a3a-363d-11ea-bb7b-265f4554af6d_story .html.

Nevins, Joseph. 2002. *Operation Gatekeeper*. New York: Routledge

———. 2007. "Dying for a Cup of Coffee?" *Geopolitics* 12(2): 228–247. https://doi.org /10.1080/14650040601168826.

Ngai, Mae M. 2004. *Impossible Subjects*. Princeton, N.J.: Princeton University Press.

Pachirat, Timothy. 2011. *Every Twelve Seconds*. New Haven, Conn.: Yale University Press.

Paley, Dawn. 2014. *Drug War Capitalism*. Chico, Calif.: AK Press.

Porter, Libby. 2014. "Possessory Politics and the Conceit of Procedure." *Planning Theory* 13(4): 387–406.

Ramos, Jorge. 2002. *The Other Face of America*. New York: HarperCollins.

Rana, Aziz. 2010. *The Two Faces of American Freedom*. Cambridge, Mass.: Harvard University Press.

Reese, Ashanté M. 2018. "'We Will Not Perish; We're Going to Keep Flourishing': Race, Food Access, and Geographies of Self-Reliance." *Antipode* 50(2): 407–424. https://doi .org/10.1111/anti.12359.

Robinson, Cedric J. 2000. *Black Marxism*. Chapel Hill: University of North Carolina Press.

Roy, Ananya. 2017. "Dis/Possessive Collectivism: Property and Personhood at City's End." *Geoforum* 80: A1–A11. https://doi.org/10.1016/j.geoforum.2016.12.012.

Rubin, Barry. 2014. *Silent Revolution*. Northampton, Mass.: Broadside Books.

Said, Edward W. 1979. *Orientalism*. New York: Vintage.

Saldaña-Portillo, María Josefina. 2017. "Critical Latinx Indigeneities." *Latino Studies* 15(2): 138–155. https://doi.org/10.1057/s41276-017-0059-x.

Sharpe, Christina Elizabeth. 2016. *In the Wake*. Durham, N.C.: Duke University Press.

Simpson, Leanne Betasamosake. 2017. *As We Have Always Done: Indigenous Freedom through Radical Resistance*. Minneapolis: University of Minnesota Press.

Smith, Linda Tuhiwai. 2013. *Decolonizing Methodologies: Research and Indigenous Peoples*. London: Zed Books.

Spade, Dean. 2011. *Normal Life*. Brooklyn, N.Y.: South End Press.

Sparke, Matthew. 2013. *Introducing Globalization*. Hoboken, N.J.: Wiley-Blackwell.

Stetson, George. 2012. "Oil Politics and Indigenous Resistance in the Peruvian Amazon." *Journal of Environment & Development* 21(1): 76–97. https://doi.org/10.1177 /1070496511433425.

Urrea, Luis Alberto. 2004. *The Devil's Highway*. New York: Little, Brown.

Valencia, Yolanda. 2017. "Risk and Security on the Mexico-to-U.S. Migrant Journey." *Gender, Place & Culture* 24(11): 1530–1548. https://doi.org/10.1080/0966369X .2017.1352566.

———. 2019a. "Inmigrante Indocumentado." PhD dissertation, University of Washington.

———. 2019b. "An Immigrant in Academia: Navigating Grief and Privilege." In Kathryn Gillespie and Patricia J. Lopez (Eds.), *Vulnerable Witness: The Politics of Grief in the Field*, 54–67. Oakland: University of California Press.

Valle Escalante, Emilio del. 2014. "Self-Determination: A Perspective from Abya Yala." *E-International Relations*, May 20. https://www.e-ir.info/2014/05/20/self -determination-a-perspective-from-abya-yala/.

Vasconcelos, José. 1997. *La Raza Cosmica*. 2nd ed. Baltimore: Johns Hopkins University Press.

Villalba, Unai. 2013. "Buen Vivir vs Development." *Third World Quarterly* 34(8): 1427– 1442. https://doi.org/10.1080/01436597.2013.831594.

Walia, Harsha. 2014. *Undoing Border Imperialism*. Chico, Calif.: AK Press.

———. 2021. *Border and Rule*. Chicago: Haymarket Books.

Wilson, Shawn. 2008. *Research Is Ceremony: Indigenous Research Methods*. Black Point, N.S.: Fernwood.

Wright, Melissa W. 2001. "The Dialectics of Still Life: Murder, Women and Maquiladoras." In John L. Comaroff and Jean Comaroff (Eds.), *Millennial Capitalism and the Culture of Neoliberalism*, 125–146. Durham, N.C.: Duke University Press.

———. 2011. "Necropolitics, Narcopolitics, and Femicide." *Signs* 36(3): 707–731. https://doi.org/10.1086/657496.

Ybarra, Megan. 2017. *Green Wars*. Oakland: University of California Press.

CHAPTER 4

Anonymous Communion

Black Queer Communities and Anti-Black Violence within the HIV/AIDS Epidemic

AARON MALLORY

> A black sense of place . . . brings into focus the ways in which racial violences . . . shape, but do not wholly define, black worlds.
> —Katherine McKittrick (2011, 947)

In 1986, Fabian Calvin Bridges, a thirty-year-old Black AIDS-positive man, was profiled in the PBS documentary series *Frontline*. The program, titled "AIDS: A National Inquiry," centered Bridges as part of a public debate on the ways Americans should respond to the HIV/AIDS epidemic. Originally, the program's production was slated to involve a number of individuals living with AIDS; however, the focus shifted to Bridges as a "noncompliant" AIDS-positive individual, which became a point to debate on individual responsibility among infected populations during the early years of the HIV/AIDS epidemic. News media and national LGBT groups labeled Bridges as a deviant sexual predator, which led to multiple confrontations with local public health officials, law enforcement, and LGBTQIA communities who responded to the potential threat of an AIDS-positive person.[1] While early portrayals of individuals suffering from the HIV/AIDS epidemic focused on victimization, Bridges's positive status as a sexual deviant highlights the social and institutional barriers that racialized gender and sexual minorities, in particular Black communities, face as they are surveilled and intervened upon based on what are perceived to be potential sexual transgressions (Esparza 2019). Bridges's portrayal on national television represents the mutually constitutive relationship between anti-Blackness and mainstream LGBTQIA communities' embrace of liberalism. For Black LGBTQIA communities, the HIV/AIDS epidemic constituted a punitive relationship, while providing mainstream LGBT communities an opportunity to articulate acceptable forms of sexual expression.

Despite Bridges's prime-time portrayal as a sexual deviant, he is a marginal figure within scholarship on the HIV/AIDS epidemic, in particular, the epidemic's relationship to racialized gender and sexual minority communities. While the popular scholarly narrative of the HIV/AIDS epidemic highlights a lack of government response to the virus, which led to the activism of white-identified gay men in New York, Los Angeles, and San Francisco (France 2016; Epstein 1996; Gould 2009), critical scholars have shown that in addition to white-identified gay communities on the East and West coasts, Black LGBTQIA communities and the U.S. South have been central to the fight against the epidemic (Moseby 2017; Cohen 1999; Bailey et al. 2019; Esparza 2019; Bost 2020; Roane 2019). Bridges's experiences demonstrate the historical centrality of knowledge produced and response to the HIV/AIDS epidemic, which is built through negative portrayals of Black people who are at risk of HIV infection. Through Bridges, we can chart the ways that liberalism is articulated in sexual regulation during the HIV/AIDS epidemic, which impacts the ways society understands the intersections of race, gender, and sexuality.

This chapter explores liberal investment in anti-Black responses to the HIV/AIDS epidemic to highlight barriers that Black LGBTQIA communities face with regard to sexual citizenship and Black sexual practices. The relationship between sexual citizenship and Black sexual practices is crucial given that the former leverages anti-Black portrayals of Black sexuality in order for white-identified sexual minorities to gain entry into normative sites of liberalism. Liberal investment in sexual expression frames preferred modes of sexual citizenship practices, limiting diversity in LGBTQIA communities and forming the grounds from which activists must fight. Therefore, in the mid- to late 1980s, ACT-UP responded not only to government retrenchment of public health services but also to liberal investment in preferred sexual practices for gender and sexual minorities (Schulman 2021). Bridges's experiences as a sexual deviant provide an example of the ways mainstream LGBT communities leverage his actions as justification for the inclusion of their communities, through a connection to anti-Black violence, which excludes Black communities. Liberal inclusion based on rights and recognition is part of what Andrew Sullivan (1996) called the "awkward acceptance" of white-identified LGBT communities into liberalism that centered sexual freedom through the sexual regulation of Black and other gender and sexual minorities. This takes place through the policing of Black gender and sexual minorities' sexual freedom as it is connected to state-driven institutional responses to poverty related to health care, housing, employment, and disability status. Stated another way, white-identified mainstream LGBT communities find a reprieve from sexual violence through the institutional regulation of Black gender and sexual minorities, which aligns these communities with anti-Black and white-supremacist practices. Bridges's experiences and portrayal provide an example of the ways anti-Blackness impacts material and imagined community formations through LGBT communities' investments in liberalism, which inform differential forms of knowledge and responses to the HIV/AIDS epidemic.

Liberalism's investment in anti-Blackness during the HIV/AIDS epidemic structures the ways Black LGBTQIA communities respond to access around HIV prevention, rates of HIV infection, and health care access. Through an analysis of Bridges's experiences, I identify anti-Black practices that Atlanta, Georgia-based Black LGBTQIA community organizations must overcome to address disproportionate rates of infection among Black populations. I argue that Bridges's story speaks not only to the ways anti-Blackness prompts Black people to be stripped of access to their bodies and sexuality but also to the ways that current organizations in Atlanta challenge barriers to community inclusion and sexual practices. By uncovering community-based organizations' contestations to anti-Black practices—practices of difference making that result in a greater propensity of Black people to be inclined toward premature death (Gilmore 2002)—this chapter expands Black geography scholarship through an engagement with queer of color critique.

This chapter employs a methodological framework, connecting the past to the present of the HIV/AIDS epidemic through Bridges's story and Atlanta-based activists, that is based in geographic-centered knowledge production. As a discipline that analyzes the relational production of space and time, geography is a system of knowledge production that considers difference as a primary mode and object of knowledge creation (Gregory 1994). From changing topographies of landscapes to local particularities of place, geography is situated around differential knowledge production. My approach combines geography with queer of color critique. Queer of color critique provides a theoretical and methodological approach to understand liberalism's investment in the HIV/AIDS epidemic through institutional responses to HIV/AIDS at the intersections of race, gender, and sexuality. Queer of color critique and geography highlight the ways anti-Blackness is central to Black LGBTQIA communities' experience of gender and sexual domination in place. The place-based convergence of race, gender, and sexuality allows for the past to be connected to the present while also demonstrating the ways anti-Blackness—as a system that reduces Black people to an object—informs sexual citizenship and Black sexuality (Manalansan 2005; Konrad 2014; McGlotten 2014; Bailey 2014). I build from queer of color critique to show the ways that Bridges's experiences around sexuality, legibility, and place provide a foundation to understand the barriers that Atlanta-based Black queer communities face during the HIV/AIDS epidemic.

Queer of color critique exposes barriers within the U.S. investment in liberalism and the HIV/AIDS epidemic to show the intimacies of anti-Blackness that Black LGBTQIA communities challenge. Black LGBTQIA communities' responses to anti-Black violence reveal a set of intimacies within the material landscapes of the HIV/AIDS epidemic. Negative portrayals and regulation of Black sexuality limit access to HIV-prevention resources and drug therapies for Black communities at risk or infected. Here, denying Black sexuality as part of anti-Black practices provides a social currency for white-identified groups to promote normative gender and sexual group formations. However, through the work of Black community-based organizations in response to the HIV/AIDS epidemic, mainstream LGBT communities' leveraging of anti-Blackness for normative inclusion into U.S. liberalisms is limited and not totalizing in scope. This is due to Black community-based organizations embracing Black sexuality regardless of negative portrayals. I focus on Atlanta-based LGBTQIA activists' response to sexual regulation to show the ways in which anti-Blackness functions, in part, as a result of intimacies developed through contestations to anti-Black violence. What emerges from this consideration is the role of place as it structures sexual citizenship and Black sexual practices. Situated in a place, Black queer communities in Atlanta engage in sexual practices, place making, and other forms of care, addressing barriers associated with the HIV/AIDS epidemic. I argue that activists in Atlanta lay bare the contours of anti-Blackness through engaging the historical barriers that Bridges faced related to Black sexuality, displacement, and health care three decades prior.

To place Bridges's experiences in conversation with local Atlanta-based Black communities, this chapter first situates Bridges's sexual transgressions in conversation with material expressions of Black sexual autonomy during the HIV/AIDS epidemic. Following this, I demonstrate the ways that liberalism's investment in the HIV/AIDS epidemic is built through the sexual citizenship practices of mainstream LGBTQIA communities and the regulation of Black sexuality. Bridges is instrumental to understanding the ways anti-Blackness is central to rights and recognition within a punitive logic that allows for white-identified LGBTQIA communities to benefit from the domination of Black people. Third, I show the ways Atlanta-based Black activists respond to the HIV/AIDS epidemic through situated place-based community building and sexual practices. This builds from Black gay cultural producers who experienced exclusion from white-identified gay communities. I take the experiences of Black gay men loving other Black gay men as a space of resistance and situate them in conversation with current Black queer community building in Atlanta.

Bridges's Story

In 1986, *Frontline* host Judy Woodruff cautions viewers that what they are about to witness is shocking and "not the typical story of someone living with AIDS and is rare" (PBS 1986). Fabian Bridges is in bed at Jefferson Davis Hospital's AIDS Ward in Houston as *Frontline* begins their portrayal of him. Bridges's relationship to the HIV/AIDS virus is typical. While working for the county flood control unit, he fell ill and was hospitalized for what he then learned were AIDS-related complications. After three months in the hospital, Bridges is well enough to leave. Bridges, without a job or home, is given a one-way ticket to Indianapolis to live with family as it is assumed he will eventually pass away. In Indianapolis, Bridges's sister, having learned about his AIDS diagnosis, denies entry to her home claiming that with a new child her family was uncertain that the disease would not spread to the rest of the family. Bridges moves around Indianapolis, between homeless shelters and the streets, until he is jailed on charges of stealing a bicycle. Bridges's AIDS-positive status causes the jail system to isolate him from the general population, which places a burden on his physical and mental well-being. At his arraignment, a sympathetic judge dismisses Bridges's charges and collects funds to give him a one-way ticket to Cleveland to be with his mother and stepfather. Once there, we learn that Bridges's mother also denies him, and he is out on the streets again.

In Cleveland, *Frontline* reunites with Bridges; however, the narrator's tone indicates a marked shift. The narrator of the *Frontline* episode crew states that Bridges "is no longer just a victim" (PBS 1986). *Frontline* producers admit that they have started to give him money due to what they perceive to be his involvement in sex work. They pay for his room and board along with other amenities to keep him off the streets. Crucially, Bridges admits to producers that he has been sexually active. In a pivotal scene, *Frontline* producers confront Bridges to ask him about his sexual transgressions, to which he replies, "I just don't give a damn." In response to Bridges's admission, *Frontline* producers notify the Cleveland Public Health Department and the president of the Cleveland City Council about Bridges's sexual transgressions. In response to this information, the Public Health Department and the City Council convene to figure out a plan to stop Bridges from having sex, with one council member likening Bridges to a "mass shooter" with the ability to infect an entire population. Esparza (2019, 271) notes that this allows a *Frontline* "panelist [to] compare HIV to a lethal weapon, branding Fabian a dangerous criminal—a biological terrorist—whose free movement threatened the general population of white middle America with a slow, painful death."

In response to *Frontline*'s revelations about Bridges's sexual transgressions, activist Buck Harris, the state of Ohio appointee for gay health, proclaims that Bridges is not part of this community and will harm him if found. Harris claims that the Cleveland LGBT community is on the lookout for Bridges in nightclubs, bars, and other LGBT community places. To justify the surveillance, Harris reiterates to the camera that Bridges's actions are irresponsible and out of line from the ways that the local LGBT community conducts itself. In an attempt to further distance himself and the local community from Bridges, Harris claims he would lynch Bridges if he found him. Although Bridges's race is never stated as a factor in the PBS documentation, the racial undertones of Harris's statement speaks to the Cleveland LGBT community's liberal investment in anti-Blackness during the HIV/AIDS epidemic. The threat of violence through lynching contributes to a white hostility against Bridges and places him as an "other" through material and imagined harms. This allows the Cleveland LGBT community to move away from Bridges as their hostility establishes a proper state regulatory response to deviant sexual practices. Harris's statement establishes race as a factor in response to deviant sexual acts.

Eventually, Bridges is able to collect Social Security Disability that was previously withheld by his mother. This allows him to leave Cleveland and return to Houston. There, during a follow-up health appointment at Jefferson Davis Hospital, Bridges is presented with a proclamation from the county public health department that states that he cannot engage in any sexual activity while he is in the city. After Bridges receives the proclamation, local law enforcement follows Bridges, hoping to entrap him in a potential sexual act. In what reads as a comedy of errors, seemingly heterosexual muscled and mustached vice police officers pose as potential clients in order to arrest Bridges for prostitution. The Houston Police Department's actions point to the extreme measures of local authorities to regulate deviant sexual acts. However, Bridges is never found to be soliciting sex. Local gay activist Ray Hill takes Bridges under his watch, where Fabian Bridges passes away four months later.

Bridges, in his depiction in this *Frontline* special, is a symbol for all that can go wrong for someone living with a positive HIV diagnosis. *Time* magazine and the *Los Angeles Times* depict his story as an example of a nomadic AIDS-positive person spreading the virus unbeknownst to the larger population. The *Times* article describes Fabian Bridges as "a gay man with AIDS, a miserable, wretched, uncaring victim-turned-victimizer who used his body as a lethal weapon" (Rosenberg 1986). Bridges's portrayal creates a position from which to articulate irresponsible sexual acts, as his admission of sexual deviation becomes justification to regulate his sexual practices. This portrayal of deviance allows for a differentiation in response to the HIV/AIDS epidemic by separating appropriate from deviant sexual acts. For example, the panel discussion between health and behavioral experts in the *Frontline* episode places Bridges outside of expected sexual practices and distances his actions from the larger LGBT community. Diego Lopez, an HIV-positive clinical psychologist and part of Gay Men's Health Crisis in New York, was pressured into explaining why Bridges was so careless. In his response, Lopez creates a distance between the actions of Bridges and the mainstream gay community that, he claims, is not reflective of Bridges's actions. Through this distancing and othering, Bridges's sexuality becomes a site from which anti-Black violence proliferates vis-à-vis the material practices of liberalism by mainstream LGBT communities as they regulate his sexuality due to perceived sexual deviances. The public disavowal of Bridges's sexual transgressions makes explicit the relationship between race and sexuality as experiences of racism are expressed through sexual regulation in favor of expanding white supremacy. In the case of Bridges, sexual regulation comes in the form of state surveillance, the unethical choice of *Frontline* producers to inform local authorities of Bridges's sexual transgressions, and county health authorities preventing Bridges from having sex. Sexual regulation is connected to anti-Blackness and informs normative expectations of sexual intercourse during the HIV/AIDS epidemic.

Additionally, Bridges's portrayal is an attempt to show the day-to-day life of someone with HIV/AIDS. Bridges experiences several different forms of marginalization prior to his encounter with PBS. The contours of his marginalization are place based between Cleveland, Indianapolis, and Houston. Denied entry to both heterosexual and homosexual communities in several different cities, Bridges's relationship to place is fraught. The actions of PBS *Frontline* enroll Bridges into a number of anti-Black acts, which expand our understanding of the heterogeneity of anti-Blackness. The potential, without visible confirmation, of sexual transgression invests Bridges into cycles of anti-Black violence through surveillance, incarceration, and sexual violence, which are structured through anti-Black relationships in place. Yet Bridges's relationship to anti-Black violence is situated through his imagined relationships to sexual actions, which make the hidden and unknown ability to have sex a central driver of his experiences.

Black Sexuality and LGBTQIA Community Liberal Formations

Bridges's story demonstrates the ways in which liberalism in the form of sexual citizenship aligns with anti-Blackness through the regulation of his supposed sexual "transgressions." HIV/AIDS criminalization laws (Gossett 2014), the lack of HIV/AIDS health-care-related resources (Sangaramoorthy 2012), the overproduction of Black sexual promiscuity (Thrasher 2018), the presence of Black men on the down-low (Snorton 2014), and the overrepresentation of heterosexual transmission among Black women (Gilbert and Wright 2003) demonstrate the ways in which Black sexuality has been pathologized and regulated and was central to producing liberal forms of sexual citizenship during the HIV/AIDS epidemic. Nero (2005) points to two factors that contribute to the use of sexual regulation. First are the middle-class aspirations of LGBTQIA communities to assimilate into the liberal project of mainstream sexual citizenship. Second are white hostilities toward Black communities. Proclamations of harm against and attempts to regulate Bridges's ability to have sex establish Black sexuality as antagonistic to the social landscapes of LGBTQIA community formations. The words of Buck Harris create borders between admissible and deviant sexual practices that define those who will be subject to policing practices, as Harris's invocation of lynching speaks to racial foundations within LGBTQIA communities. As such, LGBTQIA community formations are premised on an investment in anti-Blackness that is articulated through Black sexuality. Within these normative aspirations of white-identified LGBTQIA communities and anti-Black violence, community formations are built through the regulation of Black sexuality.

Bridges necessitates a consideration of the racial underpinnings of sexual citizenship in which his race and sexual transgressions form a basis for liberalism among mainstream white-identified LGBTQIA communities. Sexual citizenship highlights expressions of freedom as sexual minorities seek formal rights and recognitions from the state. Part of the process of receiving recognition is to establish group boundaries that become the basis of internal policing in order to align the group formation with the punitive values of the state. Lamble (2013) establishes sexual citizenship as the emergence of a group politics based in belonging and recognition of legal and social rights that are produced through the state. In exchange for rights and recognition, white-identified LGBTQIA subjects undertake the punitive elements of liberal notions of social and economic freedom. State enforcement of hate crimes and the increased use of the criminal justice system in turn prompts privileged gender and sexual minorities "to view police as LGBT protectors of sexual cit-

izenship rather than enforcers of economic, political and racial hierarches"
(Lamble 2013, 241). The goal is to seek protections from the state through policing Black sexual formations. Through Lamble's use of sexual citizenship, we
recognize that part of the emergence of a political body is the recognition that
a group is deserving of state protections through the anti-Black policing and
regulation of Black gender and sexual minorities. Sexual citizenship is racialized, regulating not only those who are deemed sexually transgressive but also
those who are outside of white-identified LGBTQIA communities.

Black LGBTQIA communities must navigate liberalism's investment in race
and sexuality, which creates a situated experience where mainstream LGBT
communities' use of sexual regulation intersects with narratives of overcoming
socioeconomic and sociopolitical determinants that define the Black experience in the United States. Bridges's experiences, as both Black and gay, point to
the need to center race as a key feature of sexual citizenship within gender and
sexual minority communities. Ferguson (2004) situates race as a key factor in
the ways group-based sexual affiliations are developed. Race, gender, and sexuality articulate with one another to center preferred forms of normative sexual practices that can then be brought into the favor of state protections in service of family and nation. Duggan (2012, 50) points to the intersection of a state
intervention on behalf of a limited understanding of sexuality as a LGBTQIA
politics that "does not contest dominant heteronormative assumptions and institutions, but upholds and sustains them, while promising the possibility of a
demobilized gay constituency and a privatized, depoliticizing gay culture anchored in domesticity and consumption." Duggan names this apolitical position of certain sexual minorities as homonormativity, in which institutions in
favor of capital are promoted through a demobilized, depoliticized LGBTQIA
culture. Race is central in that the grounds in which homonormativity can be
articulated are through investments in whiteness and anti-Black violence. For
example, Harris's claim that our community "does not engage in those type of
dangerous sexual actions" and his threats to lynch Bridges point to depoliti-
calized practices among sexual minority communities whose inclusion in state
protections is made through anti-Black violence. Through Black sexual regulation, race and sexuality articulate with one another to create a set of anti-Black
practices that define mainstream white-identified LGBTQIA communities' affiliations. Sexual regulation within mainstream LGBTQIA communities along
racial lines creates sites for state intervention against racialized deviant sexual
practices. Practices of naming Black gender and sexual minorities as deviant
allow for white-identified LGBTQIA communities to be included in U.S. economic and social freedoms through acceptable sexual practices, which eludes

a thorough understanding of Black sexuality on its own terms. This illuminates the multiple forms of marginalization that Black gender and sexual minorities face internal to the Black community and external to mainstream LGBTQIA communities whose investment in liberal inclusion creates barriers to authentic gender and sexual expressions.

While opposing Black sexuality forms the basis of group formation for mainstream white-identified LGBTQIA communities, it also illuminates a space for intervention that Black gender and sexual minority communities engage in through expanding "queer" as a political project. On one hand, Black sexuality is articulated through anti-Black racism. The violence that Bridges experiences creates nonnormative subject positions within the Black LGBTQIA community that informs the normative subject positions of white-identified LGBTQIA communities. However, on the other hand, the nonnormative subject position of Black queers intersects with other state intimacies beyond sexuality and gender that create additional barriers to normative sites like housing, employment, and other parts of society, which if taken alongside gender and sexuality have the ability to expand queer as a site of political engagement. Cathy Cohen (2001), in "Punks, Bulldaggers, and Welfare Queens," questions the sociopolitical formation of queer as singularly against heterosexuality, given that Black queer communities exist outside not only heteronormativity but also other normative sites of U.S. liberalism. For example, Black women on welfare represent a nonnormative subject position that expands queer as a political project. Cohen represents the limitations of queer subject formations against heterosexuality, contending that "a truly radical or transformative politics has not resulted from queer activism. In many instances, instead of destabilizing the assumed categories and binaries of sexual identity, queer politics has served to reinforce simple dichotomies between heterosexual and everything queer" (2001, 238). Cohen attaches race as another site of nonnormative political action that complements gender and sexual marginalization to show that race is key to the experiences of Black LGBTQIA communities. Cohen establishes gender, sexuality, and race as nonnormative subject positions that Black queer communities must address. An expansion of queerness or LGBTQIA group formations must include a consideration of the mutually constitutive relationship between gender, sexuality, and race.

To understand the ways Black sexuality expands queerness and addresses anti-Black violence, I focus on queer Black spatial production as an extension of a Black sense of place. Bridges's movements between cities, forcefully or voluntary, constitute a form of Black spatial production at the intersections of race and sexuality. A focus on sexuality and race expands the ways anti-Black violence is expressed and is contingent on historical and contested racialization and sexual practices in place. Building from a Black sense of place that calls into question the ways anti-Black violence "shape, but do not wholly define, black worlds" (McKittrick 2011, 947), anti-Black violence is articulated in and through sexuality in the form of sexual regulation and community neglect. My use of a Black sense of place points to the ways Black communities make life under conditions of anti-Black violence, through understandings of race and sexual space-making practices that inform a Black queer spatial production. If it is through gender and sexual violence that anti-Blackness finds its expression among Black people, then it is through the spatial production of Black gender and sexual minorities from which we can better understand a Black sense of place. However, for Black gender and sexual minorities, Black queer spatial production illustrates the way visible antagonisms of anti-Black violence coexist with hidden intimacies.

The volatility of Bridges's relationship to place highlights the role of hidden space as central to Black queer spatial production. My use of "hidden" to represent Black queer spatial production speaks to visible antagonisms of sexual regulation that coexist alongside the hidden intimacies of sexuality, which are central to Bridges's story. Bridges's relationship to state intimacies based in anti-Black violence is premised on his hidden sexual transgressions. Although there is no official documentation of Bridges engaging in sexual acts, the hidden potentiality of sexual acts as a Black gay HIV-positive cisgender man allows for interventions on his life at any time. The hidden potentiality of Bridges's sexuality and local government response "expose[s] how race, gender and sexuality are expressed and constituted in and through spatial landscapes, while highlighting the ways Black gender and sexual minorities' subjection to public ridicule and violence [are an] essential function in the overall erotic economy" (Bailey and Shabazz 2014, 318). Yet it is crucial to recognize that Bridges's spatial movements between places do not fully define his relationship to anti-Blackness, sexual regulation, and liberal investment in preferred sexual practices. The lack of visible documentation of Bridges's sexual transgressions underscores the reality that Black queer sexuality is largely outside of knowledge production. This unknown quality of Black queer sexuality allows for hidden sexual practices to emerge as sites to challenge the conditions that Black queer communities face under the HIV/AIDS epidemic.

The hidden spaces of Bridges's potential sexual transgressions are sites through which sexual spaces of mainstream LGBTQIA communities are normalized and whitened. Rinaldo Walcott (2005) asserts that the hidden spaces of Black gay cultural production leave a lasting impact on white-identified gay communities. The hidden spaces of Black sexuality, when made visible, are coded as white. For example, the hidden spaces of drag and gender-bending Black and Latinx ballroom communities become visible as part of larger white-identified LGBTQIA communities. Through mainstream consumption of voguing or other Black queer cultural production, white LGBTQIA communities are able to appropriate Black queer cultural production as their own. Black queerness provides a social currency for these ends as cultural consumption becomes the basis for group formation. However, the Black queer people from whom that currency is appropriated are systemically hidden as mainstream appropriations of culture do not give credit to their origins (Walcott 2005). Therefore, Black queer spatial production includes both anti-Black appropriations of Blackness and sites of Black queer sexual practices. I consider Black queer spatial practices through the ways Bridges's experiences are situated in hidden intimacies tied to his imagined and material racial and sexual relationship to place. I argue that hidden sexual practices illustrate the ways place is central to making visible Black sexual practices and the ways community-based organizations respond to the HIV/AIDS epidemic.

The proliferation of anti-Blackness through sexual regulation of visible and hidden practices of Black sexuality misrepresents the ways Black sexuality takes place. Anti-Blackness is complicit in the regulation of Black sexuality as it is narrowly understood as promiscuous, hypersexual, and lacking community diversity. Countering this, Bailey (2020, 218) argues that "sexual practices, spaces and situations in which Black gay men are engaged allow them to claim and enact sexual autonomy during this HIV crisis that disproportionately impacts them." Bailey demonstrates that the actually existing sexual practices of Black gay men under the HIV/AIDS epidemic are sites to understand the ways that the larger Black LGBTQIA community can navigate potential HIV risks. In order to understand how Black sexuality itself connects to the HIV/AIDS epidemic, I analyze the ways Black sexuality is produced in place. I show that instead of addressing the particularities of disproportionate rates of HIV/AIDS infection, Black sexual practices are sites for Black gender and sexual minority communities to respond to the HIV/AIDS epidemic. In order to address the limitations of Black sexuality in the face of the ongoing HIV/AIDS epidemic, it is necessary to understand the ways Black communities have always challenged flat depictions of sexuality through Black sexual practice. This could mean an increased focus on sexual practices like raw sex (Bailey 2019), loving one's culture as they engage in sexual practices (Jolivette 2016), or disrupting the common associations of men who have sex with men as the only communities that are sexually active and at risk during the epidemic (Coleman, Kirk, and Bockting 2014). It is important to consider the ways that Black sexual and gender expressions proliferate alongside negative portrayals of Black sexuality. I turn to the sex-positive actions of Black community-based organizations in Atlanta that have been promoting Black sexual practice as a way to intervene within the HIV/AIDS epidemic. From here, we can see the ways Black people challenge anti-Black understandings of Black sexuality and liberalism during the HIV/AIDS epidemic.

Black Queer Spatial Production: Expanding Queer Politics and Geographies of Black Sexuality

Black queer spatial production counters normative sexual citizenship practices and the suppression of Black sexuality. Bridges's experiences provide one historical account of the ways white-identified LGBTQIA communities articulate a form of liberalism based in sexual freedom through the regulation of his sexuality. Negative portrayals and policing of Black sexuality become a site from which to promote normative sexual expectations for gender and sexual minorities during the HIV/AIDS epidemic. However, the intersections between Black queer communities and their sexual and gender expressions illuminate the role of Blackness, queerness, gender, and sexuality in shaping sexual practices against anti-Black violence, sexual citizenship, and the regulation of Black sexuality. Central to understanding Black queer sexuality is the role of hidden sexual acts among Black queer people. For Bridges, the hidden potential of sexual acts outweighed considerations of the ways he experienced intimacy. Similarly, antiblackness and liberal investment in sexual practices limit the ways Black queer sexuality is lived, experienced, and understood. Therefore, the anti-Black suppression of Black sexuality is accompanied by existing hidden intimacies of Black sexual practices. For Black queer communities, responses to the HIV/AIDS epidemic are developed in these hidden situated experiences of sexual practices. Furthermore, accounting for hidden sexual intimacies requires articulating Black queer spatial production through place and an expansion of queer as a political project beyond limited forms of sexual and gender expression. Atlanta emerges as a place to understand the ways Black sexuality expands queerness within LGBTQIA communities through the response to the HIV/AIDS epidemic.

The presence of a large Black LGBTQIA population in Atlanta necessitates engaging the HIV/AIDS epidemic through Black sexuality, as this becomes a site to respond to disproportionate rates of infection. The city is arguably both the current epicenter of the HIV/AIDS epidemic and a key site for Black sexual expression in the United States. In the metro area, the Black population is 32 percent of the population but suffers from disproportionate rates of infection. Within the city there are over 36,000 people living with HIV (AIDSVu 2017). Among this population, 70 percent are Black, 6 percent are Latinx, and 18 percent are white (AIDSVu 2017). Further, 80 percent of those who are HIV-positive identify as men. Additionally, Atlanta accounts for over half of HIV/AIDS-related deaths in Georgia. Black men are five times and Black women are fifteen times more likely than their white counterparts to have a positive HIV diagnosis (AIDSVu 2017). In the midst of the HIV/AIDS epidemic, Atlanta, commonly referred to as the gay Black mecca of the United States, hosts one of the largest Black pride events in the United States, along with LGBTQIA events at homecoming (an event to celebrate historically Black colleges and universities) and a number of Black LGBTQIA formal and informal sex industries.

Atlanta community-based organizations address disproportionate rates of HIV infection through exposing the ways Black sexuality takes place. Community groups are attentive to a wider spectrum of Black sexual practices among groups who are at risk of an HIV infection. This response works to expand understandings of Black sexuality alongside other social justice movements and to address other nonnormative relationships that impact Black gender and sexual minorities. Fabian Bridges's experience around sexual regulation, for example, was also shaped by his impoverishment and the lack of housing, community, and health care he faced. Atlanta community-based organizations expand Black sexuality by taking the socioeconomic and sociopolitical contexts of individuals and groups into consideration as reflective of the ways sexual practice is socially produced. Sister Love Inc. seeks to make people aware of their risk for HIV/AIDS through their social sexual networks.

Founded in 1989 to address Black women's disproportionate rates of HIV infection, Sister Love provides a foundation from which to understand Black sexuality on its own terms by developing an intervention based on actual social-sexual practices. Sister Love situates Black sexuality within existing social formations rather than an assumed set of prescribed relationships based in proximity to HIV risk. Considering sexual social formations rather than relationship to risk provides a different point to respond to the HIV/AIDS epidemic. Although sexual identity does provide a general intervention, often missing in these group formations are the actual ways sexual acts take place, influenced through class, gender, location, and sexual identity. Sister Love implements one of the longest-running HIV-intervention strategies, the Healthy

Love party. The Healthy Love party is a group-based intervention that pro-vides sexual education based on group sexual affiliation. By contrast, the Cen-ters for Disease Control and Prevention (CDC) provides guidance to the for-mation of HIV risk groups and relies on risk group formation through sexual orientation rather than sexual practices. Rather than using CDC guidelines for risk groups based on sexual orientation, which have been found to mismatch existing sexual practices, Sister Love creates a bottom-up understanding of sexual practice (Diallo et al. 2010). Their intervention adapts safer-sex strate-gies through the contexts in which sexual intercourse takes place and seeks to intervene in existing social groups within Black communities. Sexual groups could be Black lesbians over the age of thirty or Black men who sleep with men but do not identify as gay. Sister Love establishes that people's relationships to the epidemic are contextualized within social formations and that examin-ing large sexual group formations, like men who have sex with men, does not fully approach the ways sex takes place. A key feature of Sister Love and other community-based organizations' work is their attention to the role place plays in sexual practices.

Place is central for Atlanta Black LGBTQIA communities as physical loca-tions inform sites from which Black sexuality practices can emerge. The move-ments of Bridges in response to various forms of spatial violence were based in sexual regulatory regimes operating in place. Challenging these regimes means establishing place-based sexual practices that transform anti-Black antagonis-tic spaces into sites that can be used for queer community building. Here we see a relationship between the deterministic movements of anti-Blackness and the cultural practices of Black queers that substantiate a Black queer spatial production. That is, anti-Blackness is not unassailable. Barriers in place can be worked with, not necessarily overcome, but temporarily displaced. Black LGBTQIA communities respond to anti-Blackness through place-based cul-tural practices, which create places to build alternative group formations and expand queerness. As a result, younger generations of Black LGBTQIA com-munities are shaping LGBTQIA community formation in Atlanta.

Southern Fried Queer (SFQ) seeks to bring Southern queer culture into po-litical landscapes through strategic partnerships with local organizations and business establishments. SFQ is an intergenerational, trans-positive, Black-positive, and fat-positive organization. Part of their work is creating visible spaces for political mobilization around queers in the South, in particular those in Atlanta who are transforming local communities. SFQ members host events, workshops, and other forms of cultural and community engagement that provide spaces to educate and mobilize for change in the South, especially at the intersections of being queer, Black, disabled, and low income. They produce a yearly festival in Southwest Atlanta that brings workshops, film screenings, and community building to a historically underserved neighborhood.

Through this festival, SFQ has brought queer spatial production into spaces that were formerly not queer or were even hostile to gender and sexual minorities. The festival takes place in an old industrial area south of the West End, a historically Black middle-class neighborhood, and famed Auburn Drive, forming an L-shaped intersection with Peoplestown to the east. Peoplestown was the first site of organized abandonment around public housing in Atlanta. Against the ecological gentrification around Atlanta's beltway and the introduction of craft breweries and bars, the Black and queer offerings of SFQ produce another relationship to the area. Although the site is not owned by SFQ, a DIY warehouse space has been the site for the festival and represents cultural production outside of capitalistic venue-based nightlife and the club culture of the city. This space is transformed to be Black and queer, similar to the transformation of nightclubs into drag nights or community centers into ballroom performances. Here, there is a sense that for some amount of space and time, spaces that may be hostile to queer people can be transformed. The spatial acts of SFQ transform anti-Black relationships through place making. SFQ activism shows that anti-Blackness operates as a nontotality. These spaces do not negate the ongoing violence but show how temporary transformations can take place. I take SFQ's actions as interventions within already-existing systems of anti-Blackness that advance a Black queer spatial production. Through SFQ, we find an expansion of queerness that challenges the totality of anti-Blackness in these spaces.

Atlanta as a place of Black queer sexual production allows community-based organizations to respond to the HIV/AIDS epidemic by taking Black sexuality on its own terms. The terms of Black sexual engagement involve addressing anti-Blackness as a strategy to create pathways for Black sexuality to be embraced. Central to this work is the recognition that love in the face of hate and love for one another can be the basis of Black queer group formations and that recognition of anti-Black violence can provide a foundation. For example, Bridges was denied community connection based on his sexuality and Blackness. Therefore, embracing negation as it is attached to being Black and queer in Atlanta creates alternative avenues for belonging and addressing Black sexual practices. The organizing of the Counter Narrative Project (CNP) speaks to the ways that anti-Blackness is central to finding alternative relationships. This embrace does not undo or prevent anti-Black harm, but it establishes a relationship to harm that can be the basis of inclusion. The CNP's use of social media destigmatizes the harm that anti-Blackness carries through negative portrayals of Blackness and homonormativity.

The CNP takes the Joseph Beam quote "black men loving black men is the revolutionary act" as a model for programing and advocacy (Beam 1986). The organization builds power among Black gay men in solidarity with other social and racial justice movements. The CNP argues that storytelling is critical to social change and that by amplifying the voices of Black gay men, the public narrative of Black men can change. These politics build from the revolutionary cultural renaissance of Black gay cultural production that came together during the HIV/AIDS epidemic (Beam 1986; Hemphill 2007). The goal of the organization is to center Black gay men as a group with a situated experience from which they build a critical analytic for change. Key initiatives have been the Black gay vote, harm-reduction strategies around methamphetamine use, PrEP (pre-exposure prophylaxis) advocacy and access, peer support, and various arts and culture programming. Part of their cultural change work is providing opinion pieces to local newspapers and artistic expression to challenge dominant anti-Black narratives tied to Black sexuality. In another arena, the *Revolutionary Health* YouTube series works to provide up-to-date health and scientific information about the lives of Black gay communities. Here, we see how people navigate health care access among changing HIV-prevention landscapes. *Revolutionary Health* provides a resource for Black gay men seeking assistance and access to information. This is an approach to health that addresses anti-Black practices around the stigma that Black gay men face in Atlanta.

The work of the CNP to address anti-Blackness in the sexual health of Black gender and sexual minorities centers the everyday lives of Black queer communities. Their work addresses the harms that come from social sexual group formations, the places groups come together, and the ways liberal investment in sexual regulation produce harms. This approach to addressing the visible harms creates a space to move beyond anti-Black practices of sexual regulation and limited understandings of Black sexuality. Black queer spatial production is intimately connected to addressing anti-Black practices. It is from contestations to anti-Black conditions that sites of Black queer spatial production emerge to embrace Black sexuality. This does not mean that Black sexuality disentangles itself from anti-Blackness. Instead, Black spatial practices emerge with and beyond anti-Blackness. For example, Black queer spatial production counters the forces that reduce people to a number, where only their relation to harm can be seen, and instead pushes the lived experiences of Black LGBTQIA communities as the basis of change. This not only helps current Atlanta-based Black LGBTQIA communities address barriers experienced within the HIV/AIDS epidemic but is central to understanding why Bridges's story is foundational to comprehending the struggle Black LGBTQIA individuals and communities face today.

Sexual Citizenship and Black Queer Spatial Productions

This chapter has demonstrated the ways three Atlanta community-based organizations navigate liberal investments in sexual regulation by mainstream LGBTQIA communities and the HIV/AIDS epidemic through challenging anti-Black practices of sexual citizenship and the regulation of Black sexuality. Through a historical approach using the experiences and portrayals of Fabian Bridges, I have laid bare the punitive logics at the center of anti-Blackness and the HIV/AIDS epidemic and shown how anti-Black racism finds its meaning through sexual regulation. In the archetypes of Black sexual deviance that promote normative white and homonormative sensibilities, Bridges being "othered" from a (white) LGBTQIA community lynch mob and the lack of space to call his own as he moves between cities speak to anti-Black intimacies based in his race and sexuality. Anti-Blackness is central for mainstream white-identified LGBTQIA community groups to engage in sexual citizenship. Sexual citizenship defines which sexual acts are permissible through the policing of deviant sexual activities. White-identified marginalized sexualities come together as a political body deserving of recognition through the policing of racialized others.

Sexual citizenship helps define the role of anti-Blackness in liberalism in which Black LGBTQIA communities must engage in order to find a place for Black sexual expression. Through community-based organizations like Sister Love Inc., the social sexual group formations of Black sexual practices become sites from which to contest anti-Blackness. Through Black gender and sexual minorities' sexual practices in Atlanta, Sister Love finds their HIV intervention's impact on social sexual group formations. Sister Love's work exposes the necessity of place-based struggles from which Black queer spatial practices based in sexual expression can emerge. Place is central to expanding what society knows about Black sexuality and queerness as a political project.

Black queer spatial production finds its meaning through embracing Black sexuality as it is articulated through place. SFQ addresses both the lack of material space and limited forms of Black sexual expression for Black queers in

Atlanta. Through their yearly SFQ festival, which transforms abandoned and undervalued spaces into sites of Black queer spatial production, the group expands Black queerness through repurposing inconsiderate or even hostile nonqueer spaces to the needs of the queer community. Anti-Black violence is not being overcome, but rather Black queer spatial production is emerging within these hidden spaces. What is born from Black queer spatial production is an embracing of Black sexuality, regardless of anti-Black portrayals or violence against Black gender and sexual minorities.

Finally, the activism of the CNP displays the totalizing effects of anti-Black queer violence through education and the embracing of Black sexual practices. Through work to promote self-love and community care, CNP challenges liberalism's investment in anti-Blackness while addressing the HIV/AIDS epidemic. This response is found in CNP's focus on community building through breaking and revealing silences tied to Black sexuality as a praxis of survival. What is learned from the Atlanta-based groups is that race, gender, and sexuality are mutually constituted and articulated through anti-Blackness and Black queer spatial production. In Black LGBTQIA community attempts to address anti-Blackness, race, gender, and sexuality are sites to promote Black sexual practices. This demonstrates the ways anti-Blackness shadows but does not wholly determine the everyday lives of Black LGBTQIA communities.

NOTE

1. Lesbian, gay, bisexual, and transgender (LGBT) is a historical and umbrella term that predominated before the wide circulation and institutionalization of "queer" during the mid- to late 1980s. I use LGBTQIA not to impose singular categories on gender and sexuality but to approach the vastness of these relationships beyond the umbrella term. In line with the social, theoretical, and political project of queer, my use of LGBTQIA calls into question easy gender and sexual affiliations while also critiquing gender and sexuality as the sole basis of group affiliations. Additionally, Blackness and Indigeneity always accompany the use of LGBTQIA and point to the racialized foundations of gender and sexuality, which are inseparable from queer. I use LGBTQIA with attention given to the diverse set of relationships that exceed easy categorizations. I do this to delink the common public health language of "men who have sex with men" (MSM), which dominates understandings of sexual practices within HIV/AIDS discourse and limits the empirical realities that there are more than cisgender men who are sleeping with other cisgender men as a driver of the HIV/AIDS epidemic.

REFERENCES

AIDSVu. 2017. "Understanding HIV." Emory University, Rollins School of Public Health. www.aidsvu.org.

Bailey, Marlon M. 2014. "Engendering Space: Ballroom Culture and the Spatial Practice of Possibility in Detroit." *Gender, Place & Culture* 21(4): 489–507.

———. 2019. "Black Gay Sex, Homosexual-Normativity, and Cathy Cohen's Queer of Color Theory of Cultural Politics." *GLQ: A Journal of Lesbian and Gay Studies* 25(1): 162–168.

———. 2020. "Black Gay Men's Sexual Health and the Means of Pleasure in the Age of AIDS." In Jih-Fei Cheng, Alexandra Juhasz, and Nishant Shahani (Eds.), *AIDS and the Distribution of Crises*, 217–235. Durham, N.C.: Duke University Press.

Bailey, Marlon M., Darius Bost, Jennifer Brier, Angelique Harris, Johnnie Ray Kornegay III, Linda Villarosa, Dagmawi Woubshet, Marissa Miller, and Dana D. Hines. 2019. "Souls Forum: The Black AIDS Epidemic." *Souls* 21(2–3): 215–226.

Bailey, Marlon M., and Rashad Shabazz. 2014. "Gender and Sexual Geographies of Blackness: Anti-Black Heterotopias (Part 1)." *Gender, Place & Culture* 21(3): 316–321.

Beam, Joseph. 1986. *In the Life: A Black Gay Anthology*. New York: Alyson.

Bost, Darius. 2020. "'A Voice Demonic and Proud': Shifting the Geographies of Blame in Assotto Saint's 'Sacred Life: Art and AIDS.'" In Jih-Fei Cheng, Alex Juhasz, and Nishant Shahani (Eds.), *AIDS and the Distribution of Crisis*, 148–161. Durham, N.C.: Duke University Press.

Cohen, Cathy J. 1999. *The Boundaries of Blackness: AIDS and the Breakdown of Black Politics*. Chicago: University of Chicago Press.

———. 2001. "Punks, Bulldaggers, and Welfare Queens." In Mark Blasius (Ed.), *Sexual Identities, Queer Politics*, 200–277. Princeton, N.J.: Princeton University Press.

Coleman, Edmond J., Sheila Kirk, and Walter Bockting. 2014. *Transgender and HIV: Risks, Prevention, and Care*. New York: Routledge.

Diallo, Dázon Dixon, Trent Wade Moore, Paulyne M. Ngalame, Lisa Diane White, Jeffrey H. Herbst, and Thomas M. Painter. 2010. "Efficacy of a Single-Session HIV Prevention Intervention for Black Women: A Group Randomized Controlled Trial." *AIDS and Behavior* 14(3): 518–529.

Duggan, Lisa. 2012. *The Twilight of Equality? Neoliberalism, Cultural Politics, and the Attack on Democracy*. Boston: Beacon.

Epstein, Steven. 1996. *Impure Science: AIDS, Activism, and the Politics of Knowledge*. Vol. 7. Berkeley: University of California Press.

Esparza, René. 2019. "Black Bodies on Lockdown: AIDS Moral Panic and the Criminalization of HIV in Times of White Injury." *Journal of African American History* 104(2): 250–280.

Ferguson, Roderick A. 2004. *Aberrations in Black: Toward a Queer of Color Critique*. Minneapolis: University of Minnesota Press.

France, David. 2016. *How to Survive a Plague: The Story of How Activists and Scientists Tamed AIDS*. London: Pan Macmillan.

Gilbert, Dori J., and Ednita M. Wright (Eds.). 2003. *African American Women and HIV/AIDS: Critical Responses.* Westport, Conn.: Greenwood.

Gilmore, Ruth W. 2002. "Fatal Couplings of Power and Difference: Notes on Racism and Geography." *Professional Geographer* 54(1): 15–24.

Gossett, Che. 2014. "We Will Not Rest in Peace." In Jin Haritaworn, Adi Kuntsman, and Silvia Posocco (Eds.), *Queer Necropolitics,* 31–51. Oxford: Routledge.

Gould, Deborah B. 2009. *Moving Politics: Emotion and ACT UP's Fight Against AIDS.* Chicago: University of Chicago Press.

Gregory, Derek. 1994. *Geographical Imaginations.* Hoboken, N.J.: Blackwell.

Hemphill, Essex (Ed.). 2007. *Brother to Brother: New Writings by Black Gay Men.* New Orleans: RedBone Press.

Jolivette, Andrew J. 2016. *Indian Blood: HIV and Colonial Trauma in San Francisco's Two-Spirit Community.* Seattle: University of Washington Press.

Konrad, Cynthia L. 2014. "This Is Where We Live: Queering Poor Urban Spaces in Literature of Black Gay Men." *Gender, Place & Culture* 21(3): 337–352.

Lamble, Sarah. 2013. "Queer Necropolitics and the Expanding Carceral State: Interrogating Sexual Investments in Punishment." *Law and Critique* 24(3): 229–253.

Manalansan, Martin F., IV. 2005. "Race, Violence, and Neoliberal Spatial Politics in the Global City." *Social Text* 23(3–4): 141–155.

McGlotten, Shaka. 2014. "A Brief and Improper Geography of Queerspaces and Sexpublics in Austin, Texas." *Gender, Place & Culture* 21(4): 471–488.

McKittrick, Katherine. 2011. "On Plantations, Prisons, and a Black Sense of Place." *Social & Cultural Geography* 12(8): 947–963.

Moseby, Kevin M. 2017. "Two Regimes of HIV/AIDS: The MMWR and the Sociopolitical Construction of HIV/AIDS as a 'Black Disease.'" *Sociology of Health & Illness* 39(7): 1068–1082.

Nero, Charles I. 2005. "Why Are Gay Ghettoes White." In Patrick E. Johnson, Mae G. Henderson, Sharon Patricia Holland, and Cathy C. Cohen (Eds.), *Black Queer Studies: A Critical Anthology,* 228–245. Durham, N.C.: Duke University Press.

PBS. 1986. "AIDS: A National Inquiry." *Frontline,* episode 6, March 25. https://www.pbs.org/wgbh/frontline/film/aids-a-national-inquiry/.

Roane, J. T. 2019. "Black Harm Reduction Politics in the Early Philadelphia Epidemic." *Souls* 21(2–3): 144–152.

Rosenberg, Howard. 1986. "'Frontline' AIDS Controversy: Documentary Makers' Relentless Focus on the Lethal Life Style of a Dying Fabian Bridges Puts Minneapolis Station and PBS in the Spotlight." *Los Angeles Times,* March 27. https://www.latimes.com/archives/la-xpm-1986-03-27-ca-1098-story.html.

Sangaramoorthy, Thurka. 2012. "Treating the Numbers: HIV/AIDS Surveillance, Subjectivity, and Risk." *Medical Anthropology* 31(4): 292–309.

Schulman, Sarah. 2021. *Let the Record Show: A Political History of ACT UP New York, 1987–1993.* New York: Macmillan.

Snorton, C. Riley. 2014. *Nobody Is Supposed to Know: Black Sexuality on the Down Low.* Minneapolis: University of Minnesota Press.

Sullivan, Andrew. 1996. "When Plagues End." *New York Times Magazine,* November 10.

Thrasher, Steven W. 2018. "The U.S. Has an HIV Epidemic—and Its Victims Are Gay Black Men." *Guardian*, May 30. https://www.theguardian.com/commentisfree/2018/may/30/black-gay-men-aids-hiv-epidemic-america.

Walcott, Rinaldo. 2005. "Outside in Black studies: Reading from a Queer Place in the Diaspora." In Patrick E. Johnson, Mae G. Henderson, Sharon Patricia Holland, and Cathy C. Cohen (Eds.), *Black Queer Studies: A Critical Anthology*, 90–105. Durham, N.C.: Duke University Press.

CHAPTER 5

Compassionate Solidarities

Nos/Otras and a Nepantla Praxis of Care

JUAN HERRERA

> The future belongs to those who cultivate cultural sensitivities to differences and who use these abilities to forge a hybrid consciousness that transcends the "us" versus "them" mentality and will carry us into a nos/otras position bridging the extremes of our cultural realities, a subjectivity that doesn't polarize potential allies.
> —Gloria Anzaldúa (2015, 80)

I first met David Levenson at a party. He was on the dance floor, and I quickly noticed that the man had some major moves. He danced to salsa, merengue, R&B classics, and soul with such finesse and ease. I thought to myself, who is that white man, and where did he get his moves? When I was introduced to Levenson, I realized that he was a volunteer doctor at Street Level Health Project, the free medical clinic and community resource center where I volunteered for so many years when I lived in Oakland. He told me that he loved the work at Street Level because it reminded him so much of the work he saw growing up in the 1960s—actively involved in neighborhood improvement projects in Oakland and Berkeley alike. Levenson's family was an important facet of Bay Area activism.

Levenson, like so many people at the party in honor of the eightieth birthday of one of the godfathers of the Chicano Movement, Carlos Muños Jr., were all veterans of some kind of 1960s social movement.[1] There were people of all shades and colors and different age groups, showing us how social movements are often translated to the next generation. In his youth, Levenson had been directly involved with the Black Panther Party (BPP), played on a Black Panther Band named the Lumpin, and helped his family run Committees Against Fascism, which carried out some of the major principles of the BPP. After years of studying 1960s social movements, I never expected to meet a white man who claimed to have been a part of the BPP. Yet meeting people like Levenson, a white Jewish man who was connected to Black movements of the 1960s and present-day immigrant rights projects, moved me to ask, what makes people want to mobilize collectively to care, especially across the divisions that liberalism builds between race, class, and gender?

People become engaged in social movements because they learn to care about a particular cause. Yet care often escapes the realm of the political. Following the work of feminist geographers and related fields, I challenge the notion of care merely as a private affair reserved for analysis of labor in the home or biomedical facilities. In this essay, I reflect on my work with 1960s activists in Oakland to think about how movements mobilize to care for populations. To do so, I focus on how activists experienced movements. I contend that experiences take shape in specific places and through spatialized practices. In my forthcoming book, I show how Chicano Movement activists measured the impacts of their social movement activism not solely by how many protests they attended or by how many state reforms they helped to engender. Their metric for measuring social movements was anchored in how their mobilizations helped to care for specific communities and ensured the delivery of resources for disenfranchised groups. They also highlighted how they learned to care for the broader world and for struggles taking place across the nation. Social movement activism was fundamentally a process of learning to care for specific populations and places.

Activists asserted that learning to care entailed a complex understanding of how we as human beings relate to others, relate to our environment, and navigate difference. I utilize the relational thinking of the late Chicana theorist Gloria Anzaldúa to think critically about how her work encouraged us to be attentive to the relationship between self and other, and with the environment and spirit world (2015). Anzaldúa introduced an identity category, *nos/otras*, that proposes a methodology by which to bridge divides among humans and how we relate to our environment. Anzaldúa utilized the Náhualt concept of *nepantla* to name a place or space between two colliding cultures. The term refers to a specialized set of skills that border dwellers, or *nepantleras*, develop as a result of surviving the violence of being caught between multiple systems and geographies of power (Blackwell 2010). Subjects who have the unique ability to navigate the cracks of power develop a set of strategies and tactics that enable them to move in and between prescribed societal confinements of difference. I demonstrate how this nepantla ability to see across difference helped forge a unique—and ongoing—social movement praxis of care.

As a scholar of race and social movements, I aim to challenge the focus on telling solely those stories of domination that shape racialized experiences.

As Katherine McKittrick (2011) has questioned, how do we write about issues of inequality and racism without "overtaxing the suffering Black body"? By this she means that if we solely focus on the experiences of suffering, we are left without an analysis of Black humanity. I am moved by McKittrick's assertion that instead of exclusively focusing on the geographies of domination produced through racism, we can also think about how "our racial pasts can uncover a collective history of encounter—a difficult interrelatedness—that promises an ethical analytics of race based not on suffering, but on human life" (2011, 948). An analysis of social movement caring practices, their longevity, and the way in which they structure contemporary forms of living might offer us some clues about how to move beyond this notion of overtaxing suffering bodies of color and their respective spatialities. Putting forth such an analysis of encounter requires acknowledging the role that identity categories take in shaping group dynamics and learning to work through those differences to mobilize for social change.

In this essay, I first underscore some of the important ways in which care has been employed in geography and related fields. I then outline an alternative genealogy of care that draws from social movement politics and a long tradition of BIPOC radical organizing. I highlight the work of Chicana theorist Gloria Anzaldúa to understand how her category of nos/otras shows us a critical methodology and social movement praxis of care. I underscore how social movement activists employed nepantla strategies to build a more socially just world that values the complexities of human life. They did so by building places committed to enacting a praxis of care that included educational centers, community-based organizing and politicization projects, and activist study groups to forge a commitment to social justice. This also included an internationalist relational praxis of linking their localized struggles to those of other disenfranchised groups throughout the world.

Care and the Political

Care is not exclusively delivered or experienced through social movements. In our everyday worlds, we engage and benefit from a whole array of practices of care. Political theorists Joan Tronto and Bernice Fisher define care as a "a species activity that includes everything that we do to maintain, continue, and repair our world so that we can live in it as well as possible. That world includes our bodies, ourselves, and our environment, all of which we seek to interweave in a complex, life-sustaining web" (Tronto 2013, 19; see also Tronto 1993). Although broad, most of Tronto's notions of care are intimately linked to politi-

cal theory that tethers care to state liberal politics. It also bounds care to a political nationalist framing, therefore missing the global dimensions of how care
structures forms of politics. I build on her work by highlighting how activists I
interviewed drew from a different genealogy of care. Their community-based
notions of care were a response to the uncaring practices experienced by marginalized populations in the United States. As this collection lays bare, liberal
framings and makings of poverty in fact serve to reproduce white supremacy,
a North American institutionalization of global lethal liberalism (Baldwin and
Crane 2020). In fact, most postwar activism in Oakland and the rest of the
United States sought to show that liberal orders rely on the further subordination of racialized and impoverished subjects. This made me ask, what does it
mean to care from a subject position that has been understood as the constitutive outside of liberal forms of citizenship? What new methodologies can be
learned from this unique subject position?

Care has become a kind of black box in scholarly analyses that encompasses so many aspects of human activity including state social services, child
and adult care, and biomedical procedures conducted at clinics and hospitals. Scholars have been concerned with theorizing the capacity to care and
how caring takes shape through spatialized practices (E. Power 2019; A. Power
and Hall 2018; E. Power and Williams 2020). This relates to the sites where
care takes place, including places like drop-in centers and homeless shelters
(Conradson 2003; Evans 2011; Parr 2000, 2003; Williams 2016), with respect
to health and illness (Parr 2003), or in relationship to underserved cities that
have been previously wounded (Till 2012). Scholars have also underscored the
importance of racialized workers in the delivery of child care and elder care
(Hondagneu-Sotelo 2001; Glenn 2010; Parreñas 2001).

Care takes shape within a field of power relations contoured by racialized forms of difference. It is therefore essential to understand how care is
unequally distributed based on the geographic organization of power. European colonization of the Americas created unequally positioned categories of
the human species, creating what Sylvia Wynter (2003) aptly describes as the
coloniality of being/power/truth/freedom. Katherine McKittrick, following
Wynter, demonstrates how geography powerfully shaped constructions of human difference.[2] Through colonization, our modern world was divided into
spaces designed for *us* (inhabited by secular economically comfortable European and Euro-American man) and spaces designed for *them* (underdeveloped and impoverished geographies occupied by the marginalized and BIPOC
populations) (see also Mignolo 2000; Fanon [1963] 2004; Gupta and Ferguson
1997; Wynter 2003). This organization of space constructs people of color and

the enslaved more specifically, as ungeographic, denied a sense of place, and left behind (McKittrick 2013, 9). Colonial normalization of racialized forms of difference also hardened divisions along axes of gender, sexuality, and class. In order for the oppressed to achieve a better life, or a "normal" existence, they are expected to strive to achieve entry into the spaces and modes of being designed for *us*, in other words, privilege European aesthetics and features, culture, socioeconomic standards, and forms of knowledge while disavowing those that do not fit with this mold. This teleological expectation reifies the ontological differences between *us* and *them*, thus reinforcing white supremacy and naturalizing these inequalities. McKittrick challenges this teleological imperative and instead proposes that the oppressed can choose to construct alternative forms of livelihood and spaces that value our collective humanity.

Divisions between us/them contour an unequal terrain and practice of care. Milligan and Wiles (2010) argue that care does not escape power relations and therefore we need to account for uneven geographies of care. Although these scholars assert that unequal frameworks of care exist, we are left without an examination of how race affects the making of spatialities of care. In these assessments, scholars overwhelmingly agree that "racially and ethnically marginalized groups are overburdened and under-rewarded for their care work" (E. Power and Williams 2020, 4). In sum, racialized people are framed almost exclusively as laborers in care relationships, as opposed to theoreticians and practitioners enacting alternative relations of care.

The activists I worked with took part in long-term BIPOC mobilizations that challenged the violence of liberalism by providing alternative care networks removed from the liberal state. Furthermore, these care networks challenged white supremacy and notions of capitalist accumulation that perpetuate lethal us/them divides in our modern world. These movements, therefore, provide fertile ground to envision alternative, more nuanced ways of valuing all forms of human life and trajectories.

Scholars of the Black Radical Tradition show us how Black populations, living in an illiberal anti-Black world, constructed alternative systems of care. Clyde Woods, for example, demonstrated the power of attempts by working-class African Americans to establish social democracy within a plantation-dominated economy (Woods 2017). W. E. B. Du Bois's important work provides a rich history of the alternative social organization of care for African Americans in Philadelphia (Du Bois [1899] 1969). Steven Gregory's (1998) *Black Corona* constructs a history of Black organizations and institutions in the borough of Queens in New York City in a context of African American exclusion from white institutions. Joe Trotter's (2007) study of Black Milwaukee shows a similar pattern whereby as early as the 1890s, the Milwaukee Afro-American League explicitly enunciated the philosophy of self-help and racial unity. As sociologist Alondra Nelson (2011) reveals, African Americans founded hospitals in underserved Black communities, inaugurating public health initiatives, and established schools to train Black medical professionals (25). These alternative avenues for delivering health care services and health education also reveal how social movements advance a politics or care rooted in the improvement or construction of specific places. Freedom, as Ruth Wilson Gilmore so powerfully reminds us, is a place (2017; see also Heynen and Ybarra 2020).

These anticolonial and antiracist movements—which strengthened by the mid-1900s—sought to abolish the material violence and suffering created by colonial us/them divides. According to Sylvia Wynter, these movements challenged what were thought to be truths—that divisions between colonizer and colonized, white and Black, European and native were natural due to the inferiority and eugenically *dyselected* status of the non-European (2003). She asserts that such movements unsettled the neatly naturalized categories that laid the groundwork for modern liberal humanism. Such a challenge and break of these ontological divisions between us/them as emblematized by calls such as "Black is Beautiful" and "I am Man" of Civil Rights and Black Power mobilizations laid the blueprint for how other movements challenged the normalization of divisions that liberalism builds between race, class, and gender.

Women of color feminists therefore powerfully remind us that us/them divides are not solely about race. These scholars and social movement activists critiqued approaches and responsibilities of care as it relates to their experiences as women in predominantly BIPOC spaces. These arguments were at once about their exclusion from care within the women's movement, which was predominantly white. They were also about the exclusion of gender and LGBTQ critiques in predominantly BIPOC coalitions. Women of color feminists challenged the notion of what it meant to be a "woman" while also simultaneously being "Black" or "Chicana" and also being "lesbian" or "queer." This challenge to rigid identity categories required the development of a skillful ability to weave in and out of spaces and construct alternative intersectional spaces of care. These movements built alliances across difference and challenged the neatly defined us/them organization of the world.

Building from this tradition, the activists I worked with theorized their own approaches to caring across racial, spatial, and gendered divides. This included thinking beyond their own localized experiences and enacting a more global dimension to their activism. In so doing, they challenged nationalist forms of liberalism that constricts a global framework of struggle. They also enacted a unique methodology for navigating between those differences and to mobilize a caring sensibility. This is the dynamic that I turn to next through the work of Gloria Anzaldúa. *Nos/otras* is an identity category stemming from challenges to the universalism of whiteness and the presumed singularity of any particular identity category. This challenge comes through a praxis of thinking relationally and across difference, which activists did through their social movement activism.

Nos/Otras and a Relational Approach to Challenging Us/Them Divides

In order to better understand the caring practices from what Fanon ([1963] 2004) called the wretched of the earth, I build on recent work by Latinx feminist geographers who employ theories developed by the late Chicana theorist Gloria Anzaldúa to analyze experiences of communities of color through racial, gendered, and classed relations (Cahuas 2019; Ramírez 2020). Anzaldúa wrote against the limitations of binary categories. She, for example, was concerned about divisions between men and women, white and BIPOC, straight and queer. Her writing, however, also explored how divisions between individuals that compose a similar identity category such as woman, Chicana, Indigenous, or queer can also result in feuds between equally positioned members of an identity category. She sought to theorize an identity category that would facilitate a seeing across difference and an ability to accept, celebrate, and nourish multiple perspectives and ways of being in the world.

The Spanish word *nosotras* simply means "us." Yet Anzaldúa thought critically about inserting a slash between the *nos* (us) and *otras* (others) to theorize her relational identity narrative of *nos/otras*. For Anzaldúa, an understanding of "us" can include "us" and "them" and does not have to be obsessed with reifying the divide between self and other: "We disregard the fact that we live in intricate relationship with others, that our very existence depends on our intimate interactions with all life forms" (2015, 76). This is especially the case in the United States where we live in a multicultural society and have to negotiate difference all the time. As she detailed, "We live in each other's pockets, occupy each other's territories, live in close proximity and intimacy with each other at home, school, and work. We are mutually complicitous—us and them, nosotras y los otros, white and colored, straight and queer, Christian and Jew, self and Other, oppressor and oppressed. We all of us find ourselves in the position of being simultaneously both insider and outsider" (2015, 79). She found within the identity of nos/otras an ability to negotiate the cracks between worlds, an ability to accommodate contradictory identities and social positions, and a unique methodology for navigating difference.

In Anzaldúa's conceptualization, those people who have the ability to think differently and to weave in between identity categories are called *nepantleras/os*. Following Mesoamerican Indigenous traditions, she utilizes this word to describe a threshold people, those who move within and among multiple worlds and use their movement in the service of transformation. Nepantleras construct alternative roads, creating new topographies and geographies of hybrid selves who transcend binaries and depolarize potential allies. Nepantleras are not constrained by one culture or world but experience multiple realities (2015, 82). Anzaldúa's concept of nepantla is especially useful as a framework for understanding how social movement activists mobilize to challenge us/them divides. A person who mobilizes a nepantla sensibility engages in a kind of point of contact between worlds. This entails bridging divisions between identity categories, nations, imagination and physical existence, ordinary and extraordinary (spirit) realities. Nepantleras/os mobilize to bridge the fissures among humans, to connect with each other, to move beyond us/them binaries (men and women, queer and straight, able and disabled). Nepantleros therefore endeavor to construct new places where identity differences can be appreciated and in which a nos/otras sensibility can be activated.

These new place-making practices require productive filtering: urging us to maintain our heritages' useful, nurturing aspects but release the unproductive and harmful components. According to Anzaldúa, the aim is to undertake transformative work that processes and facilitates evolving as a social group. She believed that in order to do so it was important to negotiate alliances among the conflicted forces within the self, between men and women, among the group's different factions, and among the various groups in this country and the rest of the world. It is precisely this praxis of thinking relationally and across difference that underscored so much of the activism in Oakland. Activists learned to negotiate alliances by constructing new spaces of learning and working across differences and geographical boundaries. They enacted nepantla strategies to weave in between identity categories and learn to care across difference. In so doing, they collectively built a nos/otras identity and methodology for activism. They did so by using their social movement activism to build new spaces of care, learning, and politicization.

LEVENSON AND WHITE SOLIDARITY

Solidarity is a process by which an individual becomes aligned with a cause that affects another group of people or person. It is essentially a process of creating compassion for fellow human beings and blurring the us/them divide. This was especially relevant for activists like David Levenson who came from a family deeply affected by the anti-Semitic violence. These experiences of violence equipped Levenson and his family with a unique ability to understand the violent effects of drawing deep divisions between *us* and *them*. His family survived the Holocaust, and this experience forever marked them for generations. His parents organized so they would never allow fascism to thrive again. Levenson's father was first involved in Civil Rights struggles in the South. He remembers growing up in an antiracist environment filled with interactions with different groups from across the nation. The Levensons valorized Black historical contributions to social justice struggles. Instead of merely seeing Black populations as victims of a racist system, they learned from their radical attempts to remake society and envision an alternative future.

Once the family relocated to the West Coast, the Levensons became rapidly affiliated with the BPP and other social justice causes. Levenson recalls how the BPP organized a conference to create awareness against fascism and then called for the formation of committees on a local level. Levenson's family formed the first one, the National Committee to Combat Fascism (NCCF). As he told me: "We set up a community center along the lines of what the Black Panthers did in their own communities, they had community centers where they carried out political education and community-based survival projects. We became an effectively functioning branch of the Black Panther Party but in a community in West Berkeley which was mostly a blue-collar kind of a mixed community. We functioned, as I did, as members of the Black Panther Party" (Levenson interview, August 28, 2019).[3] Levenson's family not only supported the BPP party but took part in their own community-based survival and organizing projects modeled after the party. The economic and resource inequalities that plagued many African American communities were also common among other groups. The committees against fascism sought to learn with the most oppressed groups in order to marshal better opportunities for other disenfranchised groups and for humanity more broadly. As Levenson remembered, "We took direction from the central committee of the BPP. We believed that they were sort of in the vanguard of the struggle at the time, the Black community is the most oppressed community, carried the potential to lead in the broader multi-ethnic, including white people, struggle for justice" (Levenson interview, August 28, 2019). The committee went to the same political education classes with BPP members, sold the party's newspapers, and participated in all the survival programs. Levenson's family set up a number of services modeled after the BPP, including a breakfast program, health care clinics, and education centers, even community plumbing services. They constructed a community center in a two-story building that families collectively bought in West Berkeley.

As we can learn from Levenson's examples, solidarity entailed learning to care about social justice causes by bridging the divide between self and other. Through this process, the Levenson family, along with other white, Black, and poor communities, built new community spaces and resources modeled after the BPP. Levenson demonstrates how his family deployed nepantla strategies that allowed them to weave between the cracks of identity categories and struggles in order to transcend the "us" versus "them" mentality. Through these practices, Anzaldúa believed that we could be carried into a nos/otras position bridging the extremes of our cultural realities, a subjectivity that doesn't polarize potential allies. This subjectivity also included building new community spaces that fostered a sense of collectivity. Activists constructed actually existing geographic spaces built on validating different kinds of social relations and accepting difference.

SEEING ACROSS DIFFERENCE AND PLACE MAKING

Anzaldúa's understanding of the relationship between self and geography was rooted in her analysis of how human beings interact with the environment. For Anzaldúa, geographies literally become mapped onto every aspect of a human's body and sense of self, creating what she conceptualized as geographies of selves (2015, 68). As a result of racial segregation in the United States, racial minority groups often live alongside one another. This is most true for places like Oakland, where Latinx spaces are proximal to Black neighborhoods. However, geographic proximity doesn't necessarily generate solidarity and alliances between groups. Anzaldúa reveals that enacting solidarity and alliances between different groups requires specific subjects who embody the nepantla ability to see across difference and to literally "feel" the geographies they traverse. Social movement activism provided a critical methodology by which activists worked between the cracks of identity categories or divergent political positions and engaged in a process of societal transformation.

Beatriz Pesquera came to the Bay Area from Los Angeles and grew up in a family household with a strong tradition of pride in their Mexican heritage. In retelling her background, she admitted that it was not difficult to become politicized: "As a Mexican young child coming into the U.S. was very traumatic" (Pesquera interview, August 30, 2019). She recalled that she was called a dirty Mexican and people would commonly treat her as if she was dumb. Given her light skin, some people told her she could easily pass as Italian. She, however, vehemently refused. In addition to these experiences, she credited Black radical thinkers for truly awakening her politicization: "The first way I think I became politicized was reading the autobiography of Malcom X and a book by Claude Brown *Manchild in the Promised Land*. I made the connection between African American experience and oppression and struggle and my own" (Pesquera interview, August 30, 2019). For Pesquera, her own politicization relied on a relational analysis of the effects of racism in the United States, inspiring her unique nepantla subjectivity. This politicization emerged from seeing the shared experiences of racism experienced by Mexican Americans and Black populations in the United States.

Pesquera's ability to link the oppression experienced by Mexican Americans and Blacks was fundamentally a nos/otras practice. This was not just a relational acknowledgment of shared oppression but also a call to action, or a praxis for collaborating with African American groups. She enthusiastically remembered her engagement with different groups as a student at Merritt College. There were few Chicanos around, so they didn't have their own Chicano Student Union. Pesquera and other Chicanos made an alliance with the Black Student Union and ran on what they called the Soul Ticket. She was the only woman in addition to a Black man who ran on that ticket, and she was successfully elected. As Pesquera told me,

> We had these very strong alliances. At one point we were trying to develop a Chicano Studies department and the African American students banded with us, and we locked the faculty in, the faculty senate, and we were all there together working on this. I think what's also important about that particular historical period is that we may have been focused on Chicano or Black but there were alliances. I think that's really significant to say that today given the political situation that we're facing, that we have historically struggled together. The Mexican community has struggled with other communities historically. I think that's very important to recognize, that kind of alliance. (Pesquera interview, August 30, 2019)

These forms of alliances were forged as a result of a shared geography of struggle and a social movement ethics of solidarity. By joining together, Black and Brown students had greater power to push for their demands. Through social movements, activists like Pesquera learned how to enact the nepantla ability to see a different way and to accept different opinions and perspectives and collaboratively build a space for us/them to come together within a single lens.

The proximity between Black and Brown communities in the Bay Area also meant that both groups shared the experience of overpolicing. This is one avenue that catapulted both groups into action. One of the biggest causes that activists spoke about was the Barlow Benavidez case, which galvanized the entire neighborhood. Benavidez was violently killed by a police officer who mistakenly thought he was a murder suspect. A fundamental practice of the nos/otras imperative also entails blurring the boundaries between caregiver and the person who is being cared for. Social movements fundamentally seek to empower others to be their own advocates. Andrea Benavidez, sister of Barlow, remembered how an entire group of people helped her to gain her voice as an activist against police brutality. She admits being nervous at first and wanting other people to speak for her. However, soon she became more comfortable speaking in front of large crowds. She became her own advocate and grew to love giving speeches. Andrea Benavidez now lives in Texas and credits this activism for awakening her to the ability to speak back against police brutality and to see the commonalities among different groups who experience this form of state violence. She recognizes that as someone who experienced and took part in this type of activism, she must be vigilant on its effects on other disenfranchised groups. Although she is no longer an activist, this past experience allows her to continue to deploy a nos/otras methodology for understanding the commonalities as well as differences that link Black and Brown struggles.

LEARNING TO CARE

The nepantla ability to weave between spaces and identity categories requires a deft navigation. It fundamentally calls for an educational process to understand other ways of knowing and being in the world. BIPOC student activists contested the Eurocentrism of educational systems and fought to create a more culturally relevant education. At the university level, students mobilized a Third World strike that led to the formation of departments like Ethnic Studies. But outside of the university, entire movements created more culturally relevant and revolutionary educational systems.

One of the first services that activists envisioned for the care of their community was alternative educational spaces for children and youth. A set of activists contributed to the establishment of La Escuelita (for pre-kinder) and the Street Academy (for students who had dropped out or were on the verge of dropping out from high school). Activists and teachers educated the youth not just about their own particular culture but about the local and global movements that they were linked with. Education, as activists envisioned it, would equip the next generation to be nepantleros and be able to diagnose oppression and work collaboratively to dismantle divisions.

Teachers and students both learned from these alternative educational programs. Connie Jubb came to the Bay Area from Ohio because she wanted to help with the cultural and social revolution that was happening in the region. After studying and working at Stanford at a bilingual program, she was interviewed and subsequently hired to be one of the first teachers at La Escuelita. She excitedly told me that she was interviewed not by the formal staff but by the parents themselves. Jubb loved the fact that a school would give tremendous authority in hiring to parents and open up the possibility to reimagine power relationships. For Jubb, working at the Escuelita required her to shift gears a bit in how she understood Latino culture: "I learned a lot of things through my first years at the center because I knew more about Mexico because I worked in the bilingual program and worked with Chicanos at Stanford but I didn't know so much about Latin America" (Jubb interview, August 30, 2019). At the height of 1960s social movement activism, many groups took on a strict cultural-nationalist approach that narrowly focused on nationalist framings of struggles, focusing solely on the Chicano experience for example.[4] Activists in the Bay Area, however, took on a more internationalist approach that incorporated people of many different nationalities and expanded the realm of possible collaborations. There were Anglos like Jubb and Levenson and other members who were from Latin American countries other than Mexico. Like Anzaldúa's conceptualization of nos/otras, these activists challenged constricted and closed-off constructions of identity. To do so they took up a global relational framework that linked the experiences of struggles at home with those of other nations and movements.

The school's internationalist framing introduced students to the broader world and its various revolutionary social movement struggles. Jubb recalls that on the day that she first arrived, Berta Canton, who was in charge of the program, reminded everyone that it was the anniversary of the Cuban Revolution. She asked the new teachers to work together to commemorate the important day. As Jubb remembered, "We only had a small group of kids so we ended up taking a boat ride on Lake Merritt and talking about the Granma, the ship used to begin the Cuban Revolution" (Jubb interview, August 30, 2019). In the process the students learned about the importance of the Cuban Revolution and the changes that it had offered to the island.

The Escuelita also taught students about the importance of supporting movements closer to home and the struggles of disenfranchised agricultural workers. For example, during the grape and lettuce boycott headed by the United Farm Workers, Berta Canton and the teachers collected all the grapes and lettuce that the school district gave La Escuelita. Jubb described how all the little kids hauled wagons filled with lettuce and grapes and returned them to the school district headquarters in protest. The students subsequently learned about the farm workers' struggle, how they could support their plight, and how to ultimately care about people and causes far away. Many of the teachers at the Escuelita had been directly involved with the UFW and so the students received an intimate portrayal of the movement. This sense of consciousness inspired a relational connection between Chicano struggles in rural and urban areas and engendered a nos/otras praxis of action and solidarity.

Activists linked educational experiences with community-based organizations in order to foster a greater sense of care among the students for the community in which they lived. The Street Academy was a school developed to help students get back into school and finish their high school education. The school was created to provide more individual attention to each student and to teach them an education that affirmed their cultural backgrounds. It was inspired by the activism of the time as many of the staff were involved with the Third World strike at San Francisco State. The youth were partnered with different community-based groups in the neighborhood where they conducted internships and service. They were therefore mentored by the various leaders at each of the organizations. By facilitating these connections with community organizations, the students became familiar with the various neighborhood needs. These kinds of programming initiatives helped students to make the connections to care beyond their individual needs.

In order to facilitate student learning, the teachers designed their culturally relevant rendition of the curriculum. Betsy Schultz taught science and told me how she worked diligently to bring back Aztec and Mayan knowledge. Although her focus did include Western health, she also inserted material on more traditional healing practices among Indigenous communities. In her classes she taught about the famous African American scientists and about the work of the BPP in the screening and treatment of sickle cell anemia. As a white woman, she relied on other people for inspiration in the way to frame things and especially the partner organizations. She usually mentored most of the Native American youth because the other students gravitated to mentors of their respective racial group. She relied on the community organizations to help with the mentorship of Native American youth. As Schultz recalled, "We were across the street from the Native American youth center so we got a lot of students through them. We had a lot of native students. It is still an area that is fairly native" (Schultz interview, August 27, 2019). Schultz asserted that designing a new culturally relevant education framework required active collaboration between different community groups. These interactions were central to how students were educated about the broader social movement landscape they took part in and about the multicultural nature of the community they lived in. By not only learning about these issues but also actively participating in different organizations, they learned to activate a nos/otras praxis based on relationality and care.

Culturally relevant education was not just about learning through the incorporation of Black history, Chicano literature, and Indigenous forms of knowing. Activists did not envision a kind of liberal humanisms akin to our contemporary form of neoliberal multiculturalism. Through education, activists fortified a nos/otras sensibility that allowed students to question the inequalities existing in the United States and the world and the presumed benevolence of U.S. liberal practices. It also included an analysis of inequalities at the community and global levels and the inculcation of the need to be involved in major social causes of the time. These alternative forms of education fundamentally sought to build a new culture of care and a praxis of activism framed through a relational and internationalist understanding of global inequality. This was nos/otras sensibility and praxis facilitated by diminishing the divide between "us" and "them" and creating a shared understanding of our mutual co-constitution on this earth.

ACTIVIST EDUCATION

In addition to helping to educate the next generation, activists also educated themselves. They did so by forming study groups in which, among many other topics, they engaged with Marxist theory and applied it to their own organizing and conditions of inequality. Learning through Marxism and global socialist struggles made these activists question organizing strategies centered solely on race that did not include a critique of capitalism. Analyses like this amplified their terrain of struggle and their relational understanding of inequalities and global struggles. Like in the youth and children's education, activists centered their own education to sensitize themselves about the causes that animated global struggles and that fortified their endeavors at home.

Mariano Contreras moved to the Bay Area from Los Angeles and was politicized by hanging out with his brother's college friends. He moved to Oakland and quickly got linked up with the leftist organization CASA, a Chicano group that prioritized a working-class analysis. As he learned in his work at CASA, "The Chicano Movement came and it was led primarily by students and then academia. What it lacked was a working-class perspective" (Contreras interview, August 29, 2019). Mariano and others developed this working-class perspective by learning the limitations of one of the greatest movements of the time. CASA organizers had a heavy critique of Cesar Chavez's approach in the United Farm Workers. As he told me, "That's when I was first exposed to a criticism of the United Farm Workers and Cesar Chavez because at that time he was very reluctant to organize immigrants because they couldn't vote. CASA worked to organize all workers, and you organize immigrants, you provide a service for them, and then you organize them, and the service was documentation" (Contreras interview, August 29, 2019). CASA prioritized working with undocumented immigrants in neighboring factories. They organized to protect their rights as workers and helped them to become naturalized as U.S. citizens. As Anzaldúa reminds us, "When an individual realizes that she doesn't fit into a particular collective-conditioned identity and when the tribe cannot contain all that she is, she must jettison the restrictive cultural components and forge new identities" (2015, 75). Activism is a process of building new identities and finding new positionalities by which to create broader avenues for collectively working with people. Contreras's experience with CASA opened him up to new avenues of collective organizing that also required him to think more broadly of the international and local struggles confronting marginalized communities. Being Chicano was not just about pride in Mexican American culture but also about realizing how domination works through racial, class, and national differences. In order to combat these forms of domination, collective action required better ways of linking the dynamics of all of those struggles and required the creation of new political identities, such as the Third World left that CASA identified with.

Social movement activism constantly evolved as new strands of activism emerged. This evolution of struggles was enabled by a nepantla relationality and a nos/otras praxis of bridging the gap between distinct portions of the world's population. As Contreras explained, CASA brought an anti-imperialist and working-class perspective that led to organizing and working with other groups. This meant coalitions across racial and gendered lines. This included leftist groups that were white and advanced an anticapitalist perspective, and African American women's groups that did work around the advancement and recognition of women's rights. Activists were constantly educating themselves about different causes of the time and about how global forces were taking shape throughout the world. As Contreras detailed, "There were coalitions, there were coalitions that taught us how to see, recognize principles of unity when you do work with coalitions and then abide by them" (Contreras interview, August 29, 2019).

Contreras told me many of the coalitions were facilitated by the organizing strategies of the radical left. These coalitions were built on the concept that members of the working class could rise up as a collective and change the world. They learned this by studying Marxism in collectives. As Contreras told me, "We would read it, I would pair up with somebody, and then during the study groups we would discuss it and made sure things sunk in. You know, what is to be done, all that all of it. The one that really sticks is the criticism, self-criticism" (Contreras interview, August 29, 2019). For Contreras, one of the most useful practical aspects of this Marxist teaching was the process of self-evaluation. Pesquera clarified how useful this strategy was for self-reflection and the spirit of supporting one another: "'Last month I had a task to x, y, z, I think it could have been better executed if. . . .' And I would say to you, 'You know I think that part of the work that you're doing is really great, but I may have an addition that you might want to consider.' It was done in the spirit of moving the project forward, not looking back to trash people or trash you, the idea is you wanted to move the project forward, so how do you move the project forward?" (Pesquera interview, August 30, 2019). As Pesquera narrated, activists learned to be accountable to themselves and to others, and this relational form of thinking was integral to learning to care about the self and others. Pesquera credited this approach to the Cuban Revolution, which demonstrates how activists borrowed from organizing strategies from around the world and applied them to their own local conditions. Of course, this was not always a smooth application, as Pesquera told me that some groups became far too critical and internally divided.

Entire groups of people converged to study Marxism and supported one another in collective learning. Pesquera detailed that one of the most prominent study groups was led by Henry Chan, who was himself Korean. As Pesquera told me, "He was brilliant and he led these study groups. . . . You had to be selected by your organization to go. . . . We read *Das Kapital* and we had meetings and then we had subgroups" (Pesquera interview, August 30, 2019). As she explained, these study groups focused on applying abstract theoretical concepts to daily practices of organizing work.

In the time before the internet and social media, these activists relied on magazines, newspapers, and journals to stay abreast of the major events of the time. They maintained these connections through many publications from Cuba. Pesquera especially recalled the work of the *Tricontinental Newsletter* organized by the Organization of Solidarity with the People of Asia, Africa, and Latin America. This newsletter brought together important news from these different continents in order to engender global solidarity. Activists like Pesquera looked forward to receiving their newsletter each month to stay abreast with the newest developments in revolutionary movements across the globe.

Pesquera credits these kinds of publications with helping to create modes of exchange that allowed them to bridge their activism to distant places, a key component to praxis of learning to care for the broader world.

Activists also traveled extensively to support various international causes, especially the Cuban Revolution. For Pesquera one of the most transformative and politicizing experiences was actually going on the Venceremos Brigade to Cuba:

> In that I got to see a society that functioned at a very different level. You can read all you want about this, that, and the other right. But when you're actually there on the ground experiencing the kind of solidarity, the kind of discipline, the kind of passion, that and they were building a new society. There's a lot of problems with Cuba, there was problems then, it wasn't all rosy, I didn't think everything was wonderful and everything. But it was such an amazing experience to actually see something different, and you felt it, you heard it, you lived it. (Pesquera interview, August 30, 2019)

Pesquera's intrigue with her experience in Cuba was not just about supporting the Cuban Revolution. It entailed imagining and experiencing alternative frameworks for social relations and seeing the ability to construct new forms of relating to one another as humans. This kind of imaginative potential is key to a nos/otras identity and methodology. Although she initially envisioned the people of Cuba as her subject to care for, through transnational solidarity, the interaction resulted in her own act of learning. As Connie Jubb added, "You just got this perspective on being outside of your country and in a situation where there's so many other models. It doesn't have to be that way, it doesn't have to be the way that we do things in the U.S., there's other ways of organizing a school or a group, there's other ways of human relations" (Jubb interview, August 30, 2019). The idea to care for others in such a profound way, according to Pesquera and Jubb, came from experiencing other models of doing things.

In a similar fashion, this learning from abroad was also evident in the perspectives brought by the BPP. David Levenson was interested in medicine at a young age. In fact, as a member of the BPP he had to ask the central committee permission to head off to study medicine. But prior to that, he was sent on a delegation with the BPP to China to learn about acupuncture and other forms of Chinese medicine. The BPP forged these connections with communist China as a way of supporting revolutions abroad and to learn from non-Western forms of medicine. As Levenson recalled, "Huey Newton came up to me and asked me, 'Do you want to go to China?' because China asked for, and invited, a delegation from the Black Panther Party to come" (Levenson interview, August 28, 2019). The BPP was one of the first to use acupuncture in community-based programs. As Levenson recalled, they were using it to treat opioid addictions on the East Coast. As he retold me this story, Levenson regretted that things had not turned out so favorably for the people of China as a result of the Cultural Revolution.

By learning through a global perspective activists realized that they needed to adopt a broader stance against the oppression that they saw in their local communities. As Contreras told me, "You had the antiwar movement that was taking place, the Chicano Moratorium that was saying that many of our Latino youth are being sent to Vietnam and killed. That led to the development of an anti-imperialist perspective" (Contreras interview, August 29, 2019). Many of the folks who got started in the Chicano Movement were also initiated because of their participation in the mobilizations against the War in Vietnam and in support of the United Farm Workers. And being a part of these struggles sensitized them to issues at home and abroad. As Pesquera elaborated, "The Vietnam War was also very significant in the way that we became politicized, and particularly around issues of not only the struggles of the Vietnamese people, but the fact that we were so overly represented in young men going over there and being killed or coming back pretty devastated. That was a really important aspect of our politicization and radicalization" (Pesquera interview, August 30, 2019). This kind of activism reveals that anti-imperialist struggles engendered forms of making connections between conditions at home and abroad. These connections facilitated processes of caring for others not just at home but also in faraway places linked by U.S. imperialism.

As we can see, activism was fundamentally about learning to care across difference and geography. Activists became the agents who cared for a group or a cause and in many instances also the recipients of care. For example, children and youth received educational programming. The education was also intent on bringing actionable skills to the children and youth. Children grew up learning to care for others, to understand the social movement causes of the time, and to be willing to treat others as they themselves were treated. As the activists show us, they learned to think of themselves as nepantleros of sorts, being able to not just inhabit the spaces in between or to see the relationship between us and them but also to go the extra step and initiate modes of activism to build nepantla spaces such as educational and community resource centers. These activists show us that activism is a process of building new identities and finding new positionalities by which to create broader avenues for collectively working with people. In order to do so, activists initiated a nos/otras praxis through harnessing nepantla abilities to bridge divides and sensitize themselves to the struggles of others.

Nepantla Praxes and Care

To conclude, I return to pivotal questions that animated this essay on care and the political: What does it mean to care from a subject position that has been understood as the constitutive outside of liberal forms of citizenship? What new methodologies can be learned from this unique subject position? First, activists featured in this essay show us that bringing care into the realm of the political does not mean reifying a U.S. liberalism premised on white supremacy, inequality, and suffering. Activists argued that making care political is a project of refusal of us/them divides that structure global constructions of liberalism. In so doing, these activists constructed an internationalist, anticapitalist, and globally relational framework by which to understand human difference. They also activated unique nepantla strategies to navigate differences along national boundaries, gender, race, and difference. In so doing, they set forth a form of social movement activism fueled by a nos/otras praxis of relationality. This form of relationality radically unsettles the coupling of global frameworks of lethal liberalism, white supremacy, and extractivist capitalist accumulation.

This process of unsettling requires radical forms of disruption, discomfort, and disorientation. I suggest that activists featured in this essay took part in this disorienting process. This is the same experience I felt upon my first encounter with David Levenson. I still remember that moment of seeing him on the dance floor during the birthday celebration of one of the icons of the Chicano Movement. This white man in a sea of people of color, with such eclectic moves. He stood out, but he also blended in with so much finesse. This encounter and my subsequent interview with Levenson made me think critically about a major call by Katherine McKittrick to imagine how we are tied to "broader conceptions of human and planetary life, which demonstrate our common and difficult histories of encounter." She proposes that "we might reimagine geographies of dispossession and racial violence not through the comfortable lenses of insides/outsides or us/them . . . but as sites through which 'co-operative human efforts' can take place and have a place" (2011, 960). Activism entails learning to take part in these cooperative human efforts that mobilize beyond and within rigid identity boundaries. And in so doing they help forge new identities of commonality and shared humanity, and new spaces that foster these relationships.

In this essay, I have demonstrated how "those without" have forged caring practices and traditions that are outside the terrain of liberal democracies. In fact, their construction represents the constitutive outside of these liberal democratic practices. In order to enact practices of solidarity and alliances, activists learned to care across multiple identity categories. They also learned to care across national boundaries, therefore contesting naturalized borders and hardened divisions between allegedly developed and underdeveloped countries. Anzaldúa's concept of nos/otras as navigated by nepantla subjects offers a meaningful way to understand how we maintain this caring capacity while working through differences and forming alliances. As Anzaldúa so strongly believed, "the future belongs to those who cultivate cultural sensitivities to differences and who use these abilities to forge a hybrid consciousness" (2015, 85). This hybrid consciousness must deploy nepantla strategies in order to transcend the "us" versus "them" mentality. Through these practices, Anzaldúa believed that we could be carried into a nos/otras position bridging the extremes of our cultural realities, a subjectivity that doesn't polarize potential allies.

Nos/otras is an identity and a practice that activists continue to employ. Levenson is now a doctor and works with primarily disenfranchised groups. He also volunteers during his free time to provide free medical screenings at Street Level Health Project in Oakland, where he mainly works with recently arrived immigrants and the uninsured. Pesquera went on to become a professor at UC Davis, where she taught about the Chicano Movement and other radical mobilizations of the 1960s. She also headed a program that took students to Cuba for a number of years to support and learn from the Cuban Revolution. Jubb went on to work in education and has been an advocate for culturally relevant education. Contreras owns his own printing business and is now part of the Oakland Police Board, a committee made up of residents who monitor for cases of police violence. All of them have continued to be socially active in some capacity. Levenson became a volunteer doctor during the civil wars in Central America. He also went down to support the Zapatista uprising in 1994. Contreras and his wife were involved in the anti-Apartheid movement and joined an international and multiracial group to end Apartheid in South Africa. As Levenson so eloquently told me, "I carry with me still, the true 24/7 commitment to social change. We considered ourselves revolutionary in the sense of wanting to transform the world into a better place" (Levenson interview, August 28, 2019). This is the selflessness of nos/otras, of breaking down the barriers between self and other in order to imagine a more equitable and just society and articulate a caring praxis. Instead of solely seeing BIPOC communities as laborers in the care industry, it is important to underscore the long legacy that BIPOC movements offer us to envision and work toward a more caring world. In so doing, we can envision alternatives to global lethal liberalism.

NOTES

1. Carlos Muñoz Jr. is an emeritus professor of ethnic studies at UC Berkeley. He and others led the student walkouts in Los Angeles for which he was unjustly imprisoned. He is the author of the seminal book of the Chicano Movement, *Youth, Identity, Power: The Chicano Movement.*

2. Katherine McKittrick is the preeminent scholar in what has become a field of study dedicated to analyzing the critical work of Jamaican writer and cultural theorist Sylvia Wynter. For one of Wynter's most explicit analyses of colonization and the us/them divide, see Wynter (1995). See also McKittrick (2015).

3. All interviews were conducted by the author.

4. For an extensive analysis at the limitations of a cultural-nationalist framing of Chicano Movement activism, see Blackwell (2011). See also Pulido (2006) for a geographical reading of radical activism in Los Angeles and the importance of a relational racial analysis of social movements.

REFERENCES

Anzaldúa, Gloria E. 2015. *Light in the Dark / Luz en lo Oscuro: Rewriting Identity, Spirituality, Reality.* Durham, N.C.: Duke University Press.

Baldwin, Devarian L., and Emma S. Crane. 2020. "Cities, Racialized Poverty, and Infrastructures of Possibility." *Antipode* 52(2): 365–379.

Blackwell, Maylei. 2010. "Líderes Campesinas: Nepantla Strategies and Grassroots Organizing at the Intersection of Gender and Globalization." *Aztlan: A Journal of Chicano Studies* 35(1): 13–47.

———. 2011. *¡Chicana Power! Contested Histories of Feminism in the Chicano Movement.* Austin: University of Texas Press.

Cahuas, Madelaine Cristina. 2019. "Burned, Broke, and Brilliant: Latinx Community Workers' Experiences across the Greater Toronto Area's Non-profit Sector." *Antipode* 51(1): 66–86.

Conradson, David. 2003. "Spaces of Care in the City: The Place of a Community Drop-In Center." *Social & Cultural Geography* 4(4): 507–525.

Du Bois, W. E. B. [1899] 1969. *The Philadelphia Negro: A Social Study and History of Pennsylvania's Black American Population; Their Education, Environment and Work.* Philadelphia: University of Pennsylvania.

Evans, Joshua. 2011. "Exploring the BioPolitical Dimensions of Voluntarism and Care in the City: The Case of a 'Low Barrier' Emergency Shelter." *Health & Place* 17(1): 24–32.

Fanon, Frantz. [1963] 2004. *The Wretched of the Earth.* New York: Grove Press.

Glenn, Evelyn Nakano. 2010. *Forced to Care: Coercion and Caregiving in America.* Cambridge, Mass.: Harvard University Press.

Gregory, Steven. 1998. *Black Corona: Race and the Politics of Place in an Urban Community*. Princeton, N.J.: Princeton University Press.

Gupta, Akhil, and James Ferguson, eds. 1997. *Culture, Power, Place: Explorations in Critical Anthropology*. Durham, N.C.: Duke University Press.

Heynen, Nik, and Megan Ybarra. 2020. "On Abolition Ecologies and Making 'Freedom as a Place.'" *Antipode* 53(1): 1–15.

Hondagneu-Sotelo, Pierrette. 2001. *Doméstica: Immigrant Workers Cleaning and Caring in the Shadows of Affluence*. Oakland: University of California Press.

McKittrick, Katherine. 2011. "On Plantations, Prisons and a Black Sense of Place." *Social & Cultural Geography* 12(8): 947–963.

———. 2013. "Plantation Futures." *Small Axe* 17.3(42): 1–15.

——— (Ed.). 2015. *Sylvia Wynter: On Being Human as Praxis*. Durham, N.C.: Duke University Press.

Mignolo, Walter D. 2000. *Local Histories/Global Designs: Coloniality, Subaltern Knowledges, and Border Thinking*. Princeton, N.J.: Princeton University Press.

Milligan, Christine, and Janine Wiles. 2010. "Landscapes of Care." *Progress in Human Geography* 34(6): 736–754.

Nelson, Alondra. 2011. *Body and Soul: The Black Panther Party and the Fight Against Medical Discrimination*. Minneapolis: University of Minnesota Press.

Parr, Hester. 2000. "Interpreting the Hidden Social Geographies of Mental Health: Ethnographies of Inclusion and Exclusion in Semi-institutional Places." *Health and Place* 6(3): 225–237.

———. 2003. "Medical Geography: Care and Caring." *Progress in Human Geography* 27(2): 212–221.

Parreñas, Rhacel Salazar. 2001. *Servants of Globalization: Women, Migration, and Domestic Work*. Palo Alto, Calif.: Stanford University Press.

Power, Andrew, and Edward Hall. 2019. "Placing Care in Times of Austerity." *Social and Cultural Geography* 19(3): 303–313.

Power, Emma R. 2019. "Assembling the Capacity to Care: Caring-with Precarious Housing." *Transactions of the Institute of British Geographers* 44(4): 763–777.

Power, Emma R., and Miriam J. Williams. 2020. "Cities of Care: A Platform for Urban Geographical Care Research." *Geography Compass* 14(1): e12474.

Pulido, Laura. 2006. *Black, Brown, Yellow, and Left: Radical Activism in Los Angeles*. Oakland: University of California Press.

Ramírez, Margaret. 2020. "City as Borderland: Gentrification and the Policing of Black and Latinx Geographies in Oakland." *Environment and Planning D: Society and Space* 38(1): 147–166.

Till, Karen. 2012. "Wounded Cities: Memory-Work and a Place-Based Ethics of Care." *Political Geography* 31(1): 3–14.

Tronto, Joan. 1993. *Moral Boundaries: A Political Argument for an Ethic of Care*. New York: Routledge.

———. 2013. *Caring Democracy: Markets, Equality, and Justice*. New York: New York University Press.

Trotter, Joe. 2007. *Black Milwaukee: The Making of an Industrial Proletariat, 1915–45*. Chicago: University of Illinois Press.

Williams, Miriam. 2016. "Justice and Care in the City: Uncovering Everyday Practices through Research Volunteering." *Area* 48(4): 513–520.

Wilson Gilmore, Ruth. 2017. "Abolition Geography and the Problem of Innocence." In Gaye Theresa Johnson and Alex Lubin (Eds.), *Futures of Black Radicalism*, 224–241. London: Verso.

Woods, Clyde. 2017. *Development Arrested: The Blues and Plantation Power in the Mississippi Delta*. London: Verso.

Wynter, Sylvia. 1995. "1492: A New World View." In Vera Lawrence Hyatt and Rex Nettleford (Eds.), *Race, Discourse, and the Origin of the Americas*, 5–57. Washington, D.C.: Smithsonian Institution Press.

———. 2003. "Unsettling the Coloniality of Being/Power/Truth/Freedom: Towards the Human, After Man, Its Overrepresentation—An Argument." *CR: The New Centennial Review* 3(3): 257–337.

CHAPTER 6

Refusal, Service, and Collective Agency

The Everyday and Quiet Resistance
of Black Southern Activists

PRISCILLA MCCUTCHEON AND ELLEN KOHL

I want you to say that I tried to love and serve humanity.
—Martin Luther King Jr. ([1968] 1998)

The term "activist" often brings to mind the actions of people who disrupt institutions through direct action like protesting and marching in the streets. In this chapter, we explore another facet of resistance, the everyday, quiet resistance of southern Black women and men, many of whom are religious and see their work as a part of their Christian duty to uplift their communities. We argue that their resistance to the racial, social, political, and economic structures within which they live, work, play, and pray is a radical act often overlooked by social movement scholars. We characterize their resistance as quiet and quotidian acts that are "unspoken, or unsaid, unremarked, unrecognized or overlooked" (Campt 2017, 32). The quietness of the act does not detract from the power of these actions; instead, it necessitates that as scholars we pay closer attention to the ways people contest systems of oppression, not just as individuals but as collectives. In this way, we highlight the ways these quiet, everyday acts disrupt liberal thought by constructing intentional and unintentional alternative sites for resistance that may seem unthinkable within the white liberal gaze. However, for these activists, their actions are oftentimes representative of routines present in their everyday lives.

We draw on our work with the Newtown Florist Club and Wheat Street Baptist Church. Ellen spent five years volunteering and conducting participant observation with the Newtown Florist Club (NFC), a social and environmental justice organization in Gainesville, Georgia. Priscilla spent a little over a year volunteering and conducting participant observation research at Wheat Street Baptist Church's Action Mission Ministry (AMM), an emergency food program and clothing ministry. Both organizations have, since their inception, worked to sustain the lives of the people around them through a commitment to the social justice missions of their communities. As Elwood et al. remind us in the introduction to this collection, we oftentimes look to organizations like the AMM and NFC when the failure of the liberal state affects everyone. However, neither organization has ever expected much from the liberal state. They understand that it should work for Black communities but have witnessed firsthand the continuous onslaught of racial, economic, food, and environmental injustices that occur from the neglect of the state. Still, these organizations and many like them persist and quietly work to maintain and build liberated communities. Seemingly, the state is interested in these communities only when displacing Black people is advantageous for the state's economic goals. The communities continually respond by creating their own systems of care and support. Over time, as the fabrics of the communities they serve have transformed, the NFC and the AMM have transformed with them.

This chapter focuses on everyday acts of resistance that draw from ways of being and knowing that are often overlooked as powerful tools of community engagement and social change (Pottinger 2017; Martin, Hanson, and Fontaine 2007; Horton and Kraftl 2009). First, we lay out the histories of both the NFC and Wheat Street Baptist Church's AMM. Second, we explain quiet and quotidian processes as acts of refusal. Third, we explore how service as acts of refusal, self-determination through service, collective agency and community resilience, and self-determined humanity and liberation acknowledges forms of activism that can be unthinkable to mainstream society but support, maintain, and sustain the communities these groups serve. In conclusion, we demonstrate that their quiet and quotidian acts of activism do not just provide services to their community or contest specific injustices. Instead, their work represents a quiet contestation of the systemic intersectional oppressions that structure their lives. Through their everyday acts, they are not just providing food or support for community members but working together to create a shared sense of community. Their actions exist outside the purview of what liberalism allows. They are, in part, inspired by an active faith to imagine and build a beloved community to not only survive but thrive.

History of Organizations

THE NEWTOWN FLORIST CLUB

The NFC, a social and environmental justice organization, was founded in 1950 by a group of Black women who lived in the segregated Newtown neighborhood in Gainesville, Georgia. Their social club was founded on an ethos of care. When people were sick or dying, they would shop for them, clean their house, cook for them, and watch their children. When someone in the community died, they supported the family. They also acted as flower bearers during funerals as a sign of solidarity with the family (Spears 1998). The NFC formalized what had been an informal system of care.

Over the years, the activism of the NFC expanded. They advocated for their streets to be paved and for basic services in their homes. After schools were integrated in 1969, the women of NFC created after-school activities for the community's children, who were not allowed to participate in most extracurricular activities. As their focus expanded, they maintained their original mission of caring for the sick and dying.

An ethos of care has remained an essential part of the organization. It was this mission that led them to the discourse of environmental justice. They began to notice that people in their community were dying of the same types of cancer (throat, mouth, and lung cancer) and from lupus, an autoimmune disease. They started to wonder if it was a result of the fourteen polluting industries within a one-mile radius of their homes. In response, they expanded their focus to also include environmental issues. The club continues its work advocating for social and environmental justice, but they also build community, empower youth, and address immediate concerns to Gainesville's Black community. Their work is not always loud, but it is persistent.

WHEAT STREET BAPTIST CHURCH'S ACTION MISSION MINISTRY

Wheat Street Baptist Church (Wheat Street) is a historically Black Baptist church in Atlanta, Georgia. The church was founded in 1869 on the historic Auburn Avenue, a bustling Black business and residential area once known as the Harlem of the South (Dwyer and Alderman 2008; Inwood 2011; McCutcheon 2015). In its inception, Wheat Street was led by Rev. William Holmes Borders, a Civil Rights leader known not only for his fiery preaching but for his work to make an equitable and just life for Black people in Atlanta. Across the street from Wheat Street is Wheat Street Towers, the first federally funded housing project for seniors. Wheat Street Credit Union is on the first floor (Wheat Street Baptist Church 2020). For many, Wheat Street is a reminder of the glorious past of Auburn Avenue. Its continued existence is seen as an act of survival in a neighborhood where public housing has been torn down and replaced by structures that appeal to a whiter and richer income bracket.

The increasingly aging membership of Wheat Street continually responds to changes in the community, primarily through the AMM, a registered 501(c)(3) arm of the church. The AMM includes a clothing bank and emergency food program, where volunteers cook and serve tasty food to hundreds of people twice a week. McCutcheon (2015) argues that volunteers serve "emergency soul food" that comes from the heart and is a part of their mission from God. Volunteers also direct those coming in to be served to resources including SNAP benefits, mental health services, and monthly HIV/AIDS testing. AMM is a traditional emergency food program, plagued by many of the problems that Poppendieck (1999) identifies, mainly insufficient food quantity and indignity. On the other hand, AMM is composed entirely of Black volunteers, who hope to impart on the guests they serve a humanity that they believe has been stripped from Black people.

Black Futurity and Politics of Refusal

Black people's activism has been narrowly defined, erasing the work of many people who work behind the scenes to bring about social change (Brown 2018; Simien and McGuire 2014; Robnett 1997; Barnett 1993). Oftentimes, we focus on individual leaders and their public actions, without acknowledging the everyday actions that contribute as much, if not more, to social movements. Women of color, whether by choice or by circumstance, often play different roles in social movements from men. When their work is acknowledged, it is oftentimes attributed to male leadership (Collier-Thomas and Franklin 2001; Isoke 2013; Brown 2018). This is due in part to the representation of women's work as care work, as they do what needs to be done for their families' and children's survival.

Social movement theorists have worked to identify and name these often invisible parts of social movements. Robnett (1997, 19) uses the term "bridge leaders" to identify women who worked behind the scenes to make connections within social movements and between the social movement and community members. These bridge leaders also played an important role in integrating strategies that focused on personal, individual change and consciousness with those that focused on tactical decisions to challenge state structures. Cooper (2017) defines race women as Black women who fought for social justice without overshadowing Black men, while also adopting normative values of white womanhood. Naples (1998) refers to activist mothering, or the cross-generational ways women within communities drew on their social networks to nurture their community and leverage resources from outside sources. These conceptions try to uncover the invisible work that is done in spaces that cross the public-private threshold or done in ways that are not seen as activism (Martin, Hanson, and Fontaine 2007). Importantly, all of this work is not invisible, but work that includes care or mothering is often not seen and is undervalued, particularly when the body doing the work is a Black woman's. There are also challenges to conceptions of leadership and participation that can reify gender norms and reduce women's activism to care work.

We draw on Reese's (2018) conceptions of geographies of self-reliance to complicate what it means to be an activist or participate in activism, particularly for Black men and women driven by their Christian faith. Geographies of self-reliance center "Black agency, considering how this agency becomes spatialized within the structural constraints" (Reese 2018, 408). While Reese discusses how Black people contest the processes through which food injustices arise, we contend that the geographies of self-reliance can be expanded beyond the work of food justice to other forms of social justice where "Black folks navigate inequalities with a creativity that reflects a reliance on self and community" (Reese 2018, 408). The geographies of self-reliance necessitate that we pay attention not just to the loud acts of resistance but also to quiet and quotidian acts of defiance.

To understand the role of quiet and quotidian, we draw on the work of Campt (2014, 2019). She urges attention to quiet and quotidian acts, which are often seen as invisible and unremarkable, but which she contends are not passive or invisible. Instead, quiet acts require careful listening, and the quotidian is a "practice honed by the dispossessed in the struggle to create possibility within the constraints of everyday life" (Campt 2017, 32). One way these quiet acts and quotidian processes are mobilized and enacted is through everyday practices of refusal, which not only question the current structure of society but also draw attention to the possibility of what the future can be. While the word "quiet" does rightfully indicate that someone does not hear or is not listening to the activities or activism of these communities, the someone is generally the dominant white society who ignores these everyday acts.

The politics of refusal rejects contemporary conditions and systems of oppression and instead builds on conceptions of Black futurity. Black futurity does not just look to the future but acknowledges contemporary actions that reflect, imagine, and strive for what the future can and should be. Future conditions are enacted in the present (Campt 2014). Refusal is an action, and "practicing refusal names the urgency of rethinking the time, space, and fundamental vocabulary of what constitutes politics, activism, and theory, as well as what it means to refuse the terms given to us to name these struggles" Campt (2019, 80). Acts of refusal are not just responses to authority or a new form of resistance. Instead, they are intentionally political, often social, "generative and strategic" acts that work to create movement from the old to the new (McGranahan 2016, 319). Through the act of refusal, Black activists are not only refusing to be silenced but also taking up space and (re)defining what it means to create Black geographies (Kohl 2020).

THE EVERYDAY POLITICS OF REFUSAL OF BLACK SOUTHERN ACTIVISTS

The politics of refusal and Black futurity can be operationalized in multiple ways. The act of refusal extends beyond what we normally think of as resistance and activism. It can be surviving and thriving (Reese 2019), restoration of self and community (Dunnavant 2020), an act of disengagement (Sojoyner 2017), or choosing where and when to participate (McCutcheon and Kohl 2019). It can be telling your story, so your experiences are not erased or altered (Hua 2013), or staying silent about your role for the success of the overall movement. While silence can be an important political tool, through our rewriting of histories, silence can be amplified, leaving out the important work of activists.[1] Finally, the politics of refusal can be imagining an alternative future (Kelley 2002). By practicing the politics of refusal, activists and community members are not trying to increase participation in the current system but are instead reimagining what that system can and should look like (Finney 2014; Isoke 2013; Kelley 2002; White 2011).

The politics of refusal highlights everyday resistance, which White (2018, 6) defines as "less confrontational, incurs less repression, and is usually enacted by individuals or small groups." In *Freedom Farmers: Agricultural Resistance and the Black Freedom Movement*, White theorizes past and present Black farming cooperatives through collective agency and community resilience (CACR). She notes that while CACR highlights everyday acts of resistance, even it does not account for "activities that are not disruptive but rather constructive, in the sense that the aggrieved actively build alternatives to existing political and economic relationships. The acts of building knowledge, skills, community, and economic independence have a radical potential that the term does not encompass" (White 2018, 6). While quiet, these less confrontational acts have "radical potential" (White 2018, 6) because they lean toward restoration. Restoration is both individual and community and in many Black social justice organizations is geared toward restoring humanity in oneself and one's community.

The politics of refusal connects the past and present to "unearth, invoke, reenact, and most importantly, re-envision historic legacies of struggle against injustice" (Isoke 2013, 2). The act of refusal is also deeply spatialized and performed by Black bodies in spaces they seek to transform. Humanity is at the core of this transformation, as Black people seek to create spaces in which they are allowed to be fully human and liberated, two things that are not often afforded to Black people. For Black people, this is a self-determined humanity and liberation that must be created by Black people and offered to other Black people in obvious and less obvious ways. The less obvious ways, or the acts of refusal, may take the form of "service," an act that in many cases is guided by an ethos that makes resistance difficult to parse out.

ACTIVISM AS SERVICE TO OTHERS

Service to others is an integral part of the Black religious ethos, which values communal responsibility.[2] Service to others is not a passive act; instead, it is a quiet act and a quotidian process of defiance that refuses to accept anything less than full humanity by creating places, where even just for a small moment Black people can be free, in the Black Radical Tradition (Kelley 2002), and liberated. Dr. Martin Luther King Jr.'s thoughts on service are instructive. Near the end of his famous "Drum Major for Justice" speech, he preaches about how he wants to be remembered:

> I'd like somebody to mention that day that Martin Luther King, Jr., tried to give his life serving others. I'd like for somebody to say that day that Martin Luther King, Jr., tried to love somebody. I want you to say that day that I tried to be right on the war question. I want you to be able to say that day that I did try to feed the hungry. And I want you to be able to say that day that I did try in my life to clothe those who were naked. I want you to say on that day that I did try in my life to visit those who were in prison. I want you to say that I tried to love and serve humanity. (King [1968] 1998)

For him, being a drum major for justice is tied to his mission to "feed the hungry and clothe the naked," a biblical directive from Matthew 25:35–45, in which Christ lays out a mandate for how Christians should treat the "least of these." Service to others is giving to the "least of these," while also acknowledging that those serving have been or are the least of these. For Black people, being of service to each other is an act of refusal as it acknowledges a humanity within themselves and the humanity among a community of Black people. More importantly, Black people giving of themselves to each other signals that self-determination is central to their conceptions of humanity.

Intentional and unintentional acts of service have always been a part of Black-led food and environmental justice movements. Revolutionary food and environmental justice initiatives, many of which were rooted in the Civil Rights and Black Power movements, have served as a chief part of their mission. The role of service should not be overlooked in the structure, goals, and motivations of these organizations. The Black Panther Party's free break-fast program was political. As Heynen (2009) reminds us, the Black Panther Party's free breakfast program was not just about feeding children but was also used as a tool to build Black power and Black pride in individual Black people and in the Black community at large. However, in reflecting on the Black Panther Party's free breakfast program, we oftentimes neglect the acts of service occurring in them. We highlight the revolutionary teachings of the Black Panther Party, without acknowledging that the service of food is within itself a revolutionary act. Black people serving each other meant they could control what was served, how it was served, and the meaning and intention behind it. It created places where they could not just survive but also thrive (Reese 2019).

For the members of AMM and NFC, notions of self always include their communities. The individual "I" is in conversation with the collective "we," which is clearly articulated through a shared sense of community, which challenges liberal notions of individualism. An emphasis on community and collective within the Black community is not only a reaction to white supremacy but also a way to construct joy outside the white gaze and to create spaces to not just survive but thrive (Reese 2019). It is a choice, not just something they are forced to do. For both groups, this shared sense of community becomes as important to the individual as it is to the collective. This can also be seen in the approach to activism of other organizations, such as the Black Panther Party. While the party's free breakfast program explicitly served others as part of their activism, there are countless other examples of service by Black women during the Civil Rights and Black Power movements (Williams-Forson 2006).

Service, as noted above, is self-determination. By service, we argue that giving to oneself and giving to other Black people is a part of community building both politically and geographically. This service is oftentimes framed as the backbone of the movement as Black women oftentimes used Black-owned restaurants to feed organizers and provide sites where groups could meet and strategize. Examples of these places still exist, with one of the most well-known being Paschal's restaurant in Atlanta. On its website Paschal's is described as the "'meeting place' for some of the most notable entertainers, politicians and business people, including Aretha Franklin, Dizzy Gillespie, Andrew Young, Maynard Jackson, Vice President Al Gore, and Martin Luther King just to name a few" (Paschal's Restaurant n.d.). Paschal's served Civil Rights leaders and countless Black students who attended Atlanta's historically Black colleges and universities. Oftentimes when we think about Black people serving food, it is wrapped up in a race-based and class-based hierarchy, in which Black people (in many cases Black women) are serving food to white people. However, service as an act of refusal is Black people giving of themselves to their community. In these historical examples, we argue service should not simply be categorized as the backbone of a social movement, supporting the real activist work of protesting and sit-ins. Instead, service as an act of refusal is a distinct type of activist work.

While service to others through food is perhaps more intuitive, service as an act of refusal can also be understood in the environmental justice movement. Kurtz (2007) provides a useful entry point to understanding service activism in her interrogation of gender in the public and private sphere in the environmental justice movement. She notes that women were often uniquely positioned to participate in and lead the environmental justice movement because they observed the deleterious effects of pollution on their children inside the private sphere of the home. While nurturing might not be seen as activism, these women were best equipped to identify the health effects of pollution. Perkins (2012) cautions us to not reify gender roles nor the reasons women get involved in environmental justice activism. Despite this caution, current constructions of gender give women abilities to move between the public and private realm, which grants them access to places they might otherwise not be able to gain access (Kurtz 2007).

Black feminist literature on mothering provides another avenue through which we can examine quiet and quotidian activism of service. Boris delineates mothering among Black women and white women activists. She notes that "Black activists' references to 'highest womanhood' and 'true motherhood' appeared to subvert a social script written for them by the larger culture that sought to deny them the possibility of nurturing, motherhood and family maintenance" (1989, 30). So service by Black women as understood through service to one's family in the private sphere could be considered a revolutionary act. This will become evident in our analysis of the NFC, a Black environmental justice organization founded by women who were serving Black families in their communities after a loved one had passed.

QUIET ACTS OF REFUSAL

Until her retirement in December 2014, Ms. Faye Bush would leave her home and cross DeSota Street to the house that served as NFC's headquarters. Ms. Bush, who took over as executive director in 1990, joined the NFC in 1952 when she was eighteen years old. Her mother, Maggie Johnson, was one of the eleven women who founded the organization. Despite her dedication to social and environmental justice, and her local, regional, and national recognition,

Ms. Bush does not see herself as an activist. Instead, she saw herself as someone who helps others, someone who is driven by a love for her community and a desire to care for her community (Ferris 2009). Her approach to activism reflects the quiet acts and quotidian processes that are acts of refusal. She, and the members of NFC, refuse to accept the intersectional environmental contaminants in their community (Ducre 2018). Instead, she imagines what her community can and should look like and works to make those images a reality. She and NFC members listen carefully to differentiate between their beloved community and the physical surroundings and systems of oppression that are causing them harm.

Similar to Ms. Bush, many of the older volunteers at Wheat Street have been dedicated to serving the people of Auburn Avenue for decades. Priscilla met Dr. Johnson, a longtime AMM volunteer, when she was ninety-one years old. Dr. Johnson spoke about the glory days of Auburn Avenue and her work to establish the AMM. She was a humble woman but not afraid to talk about her life and work, a life full of firsts and milestones. It is this proud humility that guides her activism at AMM as she works tirelessly to instill in others the pride she feels for herself, Black people, and the Auburn Avenue community. She trained Priscilla on her first day and impressed in her the importance of looking every guest in the eye, shaking their hands, and giving them a hug.[3] Priscilla watched Dr. Johnson follow the food limits set by the kitchen while simultaneously giving guests as much food as they would ask for as long as the food was there. Like Ms. Bush, Dr. Johnson was guided by a love for her Auburn Avenue community, which has undergone drastic changes. In some cases, guests coming in to be served were people who once attended the church on a regular basis, had fallen on hard times, and were often embarrassed to come to church on a Sunday when members would see their suffering. While Dr. Johnson would often encourage them to come to church, her ministry was intended to make guests feel comfortable and safe on Monday and Wednesday during food service.

Newtown and Wheat Street volunteers serve through quotidian processes that they have been honing for decades. They draw on long-term everyday interactions to assess the needs of their community and find new ways to address these concerns. For NFC members, the direct care of the 1950s evolved through the discourse of Civil Rights and the need for youth-based activities. In the 1990s, Newtown members learned the language of environmental justice, which enabled them to articulate their growing concerns about the connections between people dying of the same diseases and the environmental conditions in their neighborhood. Similarly, the actions of Wheat Street volunteers were often a response to the times. The leadership of the church, from its inception in the late 1800s, always knew that land ownership and food were key to them achieving their goal to support Black people. While they established institutions like a grocery store on Auburn Avenue and a farm outside of Atlanta, it was the act of bringing fresh produce to the church on Sunday that continues to be embedded in the individuals and institutions who run the AMM. For someone like Dr. Johnson, the quiet acts endure even when institutions change or no longer exist. The present-day AMM is a culmination of almost a century of activism and a realization that meeting basic needs was a necessity for a changing urban community. Both programs have expanded and evolved. However, they continue to maintain their original missions of care. Through these processes, they have worked to "create possibility within the contains of everyday life" (Campt 2017, 32). These changes reflect the quiet ways they listen to the needs of their community and adapt their activism to these needs. They continually look to the future but remember the past. The past serves as a quiet reminder of what the future can and should be.

SERVICE AS ACT OF REFUSAL

NFC members and AMM volunteers see possibility through their everyday lives as they find ways to celebrate rather than wallow in despair. Much of this is done through formal and informal acts of service. For NFC members, as Gainesville's Black community became more dispersed and access to social services increased, their direct form of service, caring for the sick and dying, took a back seat to other forms of service. Their acts of service reflect the changing needs of their community, but also the changing needs of the organization. The acts of service ranged from small, individual acts to large, coordinated acts with implications across the city. Regardless of what the act of service was, it was done with the mission to improve the conditions within their community and, as is discussed below, as constructive and restorative acts.

Individual acts of service are a hallmark of the NFC. For Ms. Bush and other members of the NFC board, this work comes from love. When asked by a reporter how she felt about being an activist, Ms. Bush responded, "An activist must always act from a place of love. When we started this organization, we would go in and bathe sick people. We did it out of love and the closeness that we have in this community. We just needed to help people, and that's what it's still about" (quoted in Ferris 2009). Their commitment to love and care is not a passive act but an act of refusal. They refuse to see their community members as dispensable; instead, they are vital members of society who deserve love and care.

While the mission of caring for their community is still integral to their

work, what it means to care for individuals has changed. At times, it is still attending funerals, when families request it, but more often than not it is providing a listening ear and a safe space for community members who are facing
hardship. NFC is often looked to as the heart of the Black community through
their service to Gainesville and the surrounding areas. "People call the Florist
Club for everything, like we're the NAACP or SCLC. . . . People just associate us
with community justice. We're going to press on and help in every way that we
can" (Faye Bush, quoted in Thomas 2008, 42). The way the community sees the
NFC is based on how they respond to community needs. If there is something
that needs to be done, they do it. They do this because they recognize that if
they fail to then no one will do it for them. They serve others in order to serve
themselves. Both groups use service to reclaim power within their community through self-determination to serve the collective. While white supremacy is a constant, it is not a constant that either organization chooses to accept.
They both see white supremacy as something that has been constructed and
therefore something that can be deconstructed. Through their consistent daily
actions, both the NFC and Wheat Street show that serving Black people and
treating them with dignity and respect are services they give to their communities, but also resistance to oppression.

Hope is a part of AMM volunteers' belief system, as it is the charitable arm
of a church that has withstood community changes. Wheat Street's motto is
"the church in Atlanta with Atlanta in its heart" (Wheat Street Baptist Church
2016). Volunteers embody the church's mission and think of themselves as "of
Atlanta" in a way that other churches are not. When talking to longtime volunteers at Wheat Street, they never disparage other large churches in the area
that receive considerably more media attention. However, Wheat Street volunteers often spoke about how their work is not for show; instead, such work
comes from a deep commitment to Atlanta, Auburn Avenue, and its people.
Caring for guests coming in to be served means meeting basic needs the city
has neglected to provide. When guests come in to be served, some volunteers
will give them soap to wash with. Though most of the guests are male, many
female guests who come in are in need of sanitary items. More often than not,
these items did not come from the AMM's budget or inventory, both of which
were often sparse. Instead, volunteers brought what they had at home and sup-
plemented the inventory as much as possible. Volunteers often harkened back
to a time when even more of the church's fellowship hall was used for service
to the community. Wheat Street takes up almost a block on Auburn Avenue,
and the fellowship hall was built to be a place to serve the community and the
church. Though much of the fellowship hall is still used today, there is an en-

tire second floor that used to provide temporary housing for residents of Auburn Avenue. There were also additional bathrooms in which AMM guests could bathe. During Priscilla's time at Wheat Street, she always felt as though they were doing as much as they could. The average age of volunteers was sixty, and it seemed impossible for them to open up temporary housing and provide baths. However, volunteers always wanted to do more, and this vision was based on a past reality.

Any acts of service done by members of Wheat Street, similar to the NFC, are intentional acts of refusal based on a history of service and an investment in community. When Priscilla was crafting her dissertation research, she was aware of the three big churches of Auburn Avenue: Ebenezer Baptist, Big Bethel African Methodist Episcopal, and Wheat Street Baptist. As she inquired about the three churches, she was immediately told that Wheat Street was the one doing the work on Auburn Avenue and had a reputation for following their mission and giving of themselves to the community, often without recognition. Service as an act of refusal should also be understood as intentionally occurring behind a cloak, at least to middle- and upper-class white people. AMM volunteers care about popularity, but audience matters. Their community is the "least of these," on Auburn Avenue, and they believe that feeding them leads to a healthy, happy, and thriving community.

SERVICE AS SELF-DETERMINATION

Self-determination is a spatial politics. In *Barbershops, Bibles and BET*, Harris-Lacewell (2004) defines self-determination as the ability of Black people to control their own lives and communities. Self-determination is rooted in a realization by many Black people and communities that government programs were never meant to truly serve Black people. While Harris-Lacewell acknowledges the importance of the community level, we draw on Reese's spatialization of self-determination. In *Black Food Geographies* (2019), Reese finds that members of the Deanwood neighborhood create self-determined communities through Black-owned grocery stores and gardens in sometimes unlikely places. For both organizations, Black people insisting on self-determined communities means insisting over almost a century on their collective right to exist and thrive in these communities.

Self-determination as a spatial ideology is evident at the AMM, in part because the emergency food program occupies a space in which the city seeks to erase any sign of Blackness. Wheat Street members often recount their many discussions and battles with city hall officials over the police department's continued harassment of Black people who are walking across the street to AMM

and are threatened with arrest for jaywalking. Ironically, much of the city's justification is their desire to keep poor Black people hidden from the many tour-
ists who visit the MLK National Historical Park. The fact that Wheat Street
continues to stand in spite of the city's attempt to erase their very presence
speaks to Wheat Street's claim that this is their community, ironic given that
much of Dr. King's mission was dedicated to serving the poor. For the members of NFC, the spatiality of self-determination can be seen in their fight for
voting rights and emphasis on the immediate concerns of their community.
Gainesville still maintains an at-large voting system, a system that has been
used to disenfranchise populations. The council member for each district must
reside in the district, but they are elected by the city as a whole. As a result,
members of NFC do not feel as if their council member represents their interests. They have challenged this system through a lawsuit based on the 1990
elections and by supporting a lawsuit brought by members of the Latinx community (*Johnson v. Hamrick* 2001).

   Self-determination is also evident in the type of space that AMM volunteers create, a space where they believe guests can be themselves while also being respectful. For AMM volunteers, this is expressed in the way they welcome
guests. When guests come into Wheat Street to be served, they sit around
tables that are reminiscent of dinner tables and are served water by volunteers. They are then served food after a church service. For many guests whom
Priscilla spoke to, the church service is their ability to worship without being
judged. For others, this church service is insulting and offensive because they
are not Christian. And then for still others, this service is a nuisance, standing
in the way of what for many is the only meal they will receive throughout the
day. However, for AMM members, the serving of food is important to them
creating and maintaining a thriving community that many of them remember.

   The desire to create a thriving community also drives members of the NFC.
This can be seen in their activism since the 1990s to move a junkyard, which is
adjacent to houses and a church in their neighborhood. When they talk about
moving the junkyard, they talk not just about what they do not want in their
community but also about what they do want: a sign surrounded by flowers
welcoming people to Newtown, biking trails instead of industry, quiet lawns
with people gardening. Just as with AMM members, they draw on the past to
create a new sense of what the future can and should be.

COLLECTIVE AGENCY AND COMMUNITY RESILIENCE

The quiet resistance of AMM and NFC can be seen in the constructive work
that builds a sense of community, connection, and knowledge (White 2018).

Historically, NFC did this because they wanted to create safe spaces where they and their children could thrive. This was done through both formal organizations, such as a young women's club, after-school activities, and an annual Fourth of July neighborhood party, and informal organizations, where people would gather in each other's yards and porches to build community. It is through the informal gatherings where Ms. Rose Johnson, the current executive director of the NFC, got her education in social and environmental justice. The older women took her in, and she learned from them by observing.

The CACR work NFC mobilizes has changed over the years. Following the end of legal segregation, Gainesville's Black population is dispersed, not concentrated in and around Newtown. A focus on youth involvement and empowerment is one way NFC maintains its leadership position in the community and expands its conceptions of community beyond the physical boundaries of the neighborhood. Through their work with youth, they see the future in the present, as Ms. Bush explains: "We're getting on in age, so if we don't teach them now. . . . We want them to be able to carry the struggle on, and I'm always impressed with the summer program. The girls are so excited and ask amazing questions. If one of them makes something happen here, it will be well worth it" (quoted in Crist 2010). For them, educating the next generation is a radical act of restoration and resiliency.

Wheat Street has always had a positive presence in the Auburn Avenue neighborhood. Wheat Street's work is steeped in the Baptist tradition, in which ministries are formalized as missions. The AMM's biweekly act of serving food is coordinated with other historically Black churches in the immediate area. When Priscilla volunteered at Wheat Street, they coordinated their efforts with both Big Bethel African Methodist Episcopal Church (AME) and Ebenezer Baptist Church. No one church was serving food at the same time as another church, and both volunteers and guests knew the schedule. While Auburn Avenue changed at the end of legal segregation, the racial makeup of the neighborhood remained mostly Black. Arguably, the most drastic changes to the neighborhood were spurred by the U.S. Department of Housing and Urban Development's HOPE VI program. The stated goal of HOPE VI was to bring more mixed-use developments to urban neighborhoods. Many argue that it instead sped up the process of gentrification. Grady Homes, Atlanta's largest housing project, was torn down less than a block away from Wheat Street. When Grady Homes was torn down, residents had nowhere to go, a struggle that was compounded by the lack of shelters in the city.

The work of the NFC and of Wheat Street has been disruptive, but also constructive and restorative. At the NFC, they want to declare not just what New-town is not (a haven for toxic pollution) but also what Newtown is (a beloved community). Through this declaration of humanity, they are contesting their community as a neglected, forgotten wasteland and instead working to create a place where members can thrive, even if the intersection of the physical, so-cial, political, and economic conditions within their community make this dif-ficult (Ducre 2018; Reese 2018). At Wheat Street, they are as invested in say-ing what Auburn Avenue is not as in saying what Auburn Avenue is. Through small acts, they are clear that Auburn Avenue is a neighborhood of people who take care of each other. While they understand that poverty exists, they fully believe that the type of poverty that they see in front of their eyes is not what and who Wheat Street or Auburn Avenue is. Their vision of Auburn Avenue is in many ways historic, as they remember it as a Black bustling space that was socially, economically, and politically prominent. All were not wealthy on Au-burn Avenue, but they lived as a community with fulfilling lives.

SELF-DETERMINED HUMANITY AND LIBERATION

Volunteers at Wheat Street's AMM and NFC are quiet activists whose work is often overlooked in part because their activism is through service. They make bold statements, through their actions and interactions, through their service, about the humanity of themselves and other Black people. We are defining hu-manity through our volunteers' actions, which means volunteers' recognition that those they serve are living, breathing souls who desire and need touch, af-fection, and conversation in the same way the volunteers do. While reaffirm-ing humanity is not something we might think of as a quiet and quotidian act, it is an act Black people have always done for themselves and each other in a world that seeks to strip this humanity from them. For AMM volunteers, a self-determined humanity means looking at guests in the eye, shaking their hands, and hugging those they know while giving them an extra squeeze at the end. Serving humanity also means getting to know guests through one-on-one conversations that can last for hours. Through these conversations, volunteers come to understand why people are in the situation of needing food and also how fragile even their own economic situations are. While hugging someone may seem small, for AMM volunteers this action indicates that they are one with their guests.

For NFC members, reaffirming humanity is a foundational principle. As mentioned in the organization's description, the club began to deliver flowers to Black people in the community after the death of a loved one. Flowers are symbolic of many funeral rituals, but one meaning they represent is that life in the soul is eternal. Given the emotions surrounding death, it is difficult for both the giver and the family receiving these flowers. We believe the act of giving flowers is representative of the humanity that members of the NFC see in the people of their community. This act of care does not end after the flowers are given; arguably the giving is the beginning of the care. A florist club that believes in a self-determined humanity and liberation wants not just to know why Black people die but ultimately to stop premature Black death.

While reaffirming the humanity of oneself and one's community might be a quiet act of refusal, it has always been a part of the work that Black communities have done. We can see this, for example, in the discourse of the Civil Rights and Black Power movements. While these movements were fighting obvious oppressions, they were also fighting the dehumanization of Black people that was a part of this oppression. The often-heard expression in many Black communities that "you are somebody" is Black people reaffirming to themselves their pride and strength in being Black. Similarly, Black theology, which is seen in many Black religious and nonreligious organizations, is focused on reaffirming humanity. Its founder, James Cone (1970), argues that ideas about liberation should come from the oppressed who are uniquely situated to see a future with liberation at the heart. However, to do so, individuals must first be liberated themselves, as individual liberation leads to community liberation. So this notion of seeing humanity in oneself and one's people is not small. However, the ways in which this happens often include these less obvious acts of refusal where reaffirming humanity is at the core.

Quiet Resistance

Many societies teach people to listen to those who are the loudest, socializing them to speak up for themselves and use their voices to convey their message. As activists and scholars, we are not immune from making these same categorizations about ourselves and the communities we work with. Often, activists and scholars strategically position particular people as the face of movements, all the while leaving others in the background. Even when the quiet work is acknowledged, it is categorized as supporting the more "important" public work being done. Moreover, history records those whose voices are heard, and they are often heralded as the heroes of movements. Rarely are there historical accounts of those who are responsible for the less public and often mundane acts that are a part of all social movements.

This chapter has interrogated the quiet and quotidian acts of Black southern environmental and food justice activists. Both organizations are rooted in the Civil Rights and Black Power movements, and fighting for change is ingrained in them. The NFC and Wheat Street's AMM do important work on a daily basis, work that is often overlooked and, when mentioned, rarely categorized as activist work. We show that the work of NFC and Wheat Street's AMM supports larger movements *and* is also in itself a radical act. These quiet quotidian acts are used to build self-reliant and self-determined communities, where Black people reaffirm themselves and their place in the community.

Acts of care, resiliency, and restoration are increasingly seen and valued in contemporary justice work. The NFC and Wheat Street's AMM centralize acts of care that are integrated within broader agendas of activism. Whether through serving food to communities or acting as pallbearers at funerals, these actions operate alongside both groups' louder activist work. Considering the totality of both groups' work, we reject the notion that Black people, Black communities, and the work they do can be neatly packaged into liberal categories that predetermine what is or isn't radical enough. We challenge ourselves and others to be quiet and listen closely; in doing so, we may be able to recognize these quotidian acts that often go unnoticed.

Telling the story of quiet and quotidian acts of service is vital to the longevity of organizations like NFC and Wheat Street. Storytelling plays an essential role in how they communicate their work to the next generation, and this act of educating *is* a radical act of restoration and resiliency. Storytelling is especially important because the organizations have aging memberships. Moreover, in both Atlanta and Gainesville, the Black population, which used to be spatially concentrated due to legal segregation, is now more dispersed. Despite this dispersion, Auburn Avenue and Newtown are still seen as the hearts of their respective Black communities. This is due in part to the work of these organizations, which continue to both care for and create space for Black communities to thrive (McCutcheon 2015; Kohl 2021). Through their work, they not only serve the collective but work to maintain a sense of the collective.

Paying attention to the quiet and quotidian highlights complex histories of resistance that go beyond singular figures and historical moments. This is evident both in the work of the NFC and Wheat Street and in the ways we pay attention to their quiet acts in our research. These orientations open a window onto what and whom we have missed by excluding everyday acts of service. These acts are not done in isolation but rather sustain and connect to larger moves to upend white supremacy and capitalism. These quiet acts represent efforts by the collective to change these systems day by day.

NOTES

1. One example of silence amplified in history is the role women from Bennett College role played in the Greensboro sit-ins. These women began planning the sit-ins, but men from nearby North Carolina Agricultural and Technical State University (A&T) began the boycotts (it is contested as to whether this was in conjunction with the women or preempted their actions). The Bennett women continued to organize, support, and participate in the sit-ins but remained silent on their role. This silence has been amplified in the retelling of this history that glorifies the Greensboro Four but writes out the women of Bennett College (Brown 2018).

2. A Black religious ethos emphasizes "notions of communal responsibility and was manifested in church-sponsored civic, educational, economic and political activity" (Taylor, Chatters, and Brown 2014).

3. For Action Mission Ministry volunteers, it is a show of respect for them to refer to those coming in to be served as guests.

REFERENCES

Barnett, Bernice M. 1993. "Invisible Southern Black Women Leaders in the Civil Rights Movement: The Triple Constraints of Gender, Race, and Class." *Gender & Society* 7(2): 162–182.

Boris, Eileen. 1989. "The Power of Motherhood: Black and White Activist Women Redefine the 'Political.'" *Yale Journal of Law and Feminism* 2(1): 25–49.

Brown, Laura. M. 2018. "Remembering Silence: Bennett College Women and the 1960 Greensboro Student Sit-Ins." *Rhetoric Society Quarterly* 48(1): 49–70.

Campt, Tina M. 2014. "Black Feminist Futures and the Practice of Fugitivity." Paper, Barnard Center for Research on Women, New York.

———. 2017. *Listening to Images.* Durham, N.C.: Duke University Press.

———. 2019. "Black Visuality and the Practice of Refusal." *Women & Performance: A Journal of Feminist Theory* 29(1): 79–87.

Collier-Thomas, Bettye, and Vincent P. Franklin (Eds.). 2001. *Sisters in the Struggle: African-American Women in the Civil Rights–Black Power Movement.* New York: New York University Press.

Cone, James A. 1970. *A Black Theology of Liberation.* Philadelphia: Lippincott.

Cooper, Brittany. 2017. *Beyond Respectability: The Intellectual Thought of Race Women.* Urbana: University of Illinois Press.

Crist, Carolyn. 2010. "Carry the Struggle Newtown Florist Club at 60." *Gainesville Times,* October 10. https://www.gainesvilletimes.com/opinion/carry-the-struggle -newtown-florist-club-at-60/.

Ducre, Kishi A. 2018. "The Black Feminist Spatial Imagination and an Intersectional Environmental Justice." *Environmental Sociology* 4(1): 22–35.

Dunnavant, Justin. 2020. "Emerging Ecologies: Archaeologies of Slavery, Landscape and Environmental Change." DOPE 2020 Plenary Panel, University of Kentucky, February 28.

Dwyer, Owen J., and Derek Alderman. 2008. *Civil Rights Memorials and the Geography of Memory.* Athens: University of Georgia Press.

Ferris, Jedd. 2009. "Flower Power—The Florist Who Saved a City." *Blue Ridge Outdoors*, January 1. https://www.blueridgeoutdoors.com/people/flash-power-the-florist-who -saved-a-city/.

Finney, Carolyn. 2014. *Black Faces, White Spaces: Reimagining the Relationship of African Americans to the Great Outdoors*. Durham, N.C.: UNC Press Books.

Harris-Lacewell, Melissa. 2004. *Barbershops, Bibles and BET: Everyday Talk and Black Political Thought*. Princeton, N.J.: Princeton University Press.

Heynen, Nik. 2009. "Bending the Bars of Empire from Every Ghetto for Survival: The Black Panther Party's Radical Antihunger Politics of Social Reproduction of Scale." *Annals of the Association of American Geographers* 99(2): 406–422.

Horton, John, and Peter Kraftl. 2009. "Small Acts, Kind Words and 'not Too Much Fuss': Implicit Activisms." *Emotion, Space and Society* 2(1): 14–23.

Hua, Anh. 2013. "Black Diaspora Feminism and Writing: Memories, Storytelling, and the Narrative World as Sites of Resistance." *African and Black Diaspora: An International Journal* 6 (1): 30–42.

Inwood, Joshua F. 2011. "Constructing African American Urban Space in Atlanta, Ga." *Geographical Review* 101(2): 147–163.

Isoke, Zenzele. 2013. *Urban Black Women and the Politics of Resistance*. London: Palgrave Macmillan.

Johnson v. Hamrick. 155 F. Supp. 2d 1355 (N.D. Ga. 2001).

Kelley, Robin D. G. 2002. *Freedom Dreams: The Black Radical Imagination*. Boston: Beacon.

King, Martin Luther, Jr. [1968] 1998. "'The Drum Major Instinct,' Sermon Delivered at Ebenezer Baptist Church." In Clayborne Carson and Peter Holloran (Eds.), *A Knock at Midnight*, 169–186. New York: Warner Books.

Kohl, Ellen. 2020. "'Some We's Weren't Part of We': Intersectional Politics of Belonging in EJ Activism." *Gender, Place & Culture* 28(11): 1606–1626. https://doi.org/10.1080 /0966369X.2020.1832968.

———. 2021. "Making the Invisible Visible: Telling Stories as Quiet, Everyday Resistance." *ACME* 21(1): 33–48.

Kurtz, Hilda E. 2007. "Gender and Environmental Justice in Louisiana: Blurring the Boundaries of Public and Private Spheres." *Gender, Place & Culture* 14(4): 409–426.

Martin, Deborah G., Susan Hanson, and Danielle Fontaine. 2007. "What Counts as Activism? The Role of Individuals in Creating Change." *Women's Studies Quarterly* 35(3/4): 78–94.

McCutcheon, Priscilla. 2015. "Food, Faith and the Everyday Struggle for Black Urban Community." *Social and Cultural Geography* 16(4): 385–406.

McCutcheon, Priscilla, and Ellen Kohl. 2019. "You're Not Welcome at My Table: Racial Discourse, Conflict and Healing at the Kitchen Table." *Gender, Place & Culture* 26(2): 173–180.

McGranahan, Carole. 2016. "Theorizing Refusal: An Introduction." *Cultural Anthropology* 31(3): 319–325.

Naples, Nancy A. 1998. *Grassroots Warriors: Activist Mothering, Community Work, and the War on Poverty*. New York: Routledge.

Paschal's Restaurant. n.d. "About Us." https://www.paschalsatlanta.com/about-us.

Perkins, Tracy E. 2012. "Women's Pathways into Activism: Rethinking the Women's Environmental Justice Narrative in California's San Joaquin Valley." *Organization & Environment* 25(1): 76–94.

Poppendieck, Janet. 1999. *Sweet Charity? Emergency Food and the End of Entitlement.* New York: Penguin.

Pottinger, Laura. 2017. "Planting the Seeds of a Quiet Activism." *Area* 49(2): 215–222.

Reese, Ashanté M. 2018. "'We Will Not Perish; We're Going to Keep Flourishing': Race, Food Access, and the Geographies of Self-Reliance." *Antipode* 50(2): 407–424.

———. 2019. *Black Food Geographies.* Chapel Hill: University of North Carolina Press.

Robnett, Belinda. 1997. *How Long? How Long? African-American Women in the Struggle for Civil Rights.* New York: Oxford University Press.

Simien, Evelyn M., and Danielle L. McGuire. 2014. "A Tribute to the Women: Rewriting History, Retelling Herstory in Civil Rights." *Politics & Gender* 10(3): 413–431.

Sojoyner, Damien M. 2017. "Another Life Is Possible: Black Fugitivity and Enclosed Places." *Cultural Anthropology* 32(4): 514–536.

Spears, Ellen Griffith. 1998. *"The Newtown Story": One Community's Fight for Environmental Justice.* Atlanta: Center for Democratic Renewal and Newtown Florist Club.

Taylor, Robert, Linda Chatters, and R. Khari Brown. 2014. "African American Religious Participation." *Review of Religious Research* 56(4): 513–538.

Thomas, Chandra. 2008. "Chandra Thomas on People Trying to Make a Difference." *Atlanta*, June 2008, 36–42.

Wheat Street Baptist Church. 2016–2022. "Wheat Street Towers.". https://www.weare wheatstreet.org/wheat-street-towers.

White, Monica M. 2011. "Sisters of the Soil: Urban Gardening as Resistance in Detroit." *Race/Ethnicity: Multidisciplinary Global Contexts* 5(1): 13–28.

———. 2018. *Freedom Farmers: Agricultural Resistance and the Black Freedom Movement.* Chapel Hill: University of North Carolina Press.

Williams-Forson, Psyche. 2006. *Building Houses out of Chicken Legs: Black Women, Food, and Power.* Chapel Hill: University of North Carolina Press.

CHAPTER 7

Storying Relations

A Method in Pursuit of Collective Liberation

MARGARET MARIETTA RAMÍREZ AND MICHELLE DAIGLE

For colonized peoples identity will be primarily "opposed to"—that is a limitation from the beginning. Decolonization will have done its real work when it goes beyond this limit.
—Édouard Glissant (1997, 17)

In this chapter, we draw from our collective collaborations that seek to envision decolonial geographies across Black, Indigenous, and people of color (BIPOC) communities to begin to theorize a relational methodology for collective liberation. In our dialogue over the years, we have gradually built a shared praxis and a method of engagement that is founded upon a radical sense of relationality (Yazzie and Risling Baldy 2018). We trace this methodology in formation through our genealogies as cisgender Mushkegowuk and Chicana women; we also trace how our understandings of liberation have formed through dialogue and relationship building between each other and a number of collaborators we have been in conversation with over the past several years. We theorize this method of radical relationality as being premised on slow relationship, trust building over time, an ethic of generosity and care, and critical attention to how we are differently situated in place.

Drawing on Black, Indigenous, and Latinx feminist theorists, we focus on the methods and practices through which an anticolonial, antiracist, and anticapitalist theory of collective liberation can emerge (Anzaldúa and Moraga 1981; Gilmore 2017; Simpson 2017; Yazzie and Risling Baldy 2018; Simpson and Maynard 2018; King 2019). This is a methodology that counters practices invested in anti-Black, anti-Indigenous and related forms of racial and gendered violence, by building radical relationality across BIPOC communities. The methods we cultivate are grounded in a storytelling praxis, as BIPOC people come together to listen to one another, to understand the distinct forms of violence that are embodied across Indigenous, Black, and Brown communities around the globe, and how those realities are simultaneously entangled in geometries of colonial capitalist power.[1] As stories are shared, relationships can grow; however, we have learned that such growth can come only with time, with the creation of spaces of flight that refuse colonial white supremacy and a willingness to reckon with the forms of violence that we are all implicated in.[2] Radical relationality as a methodology for liberation requires BIPOC people coming together to reckon with the difficult points of contention that can strain our ability to truly see one another in our desires for freedom and liberation.

We specifically focus on relationship building across BIPOC communities even though we recognize that visions of freedom articulated by Black abolition and Indigenous decolonization encompass an expansive web of relationalities with anticapitalist movements and, importantly, with other-than-human relations (Gilmore 2017; Estes 2019; Yazzie 2019). We center these relations as they are reflective of the collaborative work we have been involved in over the past several years, and more to the point, as they are reflective of the need for BIPOC communities to gather with the intention of sharing stories to truly see and understand one another and to heal from the violences that have touched our communities. While the term BIPOC is imperfect and the lexicon is constantly shifting, we utilize this term for its brevity and because we prefer it to "racialized peoples," which implies that white people are not also racialized, and so as to not reify a language of deficit, such as "formerly colonized peoples" or "dispossessed peoples." In using this term, we do not intend to reduce the plurality of Blackness, Indigeneity, and communities of color. Learning from evolving conversations in Latinx and Indigenous studies and communities that are informed by Black thinkers and organizers, we recognize how the term "people of color" can erase the plurality of experiences embodied by people who are brought together under this term, including how people are differentially racialized under umbrella ethnic identities such as Latinx, how individuals can unevenly benefit from white privilege, and how anti-Blackness is reproduced when we are complicit with or actively erase these realities. At the same time, collective liberation requires astute examinations of white supremacy and how BIPOC lives are intimately woven together through our distinct though entangled experiences of the ongoing colonial theft of our homes, relations, and humanity. For this reason, we use the imperfect term BIPOC here but specifically highlight Black and Indigenous peoples and relationalities when appropriate, for this differentiation is necessary to address particular embodied geographies and experiences.

We situate our theorizing and methodological renderings of radical relationality amid the foundational genealogies and epistemologies of Black, Indigenous, Chicana, and Third World feminisms, from which intersectional theory emerged (Combahee River Collective 1977; Anzaldúa and Moraga 1981; Crenshaw 1991; Collins 2000). As Melanie Yazzie (Diné) and Cutcha Risling Baldy (Hupa, Yurok and Karuk) state (2018), decolonization must be built through expansive relations of care that shape Indigenous life, including those that are entangled with Black and anticolonial struggles for liberation (see also Yazzie 2019). Building on this, we are also guided by the work of Black feminist theorist Katherine McKittrick (2019), who compels us to theorize liberation broadly and comprehensively, by collectivizing the ideas and strategies activated across BIPOC communities, by doing this work with care and ethical accountability. We were fortunate to be in the audience when McKittrick gave her keynote talk "Living Just Enough for the City, Volume VI, Black Methodology," delivered in September 2019 at the GenUrb: Feminist Explorations of Urban Futures conference in Toronto. In her talk, McKittrick theorizes Black methodologies of liberation and freedom in part by stressing the need to "read widely, deeply and think relationally" and urges Black and anticolonial scholars to learn from creative and interdisciplinary labor as we imagine and activate geographies of abolition and freedom. Inspired by McKittrick, and echoing her words, we seek to "theorize place as relation" by elucidating the ways of relating and living that work toward liberation. As she writes in *Dear Science*, "If we are committed to anticolonial thought, our starting point must be one of disobedient relationality that always questions, and thus is not beholden to, normative academic logics. This means our method-making may not necessarily take us where we want to go, but it will take us, as Glissant writes, to 'an unknown that does not terrify'" (McKittrick 2021, 45, citing Glissant 1997, 9). It is this form of disobedient relationality that we seek to weave through our collaborations and the method we seek to employ in and beyond this piece.

As we write elsewhere (Daigle and Ramírez 2021), the weaving of liberatory intimacies builds solid foundations for abolitionist and decolonial work, through which "tiny territories" (Gilmore 2017, 227) of mutual aid can grow into constellations that hold vast political power across space (Simpson 2017). This transformative work starts at an embodied scale as mass movements cannot be built without the mutual recognition, trust, and accountability that arise from ethical intimacies: building interrelationships is coconstitutive to more visible forms of on-the-ground political organizing (Hunt and Holmes 2015). More than this, our theorizing of radical relationality is shaped by grounded experiences with collaborators, friends, and mentors over the years, including

May Farrales (2019), Yolanda González Mendoza (chapter 3), Madeline Whetung (2019), Willie J. Wright (2020), Pavithra Vasudevan (2021), and Michael
Fabris (2017). As Nishnaabeg theorist Leanne Betasamosake Simpson articulates, "The idea of thinking in formation, or thinking with . . . comes from Indigenous intellectual practices and is also parallel to the intellectual work and
brilliance of Black feminist theorists" (2017, 37). Echoing Black feminist theorist Alexis Pauline Gumbs, Simpson proceeds to ask, "What does it mean to
'prioritize being with each other, being with the work, being with the possibilities, more than [prioritizing] the gymnastics of trying to get it right in a structure built on wrongness'" (37). We follow Simpson and Gumbs here, as we seek
to build a methodology of radical relationality while also seeking to avoid illu-
sions of seamless relationship building across BIPOC communities. This work
is fraught, complex, and at times painful, and we do not wish to reproduce or
fall back on facile metaphors of shared or overlapping oppressions. Yet as Tiffany Lethabo King so brilliantly articulates in her preface to *The Black Shoals*,
"I write to live with myself. Beyond keeping one up at night, a haunting can
grant an inheritance. My inheritance is that, as a Black person living under relations of conquest, I care about Native peoples' survival. . . . I care because the
Black radical politics that I have inherited cares about Native people. . . . It is
a Black radical politics that proceeds and moves toward Black and Indigenous
futures" (2019, xiii). King's reflections resonate with the relation that we have
been building together and with others over the past several years: we write,
think, and practice together out of a shared respect and care for each other's
lives as we live under relations of conquest. We practice from the genealogies
we have inherited, and from this shared respect and care we have built a relation of accountability to each other and to those we are in dialogue with. We
are invested in building liberatory futures with one another and our kin.

   As we think through radical relationality here, we focus on the everyday
practices and relationships that make us *feel* liberated and free, as brief as
those moments might be, while simultaneously calling attention to the spaces
in which our visions of freedom feel stifled by white possessive desires. We
are intentional in what we choose to reveal in this piece and what is not di-
vulged. While we do not intend to romanticize our relationship and dialogue
as always easy, there seems to be a possessive desire for us to perform tensions
and frictions that have emerged from our dialogue. While we refuse to do so
in this piece, for any tensions we have had are not for academic consumption, we reiterate that it is through slow and intentional relationship building
that we are able to engage with a humility and respect that enables us to an-
ticipate and navigate any tensions that may emerge. From these moments and

shared spaces of dialogue, we continue weaving pathways, routes/roots/rhizomes toward liberatory futures—this is our disobedient method.

In what follows, we draw from a conversation that was recorded in December 2018 for the Relational Poverty podcast series (Daigle and Ramírez 2019b). The intention of this chapter is to serve as an archive of these genealogies, drawing threads as we continue to weave, and collectively build a language and method of resistance and liberation. We begin by tracing the formations of our work on decolonial geographies of liberation, by recounting why and how our collaboration emerged. From there we discuss challenges and lessons we have learned along the way and how our thinking on liberation continues to take shape. In doing this, we reflect on whom we have been present with, have been thinking with, and continue to learn from. While we focus primarily on relationship building that began in academic settings, we hope that our conversation delineates how the roots of these relationships are always grounded in collaborators' respective communal and familial ties and commitments. As such, we explore how we have strategically mobilized academic spaces for relationship building, while simultaneously reckoning with the limitations of doing this work within a complicit branch of the colonial state. We end by reflecting on what work needs to be done in our respective communities and how a major part of continuing to organize toward liberatory futures is about sharing space and stories and learning how to exist in reciprocal constellation. The method we are weaving here does not take the form of an explicit model that can be easily reproduced elsewhere—this method is slow and intentional and takes time, care, and love to build. We see this piece as an archive of what we have built in our collaborations and where we are hoping to travel and as an offering of our story as a methodological example of how to build anticolonial collaboration and kinship in and beyond the academy.

Formations

MICHELLE DAIGLE (MD): Magie and I met when we were PhD students in the Department of Geography at the University of Washington. I was returning to grad school after a couple of years of working in Indigenous communities in Coast Salish territory. After several years of being immersed within Indigenous community work, I suddenly felt disconnected from the knowledge and people who had informed my thinking and political commitments over the years.

I noticed the erasure of Indigenous knowledge in different ways: in the content and the scholarship that we were reading, but also in the collective consciousness that pervaded the academic community I had joined. For example, even though we were in a geography department, there wasn't an acknowledgment of the place where we were living and working, the ancestral territories of the Duwamish nation. Those kinds of questions didn't shape seminar conversations or come up in day-to-day conversations about colonial dispossession and what responsibilities and accountabilities we might have—not just in terms of thinking about relational geographies of dispossession and how that connects different places around the world—but also what our responsibilities and accountabilities are by living on stolen and occupied Indigenous territories.

This is something that I thought about quite a bit, and there were many moments when I felt like my experiences as an Indigenous woman, coming from a community that has lived through generations of colonial capitalist dispossession, weren't centered, in many ways, within the discipline of geography. I was looking for other people to be in conversation with about these realities. This is when Magie and I started to share our concerns and to build a dialogue, as we drew on our respective experiences, including my upbringing in Cree territory in what's now widely known as Treaty 9 in northern Ontario, and hers on Ohlone territories, now named the San Francisco Bay Area. As our dialogue and relationship grew, we could see the affinities that exist between our personal experiences, the research we do, and why we do it, our visions of liberation. Or, rather, I think our relationship grew from our shared affinities. We were learning from one another, from the genealogies of theory and political work that has activated our consciousness. We also challenged each other and continue to do so by asking each other questions that aren't always easy to broach but that we've been able to do because of the relationships and trust building that we've built over the years.

MAGIE RAMÍREZ (MMR): Absolutely—our affinities and the overlaps we began to discover in the genealogies that fed us really brought us together. I started grad school in geography at the UW back in 2008, and being a first-generation graduate student I really had no idea what to expect. What I experienced in grad school was a profound culture shock that took me a long time to sort my way through. Just sitting in a grad seminar space—we all know the violences that happen in the seminar room—I was troubled by the fact that I didn't see my communities' perspectives reflected in what we were reading. And the ways that I did see them reflected were really exploitative and extractive. So I found myself, as many BIPOC students do, being the sole voice in the seminar room saying, "But what about race? But what about Indigeneity?" That sort of knee-jerk reaction when we are struggling against systemic erasure, struggling so that our epistemologies are visible and valued.

Michelle started a few years after I got to the UW, and I remember sitting in a seminar with her for the first time in 2011 or 2012 and hearing her talk about decoloniality from an Indigenous perspective. At that point I was taking a course in gender and women's studies with Michelle Habell-Pallán (2005) on Chicana feminist theory. This class was really influential for me because it gave me a language through which to understand a lot of things that I had lost from assimilation. I was exposed to writings on the borderlands, *nepantla*, and the decolonial imaginary, classic texts by Gloria Anzaldúa (1987), Emma Pérez (1999), Chela Sandoval (2000), Mary Pat Brady (2002), and other Chicana feminists. Reading these texts helped me to situate myself and my experience in theory, helped me to validate my own epistemologies. So when I heard Michelle talking about decolonization, I was thinking about it through the framework that I was really immersed in. Thinking about it from a Chicana feminist sense, thinking about the influence of the border on Mexican, Chicanx, and Latinx peoples—and how the border has created this severed sense of self, or severed positionality and consciousness, that is produced by the colonial nation-state but also carries within it this ability to build creative survival mechanisms that dispossessed peoples have to resist and survive the colonial structures that we live within (see also Herrera, chapter 5).

So when Michelle and I first started talking, I think at that point we were speaking different languages—we were using the same words but with different conceptualizations. This has been a critique of Chicana feminist theory as well, as Tuck and Yang (2012) have very precisely written, that decolonization is not a metaphor. When Michelle and I started having this dialogue, there was a reckoning for me for all the gaps in my own knowledge.

We began collaborating in 2014 when we started planning a session on decolonial geographies at the American Association of Geographers (AAG) meeting. We thought, well, we don't really see anyone in geography talking about the decolonial. So let's write a call for papers (CFP) and make something for AAGs and see what comes out of it. And we framed it as "Decolonization, Resistance and Resurgence: Enacting Alternative Geographies." That was the first title. And we had a tremendous response from that CFP.

MD: Magie and I had spent time building a dialogue between each other—but really developing a friendship, discussing ideas, and developing the trust that was needed to have conversations on decolonization and liberation. We both had blind spots. There are also difficult points of contention that arise when you're trying to grapple with what decolonization means collectively for BIPOC communities, given the divides that have been created between communities because of processes of colonization, and also through the divisiveness of particular fields in the academy, notably settler-colonial theory. Once we spent some time having these conversations and developing that trust, we decided to open it up and connect with other people who wanted to have these conversations from a grounded place.

Learnings

MD: Over the years, we've made particular commitments as we've sought to build dialogue on questions of decolonization and liberation. We've sought to center the perspectives and knowledge of BIPOC people, whose thinking is grounded in the life experiences and relationships they have with their respective communities. This became increasingly important for us after our first session at the AAG in Chicago, back in 2015. As Magie said, we received a tremendous response to the CFP. We met a number of brilliant people through this session, but there were also a number of presentations that we felt unsettled by, either because it wasn't apparent to us whether some people had relationships with the communities they were presenting on or because there was an exploitative element to their research.

Over the years, Magie and I have seen how the decolonial has been taken up within geography and within academia in general. One of the concerns, or critiques, is that a lot of this work doesn't actually seem to be grounded in respectful relationships or in relationships at all. In academia, decolonization can be framed in a rather abstract way, in a way that is disconnected from the knowledge and the people who embody anticolonial relationships and ways of being in the world. We don't take this lightly. We understand that it takes many years of relationship building before we can speak or write about particular realities related to (de)colonization.

MMR: Absolutely. This has been something that we've been developing for many years, and it wasn't until 2018 that we were actually able to sit down and start to cultivate a language—to begin to sit down and write together to think through what we mean when we say "decolonial geographies" (Daigle and Ramírez 2019a). So our intention isn't to police academic spaces but to be intentional in our own work and in the spaces we cultivate to not reproduce colonial relations and methods of knowledge extraction. To us, it is essential that the relationships we build are respectful, intentional, and accountable. This work of building relations is slow, as it needs to be.

One of the things that happened after our first session, we were approached to be part of a publication. But we didn't feel ready to be writing at that time, we didn't feel we had a language yet, so we declined. And the person who invited us to the edited collection went on to publish some of the ideas, drawing directly from knowledge in Michelle's presentation in particular. They published this piece without citing Michelle, or our session, and their work was careless, a very shallow read of Indigenous theorists that was using them as an accessorial citation more than anything. To us, this work is something that we are carrying in particular ways—it's a practice, a methodology. And we feel this is the pace that the work needs to take. We needed to have these years of consistent dialogue and conversation to really build an understanding between and among each other—between Michelle and I, and between all of our collaborators with whom we've been so grateful to engage in conversation over the years. And I really feel like every time we have written these CFPs, and every time we've created spaces for this dialogue, we've deepened our understanding.

MD: At the same time that we've been building on conversations with each other, and with other collaborators, we've both been doing the work of learning what a decolonial and liberatory politics means to the communities that we're connected to. For myself, my thinking is rooted within my nation, the Mushkegowuk nation. But increasingly, I'm also careful to acknowledge how Anishinaabe and Oji-Cree people in my community and family have informed my thinking. In other words, I've tried to be more careful about complicating rigid notions of Indigenous nationhood by thinking through the expansive kinship relationships that have cultivated my thinking on decolonization and liberation. Anishinaabe people migrated to Mushkegowuk territory. Many of them came, historically, to work in the fur trade, but they built relationships with Mushkegowuk people, and many of them remained there and became our kin and an integral part of our body politic. Even though I speak from a standpoint of being a Mushkegowuk woman, when I think of my relations, I want to acknowledge that I've also learned a lot from my Anishinaabe relatives as well. The kinship that exists between Mushkegowuk and Anishinaabe, including the tensions that were reproduced through colonial policy and interventions, has impacted my thinking on relationality—how political relationships and commitments build over time, how they are challenged yet defy colonial interventions, and the difficult and time-consuming work that goes into the relationship building that is part of Indigenous life.

So even though I use the language of the decolonial, when I think about what that actually means, I'm thinking of Mushkegowuk sociopolitical practices that are (re)building relationalities amid the ongoing conditions of colonial capitalism. I think of how generations of colonial violence have affected Indigenous life—which of course includes the assimilation policies that were implemented under the Indian Act; a long history of resource extraction, which is ongoing with mining developments that are being proposed; the systemic implementation of residential schools and the generations within my family and community that attended residential school; and also the heteronormative patriarchal assimilation policies that ruptured the leadership and the political and legal roles of Mushkegowuk and Anishinaabe women and queer and Two-Spirit people. Within this context, when I think of decolonization, I think of how Indigenous peoples can and are rebuilding our legal practices and kinship relations, and the ways that we care for one another on an everyday basis. This was my starting point when we started to build a conversation on decolonial geographies. More and more, where my thinking has gone—not that it's left that, not that that is still not a priority for me—but that I'm thinking about how that comes, then, into relationship with Black, Latinx, and anticolonial understandings of colonization, racial capitalism, and resistance and liberation.

MMR: As Michelle was saying, the relationship—we have focused particularly on BIPOC communities, and how processes of colonialism and racial capitalism have affected us in distinct ways. And that's what this relational reckoning is about—we all make meaning of the world based on our own epistemologies, our own lived experiences, the issues that are most pertinent to our communities. So in our cultivation of decolonial geographies, there is a reckoning, as Tuck and Yang (2012, 7) theorize, there are "contradictory decolonial desires" among differently marginalized peoples. And so part of this process that Michelle and I have undergone is trying to pay attention to how, within our communities, there are colonial residues that have caused us to both isolate ourselves from other communities and at times place blame.

So part of how we've developed this dialogue is also around the reckoning that needs to take place within our communities. In my case, how do non-Indigenous and non-Black Latinx peoples address the deeply entrenched racisms of anti-Blackness and anti-Indigeneity that exist in our communities, as well as the ways that Latinidad as a hegemonic project appropriates and marginalizes Blackness and Indigeneity, and how these erasures and appropriations continue to sideline Afro-Latinx and Indigenous-Latinx experiences? These are really pertinent issues that Latinx peoples need to talk about more. Related to this, how can those of us who are settlers live in better relation to those whose land we reside upon? I grew up in the San Francisco Bay Area with little awareness of whose land I was on, and it wasn't until the past few years that I've learned more about the Ohlone geographies of the Bay and how I as a Chicana settler born and raised on these territories could live in better reciprocity. The language that Michelle and I have been building is how to respectfully engage in these conversations, knowing that we are not always going to fully understand each other. We're going to make mistakes, and yet we continue building and learning because we are invested in one another's liberation.

These conversations have been one of the most fruitful exchanges that I've had in academic spaces. They have gotten me to think not only about how this informs my scholarship but also about how it shapes my accountability to people in the places that I am from and the places that I visit. We talk about how there is no language for this work—we're building the bridge as we walk across it. Like Anzaldúa wrote, "Caminiante, no hay puentes, se hace puentes al andar" (Moraga and Anzaldúa 1983, v). And so there's something really humbling about this act of building as we walk—we feel like we are trying to cultivate something that is still in formation.

MD: To build off of what you said Magie, there has also been an erasure of anti-Blackness and other forms of racial dispossession and violence in Indigenous studies and communities. Something that resonated with me in Leanne Betasamosake Simpson's book, *As We Have Always Done: Indigenous Freedom through Radical Resistance* (2017), is her chapter on "constellations of co-resistance." Her thinking in this chapter resonates with a lot of what we've been discussing over the years and what we've also learned from other people whom we've connected with, like May Farrales (2019), who works with the Filipinx community in Vancouver and more generally within so-called British Columbia. She has sought to work with her community to ask what it means to be living on stolen and occupied Indigenous lands. And what might our responsibilities and accountabilities be, even though many people from our community are here through various forms of racial dispossession as well?

One thing that resonated with me about Simpson's writing on constellations of co-resistance is that she opens up the chapter by asking, what happens when Indigenous resurgence risks—and I'm quoting her here—"replicating anti-Blackness without solid reciprocal relationships with Black visionaries who are also co-creating alternatives under the lens of the abolition decolonization and anti-capitalism" (2017, 229). As an Indigenous person, these conversations are not always easy to have within our own communities because of the divides and erasures that have been reproduced through colonial schemas, the blame placing that you referred to Magie, that happens within our own communities. I think that one of the challenges is also that there is so much work, relationship building and accountability building, that needs to happen across Indigenous communities and nations. It can become difficult to envision anything bigger than this at times, when you start thinking about these on-the-ground realities, and the concerns and challenges that are articulated by our relatives. It can be difficult to articulate the importance of building relationships with other BIPOC communities to people within our families and communities. But, having said that, I do think that more and more people are open to having these conversations and thinking critically about what our own political organizing means if it comes into relationship with other communities and political organizing led by Black people and people of color.

Simpson's work has been influential in both of our thinking. As Magie said, we drew on the idea of constellations in the piece that we wrote on decolonial geographies (Daigle and Ramírez 2019a). Due to the appropriation of Indigenous knowledge within the academy—and also how the decolonial has been appropriated within geography and in other disciplines—we hesitated in drawing on Simpson's scholarship.

Magie and I had a conversation about whether we should use the framework of constellations and what it means for us. As Simpson says, she wants people, her readers, and particularly Indigenous readers, to figure out how we can contextualize what we're learning from her work within the context of our own nation's knowledge so that we're not just drawing on how she's come to theorize resurgence or constellations of co-resistance from a Nishnaabeg perspective. If we see something in that and it speaks to us, then we have to do the work of relationship building and learning within the communities that we come from. I think that's something that we're both trying to do, right?

MMR: Absolutely. And as you said, the writing that we've been working on recently in thinking about how we theorize decolonial geographies, we definitely got a lot of inspiration not only from Indigenous feminist writings, like Simpson's, but also from Clyde Woods's (2017) and Katherine McKittrick's (2006) theorization of Black geographies. Their theorizations have been a tremendous source of inspiration in thinking about how we develop these theories, thinking about differential productions of space, drawing from Black studies, Black feminism, and the Black Radical Tradition. And also really trying to begin threading a conversation between decolonization and abolition, which is something that we tried to do in that piece (Daigle and Ramírez 2019a). And how do, not only people, but how do these movements function in constellation? How are they simultaneously working on particular issues, working toward the abolition of the carceral state, the carceral system, and the repatriation of Indigenous territories, and how are these movements working toward collective liberation? How are these movements seeking a similar future, and how can these movements work in constellation to envision futures for all of our communities, to move beyond the colonial racial-capitalist system?

MD: Yes, and I sometimes worry that when we talk about liberation or resurgence, that some people will think only about larger social movements like Idle No More or Standing Rock or Black Lives Matter and so on. Don't get me wrong—it's not that these movements are not incredibly important in activating liberatory politics. Rather, I worry about how other forms of political practices become invisibilized. In my work, I've tried to emphasize how more visible or larger forms of Indigenous activism cannot happen without the day-to-day work that occurs at the community level in different ways. This is something that Indigenous feminists and queer and Two-Spirit scholars and activists have foregrounded in their work and that I've also learned from Black and Latinx feminists as well, such as Katherine McKittrick (2011) and Ruth Wilson Gilmore's (2017) thinking. I've been thinking more about the affinities that exist between Black, Indigenous, and Latinx feminist theorizations of freedom and liberation.

To go back to what you were reflecting on, it made me think, we haven't really talked too much about the whiteness that can be embedded within conversations on solidarity building. One of the problems is that a lot of the scholarship on settler colonialism has been dominated by white scholars who tend to recenter whiteness within their conversations on settler colonialism but also on solidarity building. A great deal of settler-colonial theory has erased earlier scholarship by Indigenous scholars, who were actually talking about the same kind of processes of elimination and of settlement but maybe didn't necessarily use the language of settler colonialism.

I was on the panel that you mentioned that we organized in New Orleans in 2018 on "Geographies of Land/Liberation" with Willie Wright. I remember we had a series of reflections that were shared by a number of panelists, including

Willie Wright (2020), Melanie Yazzie (2015), May Farrales (2019), and Yolanda Valencia (2017). There was a lot that resonated with me, and I found it incredibly meaningful to have that group of people sitting together to discuss what liberation means from our respective positionalities and the communities that we come from, while also trying to reckon with how our visions come into relationship with one another. After we all shared, we opened up the space for a Q&A, and there was this unsettling silence that took over in the room. Magie, as we reflected about that afterward, I shared how I wanted to engage with ideas that some people on the panel had shared, but I knew that some of these points might feel a bit more difficult and perhaps contentious—and I also felt the gaze, I felt a white gaze, a colonial gaze, that still pervades the academy, and I hesitated in that moment to have those conversations in that space.

From there we had a discussion on what spaces are appropriate to have these kinds of conversations. Is a big venue like the AAG, an academic conference, the appropriate place to have this? Or do we need more private spaces to cultivate these conversations, similar to those we have within our own communities, where we're able to have conversations among one another without feeling like we're on display for other people in this academic space that is still very much embedded in a gaze that I still feel as an Indigenous scholar.

MMR: Yeah, that AAG session was a big learning moment, for me, definitely. I remember that same silence after everyone spoke these profound and really just powerful testimonies. The silence that followed, and like Michelle said, the gaze of the room, I felt a paralysis come over me. I went into that panel really wanting to hold space more than anything, which is why I decided not to be on the panel itself. And I think I realized, as Michelle said, that maybe that wasn't the space where we were meant to have these exchanges. The intense gaze of the audience felt very colonial, very extractive. And the density of the silence really started to consume me in that moment. We didn't know who was in that room—there were so many people, and it felt like we were putting the colonial ghosts on display without ensuring that there was going to be some accountability from those who were there to witness it. Maybe we were overly ambitious to try to have that conversation at AAGs. These are really fraught histories and geographies that we are trying to engage with, and the five of you were bringing knowledge to the table that needed to be honored. It was a very vulnerable space. And it's not really fair to open up things that can be very vulnerable and very difficult to process and articulate in that sort of setting.

I remain proud of how we cultivated that session, the five of you on that panel were really incredible. But I think that the deafening silence of the room, the density of the space after words were spoken, that was a moment that really affected me. In the aftermath of that session, I realized that maybe we needed to take a step back. And, in a sense, in the same way that we've been talking about how we've been really intentional in the pace of how we've engaged this dialogue over the years, maybe that was too big of a step to make in this public setting. The fact that it was the first time that some of the panelists were meeting each other, and to be engaging in this conversation in such a public manner—it was a learning moment for me.

MD: I think that goes to show you in many ways how this is not just an academic exercise for a lot of us who are having these conversations. We're not just there to perform our expertise on what we think the decolonial is. I see the work that I'm doing as a scholar as an extension of what I see as the larger work that needs to be done within my community. In many ways, my role within the academy is to strategically, use whatever resources or the privileges that we do have as scholars—to put that toward processes that actually matter within community. I think that's partly what shaped how the panel unfolded that day too. It's so much more difficult to have a humble dialogue about decolonization and liberation when you're thinking about what this looks like in real life, where we go from here, and how we embody a relational politics on a day-to-day basis. It's not easy.

MMR: Yes, definitely. I think that's ultimately what has brought you and I together, Michelle—that we're not just writing this because of pressure to publish. We are invested in these conversations—what they represent and how they take shape in an academic sense is part of it, but I think ultimately we're trying to build something bigger than that. It really is a form of praxis.

MD: Some of that praxis might be more visible within different academic spaces or forums. And then, I think that some of it, inevitably, is not going to be visible, and it's not supposed to be either. Right?

MMR: Yes—it's not for consumption.

The remainder of our conversation reflected on the importance of relational accountability. By drawing on our respective experiences in the North American context, we emphasized the importance of situating accountability with the Indigenous peoples, lands, and waters that we live and work on. We discussed how this framing of accountability serves as a starting point for everyone to think about ethical and responsible relationship building. We also stressed how some Indigenous peoples have sought to build dialogue within their own communities and nations, about what it might mean to welcome people into our territories according to our own political practices and law. Indeed, these are governance practices that have always continued throughout Indigenous nations, in spite of colonization, and which Indigenous peoples continue to activate as they simultaneously recognize the colonial and racial violence that have led other BIPOC peoples to be living on their ancestral territories or to have traveled to them to be in solidarity with shared struggles for land and bodily sovereignty.

Futures

The aforementioned AAG session on "Geographies of Land/Liberation" in New Orleans was a crucial learning moment for us. As Michelle recounts, she felt stifled by the gaze in the room during the Q&A portion of the session. In that moment, she made a conscious decision to not ask questions to her fellow panelists and to not probe on particular points of tension and of possible emergence. Magie, as the "chair" of the session, struggled with the performative aspect of having these intimate conversations on display and felt paralyzed by her inability to fully honor everything that was shared and navigate the role of the "audience" present. This moment, for both of us, changed the nature of doing this work and led to multiple conversations between fellow panelists and other collaborators who were in the room that day. These conversations specifically centered on the importance of continuing dialogue and relationship building, by bringing some of this work into private spaces. We discussed our frustration and concerns with white academics appropriating BIPOC theory and labor for careerist objectives, particularly when their "survey of the field"– type literature reviews are what ends up getting high "h-index" valorizations. We feel that the need to bring this work underground is also so that we can focus on building relationships between one another without having to continually mitigate a white possessive gaze that we find to dominate many academic spaces.[3] As Katherine McKittrick writes, "The story asks that we live with the difficult and frustrating ways of knowing differentially. (And some things we can keep to ourselves. They cannot have everything)" (2021, 7). More importantly, we discussed desires to create spaces where BIPOC people can come together to share ideas and strategies, where we can envision geographies of liberation, without those visions being taken up for public consumption.

Pursuits for liberation require refusals of anti-Blackness and colonial genocide, including the ways that BIPOC people resist the fetishization of trauma-based narratives and how and to whom we choose to disclose the challenges, tensions, and underlying desires of our work. At moments, freedom work must be covert and opaque (Glissant 1997; Simpson 2017; King 2019). In writing this piece, we constantly returned to these core values as we considered what to share and what not to share, as we understand our methodology to be one that is accountable to relations that are in formation, in constant renewal, built on shared practices of storytelling, healing, and organizing for our futures. The fraughtness of weaving different genealogies of decolonial thinking together further affirms the need for closed spaces that support exploratory thinking and critical generosity. At the same time, we remain hopeful of the generative potential of future public conversations and forums. Specifically, we hope to cultivate more spaces in which decolonial thinkers, including grassroots activists and artists, can share their community-based work alongside each other, to work against the silos that are reproduced through colonial disciplinary logics and practices.

Our collaboration has simultaneously led us to return to our respective work on Indigenous, Black, and Latinx liberation with renewed political commitments to the people we have learned from throughout the past several years. In doing this, we recognize the relationship building that needs to happen within each of these communities and remain committed to this resurgent and liberatory work. Alongside this, we continue to go back to our community-based work with renewed understandings of how our freedoms are contingent upon one another. For myself (Michelle), I continue to be unsettled with the ways particular framings of Indigenous sovereignty and land reclamation foreclose dialogue and relationship building with anticolonial relations, and reproduce anti-Blackness within Indigenous studies and communities. As I have previously reflected (see Attewell et al. 2018), I am particularly concerned with how settler-colonial theory reifies a land/labor binary that risks creating divisions between Indigenous and Black peoples. As Mishuana Goeman (Tonawanda Band of Seneca) articulates (2008), Indigenous space can be flattened to colonial renderings of territory that preclude relationality across Indigenous communities, but also with Black and POC relations. As Tiffany Lethabo King brilliantly articulates, Black and Indigenous peoples must build "a new grammar [that] emerge[s] at the shoals of Black and Native porous futures" (King 2019, 151). Drawing on King, I am guided by a desire for new modes of humanism that are made possible as BIPOC feminist and queer thinkers generously and humbly meet one another and become open to being shaped through our distinct yet interconnected struggles for freedom. Increasingly, I am compelled to think through the expansiveness of what it means to be Mushkegowuk, specif-

ically how Mushkegowuk life is shaped not only through our roots in the mus-
kegs but through our movement throughout space and time, and the relations
we encounter, and who shape us in transformative ways.

As for me (Magie), I am grateful that I now have Latinx colleagues in geography with whom I can grapple with many of the issues taking place in our
communities that necessarily need to be addressed. As I mentioned earlier in
this text, the anti-Black and anti-Indigenous discourses that are far too common in mestizx communities need to be challenged, both in how we inter-
nalize these colonial racisms and in how we reproduce them. Pushing back
against these discourses as they emerge around the dinner table with our parents, siblings, and other kin is a necessary part of anticolonial work. Despite
the fact that my initial engagement in decolonial theory stemmed from Chicana feminist theorists (Anzaldúa 1987; Pérez 1999), I have found myself stray-
ing from the central analytics of these literatures. I am uncertain if the borderlands, nepantla, Aztlán, the third space, and the decolonial imaginary can
offer liberatory analytics without reproducing Indigenous erasures and appropriations, as well as anti-Blackness (Cahuas 2019). Therefore, as a white Chicana, I am invested in centering the theorizations of Black and Indigenous
Latinx peoples so that *mestizaje* does not continue to be presumed in conversations of Latinx identity, and so that anti-Black and anti-Indigenous linguis-
tic and cultural practices do not continue to uphold the racisms that scaffold
mestizaje as a white-supremacist racial project. It is my work to further explore
these contentions and erasures in and beyond Latinx geographies with other
Latinx peoples, and I believe that it is through reading Black and Indigenous
thought, and respectful listening, laughing, and learning together, that we can
begin to disentangle these relations. Perhaps we need to betray Latinidad so as
to combat the toxic racisms many Latinx peoples have inherited. And to make
sure Afro-Latinx, Indigenous Latinx, queer and trans Latinx peoples are at the
forefront of our conversations, for I believe this is where we will build antiracist, antipatriarchal, anticolonial Latinx geographies that exist in relation, or in
constellation, with Black and Indigenous geographies.

As we continue to collectively weave pathways toward liberation, we are inspired by anticolonial thinkers such as Nick Estes (citizen of the Lower Brule
Sioux Tribe) (2019), Robyn Maynard (2017), and Leanne Betasamosake Simpson (2017), who ground their theorizations of Indigenous and Black liberation
within the roots and routes that give rise to their desires for freedom, while
also attending to how their genealogies and lives are intimately entangled with
those of other BIPOC communities around the globe. We are also guided by
examples of anticolonial thinkers coming together to share stories and col-

laboratively envision collective liberation (Tuck and Walcott 2017; Simpson and Maynard 2018; Simpson and Brand 2018), while also being deeply thankful and invigorated by brilliant theorists such as Tiffany Lethabo King (2019) who are tracing the entanglements of anti-Blackness, Indigenous genocide, and white supremacy as well as the deep histories and interactions that have always enlivened radical relationality across BIPOC communities. We are energized by these writings and the conversations and relationships that continue to emerge. It is through continued conversation and the sharing of space, food, song, and story that we find constellations of radical relationality emerging. While the act of engaging in slow, private, and intentional exchanges may seem simple, we find that it is a necessary part of finding roots, routes, and rhizomes (Glissant 1997) toward liberatory futures, and, following Glissant's words from the epigraph, a valuable piece of moving beyond frameworks of opposition and into relation.

NOTES

1. We draw on the framing of "Brown" from José Esteban Muñoz's posthumous text *Sense of Brown* (2020) to signal shared experiences of colonial violence across the Global South, well aware of the imperfection of the term. Brown, Muñoz writes, because "the world is and has been brown and has been so despite the various blockages that keep us from knowing or being attuned to brownness. This is to argue that lives are still organized and disorganized by harsh asymmetries that systemically devalue classes of singularities . . . a brown commons [is] . . . not only a shared indignation but also a process of thinking and imagining otherwise in the face of shared wounding" (5–6).

2. We draw on Leanne Betasamosake Simpson's (2017) theorization of flight and constellations in this piece, the latter of which we reference below. Simpson anchors her thinking on constellations within Nishinaabeg cosmologies and draws on Cree media maker and writer Jarrett Martineau's (2015) work on affirmative refusal as well as on Stefano Harney and Fred Moten's (2013) work on fugitivity to reflect on how constellations of co-resistance provide a flight "out of settler colonial realities into Indigeneity" (Simpson 2017, 217). As we have previously written (Daigle and Ramírez 2019b), Simpson centers relationship building between Indigenous and Black communities and asks Indigenous peoples whom we should be in constellation with in our pursuits for freedom. She cautions that Indigenous resurgence risks "replicating anti-Blackness without solid, reciprocal relationships with Black visionaries who are also co-creating alternatives under the lens of abolition, decolonization, and anti-capitalism" (Simpson 2017, 228–229).

3. We draw this from George Lipsitz's writings on "the possessive investment in whiteness" (1995). While Lipsitz's work addresses how white supremacy functions in society writ large, we have occasionally encountered an insatiable desire of white academics to consume BIPOC theories and experiences, to the extent that at times white academics demand entry, demand the right to be a part of (or at least to witness) our

conversations. We refuse this possessive gaze, refuse to cater to these colonial desires to consume our stories.

REFERENCES

Anzaldúa, Gloria. 1987. *Borderlands / La Frontera*. San Francisco: Aunt Lute.

Anzaldúa, Gloria, and Chela Moraga. 1981. *This Bridge Called My Back: Writings of Radical Women of Color*. Watertown, Mass.: Persephone Press.

Attewell, Wesley, Michelle Daigle, Genevieve Clutario, May Farrales, Stevie Ruiz, Christine Peralta, Dory Nason, and Iyko Day. 2018. "Alien Capital: Asian Racialization and the Logic of Settler Colonial Capitalism." *AAG Review of Books* 6(3): 192–205.

Brady, Mary Pat. 2002. *Extinct Lands, Temporal Geographies*. Durham, N.C.: Duke University Press.

Cahuas, Madelaine. 2019. "Interrogating Absences in Latinx Theory and Placing Blackness in Latinx Geographical Thought: A Critical Reflection." *Society & Space*, January 23. https://www.societyandspace.org/articles/interrogating-absences-in-latinx-theory-and-placing-blackness-in-latinx-geographical-thought-a-critical-reflection.

Collins, Patricia Hill. 2000. *Black Feminist Thought: Knowledge, Consciousness, and the Politics of Empowerment*. Oxford: Routledge.

Combahee River Collective. 1977. "A Black Feminist Statement." In Zillah Eisenstein (Ed.), *Capitalist Patriarchy and the Case for Socialist Feminism*, 210–218. New York: Monthly Review Press.

Crenshaw, Kimberlé. 1991. "Mapping the Margins: Intersectionality, Identity Politics, and Violence against Women of Color." *Stanford Law Review* 43: 1241–1300.

Daigle, Michelle, and Margaret Marietta Ramírez. 2019a. "Decolonial Geographies." In *Antipode* Editorial Collective (Ed.), *Keywords in Radical Geography: Antipode at 50*, 78–84. Oxford: Wiley.

———. 2019b. "On Relationality as Constellation: A Conversation on Decolonization and Liberation." *Relational Poverty Network* (podcast), January 24. http://depts.washington.edu/relpov/on-relationality-as-constellation-a-conversation-on-decolonization-and-liberation/.

———. 2021. "Space." In K. W. Tompkins (Ed.), *Keywords for Gender and Sexuality Studies*, 216–220. New York: New York University Press.

Estes, Nick. 2019. *Our History Is the Future: Standing Rock versus the Dakota Access Pipeline, and the Long Tradition of Indigenous Resistance*. London: Verso.

Fabris, Michael. 2017. "Decolonizing Neoliberalism? First Nations Reserves, Private Property Rights, and the Legislation of Indigenous Dispossession in Canada." In Maja Hojer Bruun, Patrick Joseph Cockburn, Bjarke Skaerlund Risager, and Mikkel Thorup (Eds.), *Contested Property Claims: What Disagreement Tells Us about Ownership*, 185–204. New York: Routledge.

Farrales, May. 2019. "Repurposing Beauty Pageants: The Colonial Geographies of Filipina Pageants in Canada." *Environment and Planning D: Society and Space* 37(1): 46–64.

Gilmore, Ruth Wilson. 2017. "Abolition Geography and the Problem of Innocence." In

Theresa Gaye Johnson and Alex Lubin (Eds.), *Futures of Black Radicalism*, 225–240. London: Verso.

Glissant, Édouard. 1997. *Poetics of Relation*. Ann Arbor: University of Michigan Press.

Goeman, Mishuana. 2008. "From Place to Territories and Back Again: Centering Storied Land in the Discussion of Indigenous Nation-Building." *International Journal of Critical Indigenous Studies* 1(1): 23–34.

Habell-Pallán, Michelle. 2005. *Loca Motion: The Travels of Chicana and Latina Popular Culture*. New York: New York University Press.

Harney, Stefano, and Fred Moten. 2013. *The Undercommons: Fugitive Planning and Black Study*. New York: Minor Compositions.

Hunt, Sarah, and Cindy Holmes. 2015. "Everyday Decolonization: Living a Decolonizing Queer Politics." *Journal of Lesbian Studies* 19(2): 154–172.

King, Tiffany Lethabo. 2019. *The Black Shoals: Offshore Formations of Black and Native Studies*. Durham, N.C.: Duke University Press.

Lipsitz, George. 1995. "The Possessive Investment in Whiteness: Racialized Social Democracy and the 'White' Problem in American Studies." *American Quarterly* 47(3): 369–387.

Martineau, Jarrett. 2015. "Creative Combat: Indigenous Art, Resurgence, and Decolonization." PhD dissertation, University of Victoria.

Maynard, Robyn. 2017. *Policing Black Lives: State Violence in Canada from Slavery to the Present*. Winnipeg: Fernwood.

McKittrick, Katherine. 2006. *Demonic Grounds: Black Women and the Cartographies of Struggle*. Minneapolis: University of Minnesota Press.

———. 2011. "On Plantations, Prisons, and a Black Sense of Place." *Social and Cultural Geography* 12(8): 947–963.

———. 2019. "Living Just Enough for the City, Volume VI, Black Methodology." Keynote, GenUrb: Feminist Explorations of Urban Futures, Toronto.

———. 2021. *Dear Science and Other Stories*. Durham, N.C.: Duke University Press.

McKittrick, Katherine, and Clyde Woods (Eds.). 2007. *Black Geographies and the Politics of Place*. Toronto: Between the Lines.

Moraga, Chela, and Gloria Anzaldúa. 1983. *This Bridge Called My Back: Writings by Radical Women of Color*. 2nd ed. New York: Kitchen Table / Women of Color Press.

Muñoz, José Esteban. 2020. *The Sense of Brown*. Durham, N.C.: Duke University Press.

Pérez, Emma. 1999. *The Decolonial Imaginary: Writing Chicanas into History*. Bloomington: Indiana University Press.

Sandoval, Chela. 2000. *Methodology of the Oppressed*. Minneapolis: University of Minnesota Press.

Simpson, Leanne Betasamosake. 2017. *As We Have Always Done: Indigenous Freedom through Radical Resistance*. Minneapolis: University of Minnesota Press.

Simpson, Leanne Betasamosake, and Dionne Brand. 2018. "Temporary Spaces of Joy and Freedom." *Literary Review of Canada: A Journal of Idea*s, June. https://review canada.ca/magazine/2018/06/temporary-spaces-of-joy-and-freedom/.

Simpson, Leanne Betasamosake, and Robyn Maynard. 2018. "Leanne Betasamosake Simpson in Conversation with Robyn Maynard." CKUT 90.3FM, April 23. https://

soundcloud.com/radiockut/leanne-betasamosake-simpson-in-conversation-with
-robyn-maynard.

Tuck, Eve, and Rinaldo Walcott. 2017. "A Conversation between Eve Tuck & Rinaldo Walcott." *The Henceforward* (podcast), May 17. http://www.thehenceforward.com
/episodes/2017/5/17/episode-13-a-conversation-between-dr-eve-tuck-dr-rinaldo
-walcott.

Tuck, Eve, and K. Wayne Yang. 2012. "Decolonization Is Not a Metaphor." *Decolonization: Indigeneity, Education & Society* 1(1): 1–40.

Valencia, Yolanda. 2017. "Risk and Security on the Mexico-to-U.S. Migrant Journey: Women's Testimonios of Violence." *Gender, Place & Culture* 24(11): 1530–1548.

Vasudevan, Pavithra. 2021. "An Intimate Inventory of Race and Waste." *Antipode* 53(3): 770–790.

Whetung, Madeline. 2019. "(En)gendering Shoreline Law: Nishnaabeg Relational Politics along the Trent Severn Waterway." *Global Environmental Politics* 19(3): 16–32.

Woods, Clyde. 2017. *Development Arrested: The Blues and Plantation Power in the Mississippi Delta*. New York: Verso.

Wright, Willie Jamaal. 2020. "The Morphology of Marronage." *Annals of the American Association of Geographers* 110(4): 1134–1149.

Yazzie, Melanie K. 2015. "Solidarity with Palestine from Diné Bikéyah." *American Quarterly* 67(4): 1007–1015.

———. 2019. "U.S. Imperialism and the Problem of 'Culture' in Indigenous Politics: Towards Indigenous Internationalist Feminism." *American Indian Culture and Research Journal* 43(3): 95–117.

Yazzie, Melanie, and Cutcha Risling Baldy. 2018. "Introduction: Indigenous Peoples and the Politics of Water." *Decolonization: Indigeneity, Education & Society* 7(1): 1–18.

CONTRIBUTORS

MICHELLE DAIGLE is Assistant Professor of Geography and Indigenous Studies at the University of Toronto. She is Mushkegowuk (Cree), a member of Constance Lake First Nation in Treaty 9, and of French ancestry. Broadly, her research examines colonial capitalist dispossession and violence on Indigenous lands and bodies, as well as Indigenous practices of resurgence and freedom. Her current research project examines the relational and embodied impacts of state-sanctioned environmental violence reproduced through mining extraction in Treaty 9.

SARAH ELWOOD is Professor of Geography at the University of Washington and cofounder of the Relational Poverty Network with Victoria Lawson. She teaches GIS and digital geographies. Her research contributes to relational poverty studies, critical GIScience and digital geographies, visual politics and mixed methods, and urban geography. She is coeditor of *Relational Poverty Politics: Forms, Struggles, and Possibilities* (2018), *Crowdsourcing Geographic Knowledge* (2012), and *Qualitative GIS* (2009).

YOLANDA GONZÁLEZ MENDOZA is Assistant Professor of Geography and Environmental Systems at the University of Maryland Baltimore County. She is a Latinx feminist geographer whose teaching and research interests include migration, race, borders, communality, and theories from the South. Her most recent research focuses on understanding how those made illegal by the law—undocumented Mexican immigrants and Mexican immigrants in general—experience risk and produce safe spaces as they navigate displacement in Mexico and segregation and multiple borders in the United States. More specifically, her work asks, how do undocumented Latinx immigrants thrive in places made for their failure in the United States?

ANA P. GUTIÉRREZ GARZA is Lecturer in Social Anthropology at the University of St. Andrews. She is an economic anthropologist who specializes in migration, gender, race and ethnicity, care, and labor. Her first book explores the lives of Latin American women who exchange care and intimacy for money while working as domestic and sex workers in London. It examines the role that care as a labor practice as well as an ethical practice has in the lives of migrant women. In 2014, 2015, and 2016 she developed stints of fieldwork in Tulsa, Oklahoma, where she has analyzed networks of care and cooperation among undocumented migrants from Mexico. Her interest in care continued with her second long-term research project (2015–2018) among a housing social movement in Madrid, where she analyzed the role that collective forms of care and advice have as a mechanism to counteract the lack of empathy and welfare cuts implemented by the neoliberal austerity policies in Europe.

JUAN HERRERA is Assistant Professor of Geography at the University of California, Los Angeles. He is a human geographer who specializes in social movements, spatial theory, race, queer of color critique, and women of color feminisms. His first book explores how social movements produce spaces of resistance anchored by institutions that care for racialized poor. He teaches courses on space and power, race, Latinx geographies, and transnational migration.

ELLEN KOHL is Assistant Professor of Environmental Studies at St. Mary's College of Maryland. She is a human geographer whose primary research and teaching interests are at the intersections of race, environmental policy, and place. Her research examines how compounding sociospatial processes, developed and perpetuated by urban and environmental policies, contribute to places of persistent environmental injustice in the United States.

VICTORIA LAWSON is Professor of Geography at the University of Washington, Director of the UW Honors Program, and cofounder of the Relational Poverty Network with Sarah Elwood. She teaches critical poverty studies and feminist care ethics. Her research focuses on relational poverty analysis and feminist theorizations of politics to explore pluriverse forms of politics that refuse liberal poverty governance. She is most recently coeditor of *Relational Poverty Politics: Forms, Struggles, and Possibilities* (2018).

JOVAN SCOTT LEWIS is Assistant Professor of Geography and African American Studies at the University of California, Berkeley, where he also coleads the Economic Disparities research cluster at the Haas Institute for a Fair and Inclusive Society. Jovan's research focuses on the qualitative experience and histories of raced poverty through the framework of repair in the Caribbean and the United States.

AARON MALLORY is Assistant Professor of Geography at Florida State University. A child of Detroit auto workers and southern raised, he has an inherent commitment to positive social change that led him to pursue a BA in political economy at the Evergreen State College. Prior to pursuing graduate school, Aaron worked as a community organizer for a public health care and prevention organization in Inglewood, California. This experience working to address health disparities in low-income communities of color led Aaron to pursue a PhD in geography, where he combines his research in health, HIV/AIDS prevention, and Black LGBTQ communities together in an interdisciplinary setting. His research interests are health geography, feminist knowledge production, Black studies, and queer theory.

PRISCILLA MCCUTCHEON is Assistant Professor of Geography at the University of Kentucky. Priscilla is also affiliated with the African American and Africana Studies Institute at UK. Priscilla's research focuses on Black faith-based food and sustainable agricultural programs in the U.S. South. She is currently conducting archival research into food programs of the Black Power and Civil Rights movements that include Fannie Lou Hamer's Freedom Farms and the National Council of Negro Women Hunger Campaign.

MARGARET MARIETTA RAMÍREZ is Assistant Professor of Geography at Simon Fraser University. Her work explores how the creative cultural practices of people of color produce urban space, how they are policed and co-opted as cities gentrify, and how these same creative geographies are taken up to resist urban redevelopment.

CHANDAN REDDY is Associate Professor in the departments of Gender, Women and Sexuality Studies and the Comparative History of Ideas at the University of Washington, Seattle. He is coeditor (with Jodi Byrd, Alyosha Goldstein, and Jodi Melamed) of the special issue "Economies of Dispossession: Indigeneity, Race, Capitalism," *Social Text* (Spring 2018). His book *Freedom with Violence: Race, Sexuality and the U.S. State* (2011) won the Alan Bray Memorial Award for queer studies from the MLA as well as the Best Book in Cultural Studies from the Asian American Studies Association, both in 2013. He is currently at work on a new book project titled *Administrating Racial Capitalism.*

INDEX

AAG (American Association of Geographers), 168–169, 174–176, 177

abolition: of lethal liberalism(s), 19; of poverty concept, 51, 63, 65; of poverty studies, 8, 17, 18, 21, 49

academia: accountable relationality in, 63–65, 164–167, 169–174, 176, 177–180; authorship in, 13, 14–16; white/colonial gaze in, 175, 177, 180n3; white epistemologies in, 51, 57, 59–63. *See also* space(s): academic

academic space(s). *See* space(s): academic

accountable relationality: in academia, 63–65, 164–167, 169–174, 176, 177–180; in activism, 133; in collective authorship, 15–16; in poverty studies, abolition of, 51–52; relational politics and, 20–21. *See also* relationality

Action Mission Ministry (AMM). *See* Wheat Street Baptist Church

activists and activism: care and, 118–120, 121, 122–123; LGBT+, 96, 98, 100, 104, 108–113; beyond liberalism, 5; nepantla strategies of, 124, 126, 136–138; quiet, 141–142, 147–149, 154–156, 157–158; of racialized communities, learning from, 8–12, 19–21; relationality and, 123–124; scholarly, 16–17; solidarity across different groups of, 127–128, 132–133; visible versus invisible, 174. *See also specific individuals and groups*

ACT-UP (AIDS Coalition to Unleash Power), 96

African American communities. *See* Black communities

Alexander, Michelle, 56

Amelia (Educare participant), 33

American Association of Geographers (AAG), 168–169, 174–176

AMM (Action Mission Ministry). *See* Wheat Street Baptist Church

Anishinaabe people, 170–171

anti-Blackness: in academia, 57; de-Indianization and, in racial capitalism, 71, 84; gender and sexuality in, 6, 19; of HOPE VI developments, 62; in LGBT+ communities, 95–99, 100–101, 102–107, 109, 110–113; "people of color" term and, 163; racialized communities and, 16, 171–173, 178–179; relationality as counter to, 163, 171–173, 177–180. *See also* white supremacy

Anzaldúa, Gloria: on bridge building, 172; influence of, 168; on nepantla and nos/otras, 117, 118, 119, 123–124, 129, 137; on solidarity, 126, 132

Arday, Jason, 57

As We Have Always Done (L. B. Simpson), 172

Athena Co-Learning Collective, 14

Atlanta, Ga.: Black communities in, 148–149, 158; LGBT+ communities in, Black, 97–99, 107–113; Wheat Street Baptist Church in, 143–144, 152–153, 155

Auburn Avenue. *See* Wheat Street Baptist Church

Bailey, Marlon M., 106

Balderrama, Francisco E., 29

Barbershops, Bibles and BET (Harris-Lacewell), 153

Beam, Joseph, 111

Benavidez, Andrea, 128

GEOGRAPHIES OF JUSTICE AND SOCIAL TRANSFORMATION

CPSIA information can be obtained
at www.ICGtesting.com
Printed in the USA
LVHW041148280623
751003LV00003BA/140